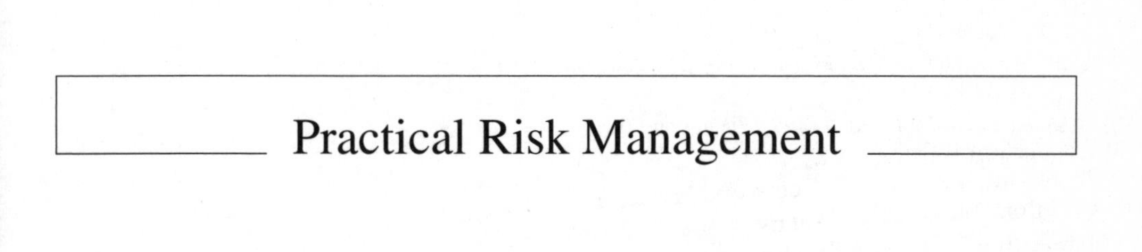

Practical Risk Management

Wiley Finance Series

Practical Risk Management: An Executive Guide to Avoiding Surprises and Losses
Erik Banks and Richard Dunn

Risk-adjusted Lending Conditions: An Option Pricing Approach
Werner Rosenberger

Exchange-Traded Derivatives
Erik Banks

Option Theory
Peter James

The Simple Rules of Risk: Revisiting the Art of Risk Management
Erik Banks

Capital Asset Investment: Strategy, Tactics and Tools
Anthony F. Herbst

Brand Assets
Tony Tollington

Swaps and Other Derivatives
Richard Flavell

Currency Strategy: A Practitioner's Guide to Currency Trading, Hedging and Forecasting
Callum Henderson

The Investor's Guide to Economic Fundamentals
John Calverley

Measuring Market Risk
Kevin Dowd

An Introduction to Market Risk Management
Kevin Dowd

Behavioural Finance
James Montier

Asset Management: Equities Demystified
Shanta Acharya

An Introduction to Capital Markets: Products, Strategies, Participants
Andrew M. Chisholm

Hedge Funds: Myths and Limits
Francois-Serge Lhabitant

Securities Operations: A guide to trade and position management
Michael Simmons

Modeling, Measuring and Hedging Operational Risk
Marcelo Cruz

Monte Carlo Methods in Finance
Peter Jäckel

Building and Using Dynamic Interest Rate Models
Ken Kortanek and Vladimir Medvedev

Structured Equity Derivatives: The Definitive Guide to Exotic Options and Structured Notes
Harry Kat

Advanced Modelling in Finance Using Excel and VBA
Mary Jackson and Mike Staunton

Operational Risk: Measurement and Modelling
Jack King

Advance Credit Risk Analysis: Financial Approaches and Mathematical Models to Assess, Price and Manage Credit Risk
Didier Cossin and Hugues Pirotte

Interest Rate Modelling
Jessica James and Nick Webber

Interest-Rate Option Models: Understanding, Analysing and Using Models for Exotic Interest-Rate Options (second edition)
Riccardo Rebonato

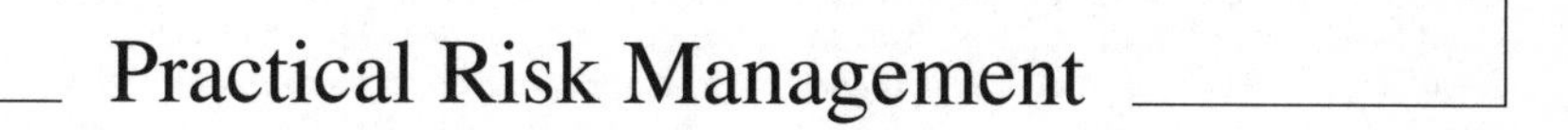

Practical Risk Management

An Executive Guide to Avoiding Surprises and Losses

Erik Banks and **Richard Dunn**

Telephone (+44) 1243 779777

Email (for orders and customer service enquiries): cs-books@wiley.co.uk
Visit our Home Page on www.wileyeurope.com or www.wiley.com

Reprinted December 2003

Other Wiley Editorial Offices

John Wiley & Sons Inc., 111 River Street, Hoboken, NJ 07030, USA

Jossey-Bass, 989 Market Street, San Francisco, CA 94103-1741, USA

Wiley-VCH Verlag GmbH, Boschstr. 12, D-69469 Weinheim, Germany

John Wiley & Sons Australia Ltd, 33 Park Road, Milton, Queensland 4064, Australia

John Wiley & Sons (Asia) Pte Ltd, 2 Clementi Loop #02-01, Jin Xing Distripark, Singapore 129809

John Wiley & Sons Canada Ltd, 22 Worcester Road, Etobicoke, Ontario, Canada M9W 1L1

Wiley also publishes its books in a variety of electronic formats. Some content that appears in print may not be available in electronic books.

Library of Congress Cataloging-in-Publication Data

Banks, Erik.
Practical risk management : an executive guide to avoiding surprises and losses / Erik Banks and Richard Dunn.
p. cm.—(Wiley finance series)
Includes bibliographical references and index.
ISBN 0-470-84967-3 (alk. paper)
1. Risk management. 2. Business enterprises—Finance. I. Dunn, Richard.
II. Title. III. Series.
HD61.B36 2003
658.15′5—dc21 2003050191

British Library Cataloguing in Publication Data

A catalogue record for this book is available from the British Library

ISBN 0-470-84967-3

Typeset in 10/12pt Times by TechBooks, New Delhi, India
Printed and bound in Great Britain by MPG Books Ltd, Bodmin, Cornwall
This book is printed on acid-free paper responsibly manufactured from sustainable forestry in which at least two trees are planted for each one used for paper production.

Contents

Acknowledgments

We would like to take the opportunity to thank a number of people who have helped us with this project. First, great thanks are due to Samantha Whittaker, our publisher at John Wiley, for her enthusiastic support of the project at the outset and her ongoing support throughout the process. Thanks are also due to Carole Millett, editorial assistant, Samantha Hartley, Production Editor, and to the John Wiley marketing and production teams.

Various finance professionals were kind enough to read through drafts of this book and give us useful feedback. We are grateful to Martin Loat, Lisa Polsky, Pascal Scemama, Steve Schulman and Phil Tazza for their helpful comments, criticisms and suggestions for improvements. We would also like to acknowledge Chris Hayward's efforts in developing the initial concepts behind the maximum loss framework discussed in the book. Thanks are also due to many others at Merrill Lynch who gave us support and opportunities over many years.

Last, but certainly not least, we would like to thank Milena and Sabrina for their patience and support during the writing of this book!

We are always eager to receive suggestions or queries from our readers. You may correspond with us at practicalrisk@netscape.net.

E. Banks and R. Dunn
December 2002

Biographies

Erik Banks has held senior risk management positions at several global financial institutions, including XL Capital, where he was Partner and Chief Risk Officer of the Bermuda reinsurer's derivative subsidiary, and Merrill Lynch, where he spent 13 years managing credit and market risk teams in Tokyo, Hong Kong, London and New York. Mr. Banks, an Adjunct Professor of Finance at the University of Connecticut, has written various books on risk management, emerging markets, derivatives, merchant banking, and electronic finance.

Richard Dunn became the youngest member of Merrill Lynch's Executive Committee in 1998. Concurrent with this appointment he was made Head of Market and Credit Risk and was instrumental in the Wall Street "bail out" of LTCM. Prior to this Mr. Dunn was Co-Head of Merrill's Equity Division, Head of European Debt, and Head of Asian Debt and Equity. His training was in debt and equity derivatives. Mr. Dunn holds a Masters in Economics from the London School of Economics, speaks Japanese, French and Italian, and is an avid snowboarder.

Introduction: Financial Risks and Avalanches

Since 1990 financial risks have wiped out tens of billions of dollars of shareholder savings, forced several major companies into bankruptcy and thrown tens of thousands of families into disarray through job losses. This is our collective scorecard on managing financial risk.

We can do better.

So whom do we hold accountable for this?

The people we have entrusted with our money. We must also not forget those we have entrusted with overseeing them.

How do we know that these individuals are truly qualified and aware of their responsibilities, and what questions can we ask to make sure they are?

If you are a board director, CEO, CFO, chairman, president, senior manager, senior regulator, partner in an accounting firm or senior employee in a rating agency, you have a significant accountability to shareholders. Among other things, you must know enough about financial risk to make the right decisions. But do you feel that you are properly equipped to deal with the subject?

These questions were the genesis of this book. They came to us while snowboarding down mountains in the Himalayas. Was it the threat of avalanches, those "once in a blue moon" events that are likely to kill? Was it that we were entrusting our lives to a guide? It must have felt suspiciously similar to the way shareholders feel about entrusting their capital for you to manage in the dangerous corporate terrain. Did you know that avalanches are most likely to occur on slopes with gradients of 35 to 42 degrees? There exists a whole body of avalanche science and formal avalanche expert accreditation. The best guides spend a lifetime learning about snow formation, mountain terrain and weather conditions in order to travel safely.

So where is the science on financial market avalanches? Do we understand why they occur? Is there an accreditation system or formal training for those held accountable?

Well, there is no credible accreditation system. There are journalistic books about some of the better known financial disasters. There is a fabulous body of work detailing the various financial products and their accompanying mathematical formulas. And the more enlightened universities have been featuring financial product seminars for the past 15 years. But that is all. So where do you turn to if the books are too complex and detailed, past disasters are rehashed in a sensationalist manner by journalists who were not in the midst of them and you cannot dedicate the time to go back to school?

We recently decided to take some time off. We have both spent our careers managing business and financial risk for the shareholders of large financial organizations. During almost two decades the technology of creating and managing complex risk has exploded and we have both had a lot of fun being part of some of the most creative developments that the financial markets have ever seen. It is now time to give something back.

Driven by the fear of avalanches and the lack of "mountain guides", we set our sights on writing a book to help senior managers, board members, regulators, accountants and institutional shareholders better understand and manage financial risk. We start by analyzing a few recent financial disasters we observed first-hand. From these we develop a basic definition of financial risk and analyze the measurement techniques currently available. In the second part of the book we use these tools to develop a framework of risk control for an institution.

The book is based on our experience working in large and complex financial groups. However, it remains equally relevant for investment funds, smaller companies and non-financial organizations. It is also relevant for those operating in different parts of the world – financial risks have no boundaries. We hope that it stimulates ideas for the reader and provides a basis for dialogue around a better understanding of financial disasters, better governance and transparency of risk, better awareness of roles and responsibilities. Above all we hope that it prevents a few financial avalanches.

Happy snowboarding!

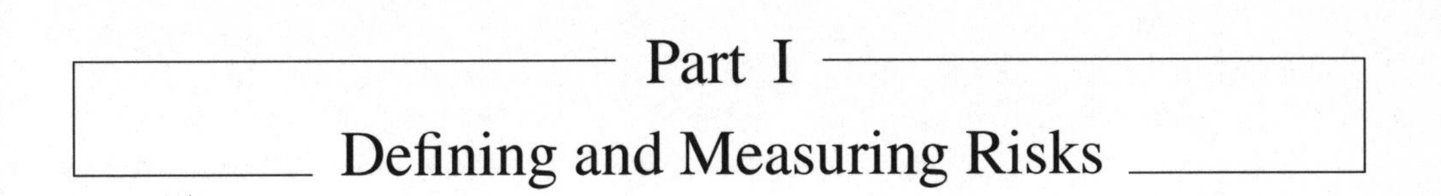

Part I

Defining and Measuring Risks

1 Losses: One-Hundred-Year Floods that Happen Every Three Years

In early 1995 people were glued to their television sets watching the aftermath of a very large earthquake in the city of Kobe in western Japan. Little did they suspect the deep-seated implications of this event on the financial markets in general, and on the Bank of England in particular. The earthquake caused a major sell-off in the already weakened Japanese stock market. As a result Baring Brothers, the venerable British merchant bank, lost such a large (and at the time unquantifiable) amount of money that it had to be sold to a Dutch bank for a symbolic £1. In late September 1998 the financial world looked on the verge of a serious precipice: the Russian government had defaulted on its rouble-denominated debt, Long Term Capital Management (LTCM), a hedge fund, was being bailed out by Wall Street, and financial stocks had lost half of their market value. Alan Greenspan, Chairman of the US Federal Reserve Board, noted that "[t]he most virulent phase of the crisis has infected our [U.S.] markets as well. Concerns about business profits and a general pulling back from risk taking in the midst of great uncertainty around the globe have driven down stock prices and pushed up rates on the bonds of lower-rated borrowers. Flows of funds through financial markets have been disrupted."[1] In the aftermath of this international crisis many major financial institutions were forced to disclose very large losses and lay off hundreds, even thousands, of workers. Early in 2002 Ireland's largest bank, Allied Irish Bank (AIB), announced that a trader in its Baltimore-based subsidiary had lost $691 million – or 16% of AIB's capital base. After significant regulatory scrutiny the bank was compelled to overhaul its management structure and re-examine all of its control processes. In late 2002 Natexis, the investment bank of Banques Populaires in France, declared that it had experienced "heavy" losses from derivatives trading.

During such events many people lose their jobs. Apart from the executives involved, innocent employees and their families are often affected. The reputation of the financial system is temporarily impaired as the general public, media and politicians call into question its stability and governance. The primary role of the financial system is to recycle money by borrowing and lending, or by introducing borrowers and investors. As soon as confidence in the system is questioned, the risk premium charged for these activities increases. These "hundred-year floods" therefore ultimately lead to an increased cost of capital. Someone pays for this. If it is not the shareholders of financial stocks it has to be the borrowers or investors, the pension funds, companies, governments and, ultimately, the consumer.

To understand the dynamics at work, it is useful to analyze a few of these incidents in more detail.

[1] Testimony before the US Senate, September 23, 1998.

1.1 BARINGS: FLAWED CONTROLS

Barings was a venerable British merchant bank with an aggressive and well-respected futures business. During the early 1990s, Nick Leeson, a Barings settlement specialist working in London, was transferred to the bank's Singapore office to oversee settlements in Asia. After a short while he was given the additional job of running the bank's futures brokerage. He soon made his mark by establishing a strong presence on the floor of the Singapore International Monetary Exchange (SIMEX, now part of the Singapore Exchange) and reporting strong profits. In fact, Leeson was so successful that he ended up as a "poster child" for both Barings and SIMEX management, featuring on the cover of the Exchange's annual report.

A futures broker uses its exchange membership to accept customer orders and execute them on the exchange. The customer gets charged a brokerage fee and posts margin money or securities against positions on the exchange. The broker monitors these positions as markets move and makes calls for, or returns, margin accordingly. Exchange margin requirements are fairly conservative, enabling the exchange to ride safely through most crises. Properly run, the futures brokerage business may not carry high profit margins but should be fairly low risk. Occasionally a clerk makes a mistake in executing a customer order or a customer disputes a trade. Client disputes normally get resolved promptly. Clerical errors can result in a position being held by the broker, but there are usually strict rules and these, too, get closed immediately. Starting in late 1992, Leeson ended up with such error positions in the Japanese Nikkei stock index. Instead of closing them out immediately, he maintained them in an unauthorized, off-system "error account" (the famous "88888" account) in which he would trade these positions in order to try and make back losses. This is usually a losing strategy. Indeed, Leeson's position, and associated losses, grew consistently: by the end of 1993 he had lost £24 million; by September 1994 the figure had grown to £56 million and continued escalating into early 1995 as he increased his unauthorized bets in the hope of again making up losses.

As a result of his good internal credentials Leeson managed to obtain cash from head office to fund the SIMEX margins on his unauthorized positions. Through the latter part of 1994 he secured £144 million of funding for margin, and between January and February 1995 a further £750 million (equal to 1.7 times Barings' total capital) – all without a proper reconciliation of positions by head office or local controllers. Eventually, however, the positions, losses and margin calls became too large to disguise. In early 1995, as a last ditch attempt to conceal his activities, Leeson sold a vast amount of **straddles**[2] (put and call options with the same strike price) to raise money and alleviate the margin funding pressure; this strategy of selling straddles creates a liability to the seller and demands a very tranquil market in order not to lose money. Unfortunately, on January 17, 1995, an earthquake measuring 7.2 on the Richter scale struck the city of Kobe. This severely rocked the Japanese stock market, and destroyed Leeson's last attempt at salvaging his position. As markets tumbled and volatility spiked in the week following Kobe, Leeson's straddles lost £69 million; several weeks later another steep drop in the Nikkei (and a rally in Japanese government bonds, where Leeson also held positions) created an additional £144 million loss – at that point he fled to Malaysia and was eventually arrested in Frankfurt. In the meantime, Barings had lost all credibility in the financial markets and could not survive independently.

A sale of the company was arranged under the watch of the Bank of England without anyone being able to ascertain the potential liability of the positions held in the fictitious

[2] Terms in **bold** are further referenced in the glossary appearing at the end of the book.

"88888" customer account. Several bank consortia tried to grapple with the extent of Barings' potential liabilities but were unable to get comfortable and refused to fund the institution as a going concern – particularly as the Bank of England was unwilling to step in and cap the bank's liabilities. ING ultimately gained exclusive rights to bid on Barings and was able to quantify certain downside scenarios; following its analysis it bid £1 to assume all outstanding liabilities, and was awarded control. Once the dust settled the extent of the damage, and the value of Barings, became clearer: Barings' capital of £440 million was depleted by £860 million of losses, creating negative net worth of £420 million. ING injected an additional £240 million, valuing their acquisition at £660 million.

In the aftermath, it became very clear that controls, governance and management oversight had failed: Leeson had full authority over front- and back-office functions and could create financial fiction; the financial control, treasury and risk functions never queried Leeson's demands for margin or the source of Leeson's impressive profits – reported gains of nearly £55 million over two and a half years. These should have set off alarm bells, as such returns may have been well in excess of what could have been achieved in this "low"-risk futures execution business in Singapore. Local and product management also never assumed direct responsibility for understanding the nature of Leeson's activities – as long as he was profitable, he was left to his own devices. This was a classic misjudgement – one that occurs time and time again.

1.2 LONG TERM CAPITAL MANAGEMENT: TOO MUCH LEVERAGE, TOO LITTLE LIQUIDITY

Long Term Capital Management (LTCM) was the outgrowth of the proprietary arbitrage trading desk at Salomon Brothers, the US investment bank that now forms part of Citigroup. After the US trading bond scandal of 1991 (where certain Salomon traders bid for too much of a Treasury securities issue, in contravention of established rules), John Meriwether, the Vice-Chairman of Salomon who also headed the arbitrage unit, left the firm. Many ex-colleagues, as well as Nobel laureates Robert Merton and Myron Scholes, soon joined him. Together they raised money from investors to continue their trading strategies within the confines of a fund; many of these early strategies sought to take advantage of small discrepancies between financial asset prices – discrepancies that the team believed would ultimately "revert" to certain historical levels. By 1994 they had $7 billion of capital and by 1997 investors in LTCM had enjoyed amazing returns on their initial investments, including 43% in 1995 and 41% in 1996, and a still respectable 17% in 1997.

With good performance comes the headache of having to manage more money as profits are reinvested. In order to maintain a good track record a fund manager has to generate at least equal appreciation on this ever-growing pool of money – therefore the more successful a fund is the more successful it needs to be. At some point though most investment strategies can no longer absorb a greater allocation of money and provide the same returns without assuming more risk. Indeed, the more money LTCM made the more it was facing an uphill battle to sustain the returns to which investors had become accustomed. By 1996 the fund was therefore, not surprisingly, closed to new investors. At the same time as LTCM was proving to be a success, many banks and investors were also allocating increasing amounts of capital to similar trading strategies managed by others. There was now a lot of money chasing after similar investment ideas. LTCM was no longer alone.

Through its own success LTCM was managing more and more money. Yet the market place was becoming more competitive and returns on the partners' traditional investment expertise were shrinking. Its ability to produce the same performance for equal amounts of risk was declining. Realizing this, LTCM decided that it was in the best interests of its investors to return some of their capital. In 1997 LTCM returned $2.7 billion to investors, representing an average annual return on capital of 33.5% from inception. But in returning the capital, risk positions were not lowered, causing leverage in the fund to increase dramatically and ultimately exacerbating the liquidity problems that followed. In addition traders at the fund continued the search for new ways to provide attractive returns. The predominantly fixed income specialists at LTCM turned their attention to investment ideas in the equity markets with which they were arguably less familiar. When a fund starts to deviate from its original investment expertise we refer to this as **style drift**.

We digress momentarily to discuss the risk complexities and characteristics that define funds such as LTCM – this helps us illustrate several key points on the topics of leverage, liquidity and risk. The fund managed by LTCM is commonly known as a hedge fund, a fund that can buy, sell and borrow a broad range of securities. The main difference between hedge funds and traditional equity or bond mutual funds or unit trusts is the ability to pledge their investor funds to borrow more money, borrow securities or create contractual arrangements – each of which can allow the fund to manage more than its original capital. For example the fund could buy stock in IBM, pledge its IBM shares to a lender in exchange for borrowed money and purchase another 50% of IBM shares. The fund now owns 150% of its original investment in IBM stock. As the price of IBM rises and falls it will gain or lose around 50% more than if it had only bought the first lot of IBM stock. These techniques create **leverage** on the fund's capital and alter the return profile. Investment strategies used by hedge funds can be more complex, nonetheless it is easy to picture how they can end up managing several multiples of their capital.

As portfolios become complex with a multitude of investment strategies, multiple financial instruments across several markets and in different currencies, the notion of a total amount invested by a fund manager becomes hard to relate to in simple terms. Returning to the example above, the fund manager is bullish on IBM shares but also happens to believe that the yen is going to weaken against the dollar over the next three months. Instead of purchasing more IBM shares with the money borrowed she decides to enter into a contractual obligation in which she agrees in three months' time to deliver yen in exchange for receiving dollars at a conversion rate set today. In order to back up her obligation under this foreign exchange contract her counterparty requires the creation of a lien on money in the fund. The amount is agreed at all times to be sufficient to pay the obligations under the contract in the eventuality of a premature exchange of the specified yen and dollars. In addition the counterparty has requested a cushion of 1% of the dollars to be exchanged. The fund's investments now amount to 100% of its capital in IBM stock, which in turn has been pledged to a lender in exchange for borrowed money and a contract to deliver in three months' time agreed amounts of yen in exchange for dollars, against which some or all of its borrowed money has been pledged.

So how should one measure risk in this portfolio? The various elements cannot easily be added. Adding, for example, the amount of IBM stock to the notional amount of dollars to be received under the foreign exchange contract, and subtracting the money that is borrowed and the yen due, is meaningless and certainly not representative of the actual risk carried by the fund. A better way to understand the portfolio is to analyze what happens under various scenarios. As the price of IBM and the yen/dollar rate change on a daily basis the fund has commitments to live up to. If IBM falls the lender requires part of its loan to be reimbursed in order to maintain a constant ratio of loan to value of IBM stock. As the yen strengthens the foreign exchange contract obliges more money to be pledged. If both scenarios happen together the fund has to simultaneously repay loans and pledge more money. If there is no money left in the fund and it cannot borrow more, the only course of action would be to sell IBM shares. Simulating the behavior of a portfolio in such a manner is referred to as **scenario** analysis. It provides one possible measure of risk for this portfolio and the obligations that may be created *relative* to an ability to raise money to satisfy them. The ability to raise money will in turn be determined by the type of, and market for, the investments held as well as access to funding – a concept that we shall refer to as liquidity, in essence a mini balance sheet of risk! This is where financial management becomes an art rather than a science. Nonetheless, the reader should be able to sense that there is an optimal amount of risk above which a fund manager is inappropriately managing investor funds given its liquidity profile. The art is really in the measures of risk and liquidity. Perfecting this art is critical for CEOs, government officials, regulators, fund managers, investors and lenders.

Returning to our review of LTCM, though the fund had some of the most sophisticated analytics and arguably some of the smartest people in the financial industry, it critically misjudged the risk relative to the liquidity of its investment strategy. The fund held a few very large positions – such as **swap spreads** (the yield difference between a risky credit and a risk-free benchmark), **equity volatility** (the relative level of turbulence in an equity market) and stocks – the liquidity characteristics of which were not properly understood. The time horizon over which it could raise money via the sale of part or all of each of these positions was poorly judged, especially for investments held in the equity markets. In addition, the degree to which these varied positions would all behave in a similar fashion was critically underestimated. Under times of stress, historically quite diverse strategies in a portfolio can sometimes all behave in the same way – **correlations**, or the price relationships that exist between assets, can change dramatically when markets start panicking. For example, when stock markets crash investors often sell everything they own: the good and the bad, the baby and the bath water. Several of the supposedly unconnected LTCM trading strategies simultaneously created the need to repay loans, raise money and pledge more assets. The inability to raise money or free up assets to pledge in line with its growing obligations was the demise of LTCM. It was running too much risk relative to its liquidity profile. We discuss the important topic of liquidity risk at greater length in Chapter 3. It must be added that in addition some market professionals generally knew the LTCM strategies and the size of their investments. Once news of their troubles spread these positions were pushed around by traders in a massive game of Wall Street poker, further exacerbating LTCM's problems.

LTCM was not the only culprit in this debacle. Lenders also need to concern themselves with the risk of a fund's investment strategies relative to its liquidity profile. As described earlier, lending to a fund is typically effected via the fund giving a lien on a specific amount of money, several specific securities or contractual obligations. In the event of default, the lender relies on the ability to collect on the pledged asset(s) to repay a loan. By the time a sale can be arranged the instrument may be worth less than the loan. Lenders therefore typically demand a cushion that is referred to as the **haircut** on the loan. The amount requested will vary according to the liquidity of the pledged instrument as well as the type of loan. With a sufficient haircut the lender can normally feel comfortable. However, other lenders may have taken the same or similar instruments in pledge, making the aggregate haircut for all lenders to a single fund potentially insufficient. Funds rarely divulge information about their holdings for fear that other professional investors will use the information. Lenders are thus only aware of the sliver of the portfolio they have lent against and some general risk and net asset value statistics. They are blind as to the contracts that others have entered into with the fund, even though this critically affects their risk profile. Lending to hedge funds is therefore another big game of financial poker. Returning to LTCM, many of the top lenders found themselves holding the same pledges. Some further exacerbated the problem by taking insufficient haircuts on their specific loans in the interest of doing more business with the traders at LTCM. The latter, it must be said, were masterful in the art of playing lenders off against one another in exchange for business. This further encouraged an overleveraging of the portfolio and led to lenders panicking when news of problems surfaced.

With style drift, a misjudgement of risk relative to liquidity, lenders with insufficient collateral, competing traders sniffing blood in a market place which was reeling from events in South East Asia and Russia and a fall out in global credit markets, the ensuing LTCM debacle today seems quite explainable.

1.3 MERRILL LYNCH: TOO MUCH RISK, NOT ENOUGH GOVERNANCE

Merrill Lynch took the lead in arranging the Wall Street bail out of LTCM. But it was not without many problems of its own. By the end of 1998 the company had absorbed losses in excess of 10% of its capital base. Merrill Lynch, having its origins in the provision of brokerage services to "retail" customers, prided itself on being a client-driven firm. In the minds of much of senior management, originating from the retail brokerage side of the business, Merrill Lynch was not a large risk taker. They did not, therefore, have to spend too much time on this complex topic.

Merrill Lynch consists of three main business lines: wealth management and advice for individuals, an asset management business and a capital markets unit centered on private and public institutions. The business for private clients typically carries small amounts of market or credit risk. Margin loans are healthily backed by stock positions, a small book of working capital loans is adequately secured by plant and equipment resale values, and a small book of real-estate loans to clients is secured by real estate and other investments pledged to Merrill Lynch. A couple of exceptions fell foul of these strict rules, but the clients in question were very well known to the highest echelons of senior management. The asset management business at Merrill Lynch was essentially built on the ability to sell US mutual funds through the 15 000 brokers. Since the money that was entrusted belonged to clients, management did not concern itself with the underlying client market or credit risk. This perception did not change materially with the 1997 acquisition of Mercury Asset Management, the dominant UK asset manager.

On the capital markets side there are three businesses: equity markets, debt markets and advisory. Until the acquisition of Smith New Court in 1995, Merrill Lynch would seldom end a day with substantial secondary equity positions, such was the flow throughput at the largest US broker! Growth in the convertible bond universe and the addition of Smith New Court with its dominant presence in the UK and South East Asia altered this, but risk taken remained relatively small and very disciplined. It was only in the mid-1990s that Merrill started becoming a more active risk taker in equity derivatives, selling equity option products to institutional and retail clients and thereby exposing itself to increased market turbulence (as in 1997 and 1998). In underwriting new equity issues the company would sometimes be left with unsaleable product. This would, however, quickly gain the attention of senior management, hourly phone calls would be the norm and the position would usually be disposed of fairly shortly. The advisory business, being primarily selling advice on mergers or acquisitions, would not in itself create any residual risk positions, though it would lead to transactions being executed in the debt or equity divisions. (The exception to this were tax-motivated transactions that Merrill Lynch constructed for clients – many of which were subsequently successfully challenged in the courts by the US Internal Revenue Service.)

The debt business at Merrill Lynch had started out predominantly offering private clients tax-advantaged municipal bonds and certificates of deposit to enhance the yield on their short-term fixed income investments. By 1990 Merrill Lynch had taken on the institutional debt leaders such as First Boston and Salomon Brothers to create what was to become the dominant debt house for the next decade. The leaders of this division were very talented and charismatic – with very loyal employees to boot. The debt business had grown to encompass derivatives, underwriting and trading of government, corporate, municipal, mortgage and asset-backed obligations as well as foreign exchange. Debt profitability and its presence outside the US had grown faster than in the equity division. It also carried increasing amounts of risk. The division had become fairly autonomous and was proud of this. For five years starting in 1992 senior management began a concerted effort to rein it in. This resulted in the departure of the two most critical leaders. Management of the division was eventually entrusted to a co-head structure of two individuals who often found it difficult to see eye to eye. Absent the charismatic senior executives, knowledge of debt markets at the executive level declined at a time of increased product complexity and client enquiry. Senior executives found it easier to spend time on the private client business, the latest equity underwriting, the league tables or the merger of the moment.

Times had been good at Merrill Lynch. The general decline in interest rates in 1993 had brought in bumper profits: most players, including Merrill, had correctly anticipated the lowering of interest rates by the central banks and decided to fund long-term assets with short-term borrowings – locking in nice profits. Though 1994 was a tough year for the financial industry with rising interest rates, derivative blow-ups and emerging market dislocations, the firm continued to do well. Merrill's presence in Latin America was too small for the Mexican crisis to severely affect its results and it managed, at least for a time, to avoid any of the derivative mishaps that impacted some of its peers. Annual after-tax earnings were increasingly rapidly: from $1.1 billion in 1995, to $1.6 billion in 1996 and $1.9 billion in 1997 – all representing better than 20% returns on equity. (When times are good, we all have a tendency to go home feeling good, overestimating our contribution to these good results and forgetting to ask the tough questions needed to truly understand what is driving the numbers.) Each record year ended with managers at Merrill Lynch being handed down ever-increasing budgetary targets. In response to this, the fixed income and equity traders were running greater risk, particularly in credit, emerging and derivatives markets. Traders of credit and emerging market instruments were carrying more and higher yielding positions on their books. The signs of the build up of these risks were visible. Assets on Merrill Lynch's balance sheet had grown to accommodate this risk as had the use of off-balance sheet vehicles. To fund part of this growth, issuance of debt instruments increased dramatically, in particular, commercial paper (CP). In 1997 Merrill Lynch was the second largest issuer of CP after General Electric, with $34.3 billion of outstandings. Much of the increased profitability was thus driven by good markets and increased credit exposures, generating increased interest income over Merrill Lynch's cost of funds. Indeed, some of Merrill Lynch's debt activities centered on taking advantage of the spread between its public debt ratings and this portfolio of lesser credit securities. In many ways Merrill Lynch had started to resemble a hedge fund!

Aware of this increased risk profile, the co-heads of the fixed income division made a presentation to senior management exposing the nature and magnitude of their high yield and emerging market positions. A fairly elaborate study was laid out estimating how much money could be lost or made under various scenarios. It included an unlikely scenario under which over a billion dollars would be lost if the credit and emerging markets imploded. The presentation did not advocate any action but was designed to ensure knowledge of these exposures reached the top of the organization. This study did not result in any material reduction in financial risk.

Several months later, the unlikely events portrayed in the presentation had become reality and the losses were in line with the study. In addition, Merrill Lynch was under public scrutiny for its dealings with LTCM. Senior management pulled the trigger on an emergency plan to quickly raise money and reduce exposures. Fixed income trading and corporate risk management personnel were dismissed, over 3000 people were fired, risk taking in credit instruments at Merrill Lynch was curtailed and the risk process entirely redesigned. At the time of writing Merrill Lynch borrows less than $6 billion in the CP market, features a new risk control process and a much stronger governance structure, including an explicit risk mandate and regular reporting to senior executives. But the changes came at a high price: shareholders lost in excess of 10% of the capital base between 1997 and 1998, the firm's reputation had been damaged and employee morale severely affected.

1.4 FAILURES IN THE RISK PROCESS

The incidences of Barings, LTCM and Merrill Lynch are not, unfortunately, unique. There are many other examples of failures in the risk process we can draw on: the sale of risk products that was instrumental in the eventual downfall of Bankers Trust (and its subsequent sale to Deutsche Bank in 1999); the nearly $1 billion of equity derivative losses[3] and $680 million in LTCM-related losses that cost the CEO of UBS his job in late 1998; the unauthorized foreign exchange trading that caused AIB's US subsidiary to lose $691 million; the lack of separation between front- and back-office duties that led to losses of $1 billion at Daiwa Bank and $2.5 billion at Sumitomo Corporation; the thousands of small, but ultimately costly, operational risk errors that caused major financial institutions to lose an estimated $7 billion (and probably much more) in 1998–1999,[4] and so on.

What is amazing about these events is not only the speed and ferocity with which they occur, but the fact that these supposed "hundred-year floods" seem to occur every two or three years. We need only consider the examples in Table 1.1, which highlight severe market dislocations over the past 15 years.

Taking this down to the company level, Table 1.2 highlights a small sampling of known significant losses that have occurred within sectors or institutions over the same period.

Since "hundred-year floods" are not actually meant to happen every few years, other forces were, and are, at work. Closer examination suggests either that an exogenous event sparks off a crisis that one or many institutions are ill equipped to handle or that some institutions simply trip over themselves. In any event a breakdown in risk control processes is typically at the heart of the resulting problem. As we have explored through the analysis of the three

[3] Including approximately $440 million of losses booked in 1997 (which played a part in the sale of the bank to smaller rival Swiss Bank Corporation), along with $540 million of losses recognized as part of the post-merger "clean up".

[4] Results of a 110-institution survey conducted by PriceWaterhouse Coopers ("Operational Risk: The New Frontier").

Table 1.1 Severe market dislocations

Year	Market dislocation
1986/9	Latin debt crisis
1987	Global stock market crash
1989/91	US savings and loan crisis
1990	Junk bond crash
1992	European currency crisis
1994/5	Mexican peso crisis, US interest rate spike
1995	Latin currency crisis
1997	Asian currency crisis
1998	Russian default, hedge fund crisis, credit crunch
2001/2	Technology, media, telecom stock market plunge

Table 1.2 Individual institution losses

Entity	Loss
UK Local Authority Swaps (1986–1988)	$750 million swap losses
Prudential Securities (1980s–1990s)	$1 billion+ limited partnership lawsuit losses
Drexel Burnham Lambert (1990)	Varied counterparty losses
Allied Lyons (1991)	$225 million FX options loss
Showa Shell Seikyu (1993)	$1.2 billion forward foreign exchange loss
Procter and Gamble (1994)	$195 million leveraged interest rate product loss
Codelco (1994)	$200 million copper futures loss
Askin Capital (1994)	$600 million mortgage derivative/financing loss
Air Products and Chemicals (1994)	$113 million interest rate/currency derivative loss
Metallgesellschaft (1994)	$1.3 billion oil futures loss
Kashima Oil (1994)	$1.5 billion currency derivative loss
Orange County (1994)	$1.8 billion leveraged interest rate product loss
Glaxo (1994)	$190 million asset-backed/derivative loss
Chemical Bank (1994)	$70 million currency derivative loss
Kidder Peabody (1994)	$350 million "phantom" US Treasury trading loss
Capital Corporate Federal Credit Union (1995)	$126 million mortgage derivative loss
Barings (1995)	$1.2 billion index and interest rate futures loss
Daiwa Bank (1995)	$1.1 billion bond trading loss
Wisconsin Investment Board (1995)	$95 million currency/interest rate derivative loss
Postipankki (1995)	$110 million mortgage derivative loss
Deutsche Bank Investment Management (1996)	$710 million unregistered securities loss
Sumitomo Corporation (1996)	$2.5 billion copper futures loss
National Westminster Bank (1997)	$144 million interest rate derivative mispricing loss
Long Term Capital Management (1998)	Varied market losses
Major international banks (1997/8)	Very large market losses
Allied Irish Bank/Allfirst (2002)	$691 million foreign exchange loss
Natexis (2002)	"Heavy" derivative trading losses

Source: Adapted from Banks (2002).

sample events earlier in this chapter, such a breakdown can usually be traced to:

- *Poor senior management decision making* in relationships to risk issues.
- *Lack of risk governance* within the organization, including absence of senior management involvement and accountability.
- *Unclear risk appetite* and a lack of discipline in defining risk as a limited resource within the corporate finance attributes and strategy of a company.

- *Inadequate liquidity management*, including lack of focus on risk relative to liquidity.
- *Insufficient checks and balances* around risk, profit and loss and business process.
- *Avoidance of common sense solutions* in favor of "automated risk management techniques".
- *Flawed risk infrastructure*, including weak risk data, processing and reporting mechanisms.

With Barings there were poor senior management decisions, flawed corporate governance, lack of segregation between front- and back-office functions, inadequate checks and balances and a weak control infrastructure. With LTCM there were poor decisions and a lack of risk discipline and liquidity management – especially as the fund ventured into new investment territory. There was also a failure to understand concentration and liquidity risks and an unwillingness to override some of the sophisticated analytical infrastructure with common sense. Those that lent to LTCM were plagued by insufficient understanding of the risks, a lack of checks and balances when it came to risk versus reward in dealing with the fund, and inadequate infrastructure that prevented accurate computation of daily exposure across complex and multi-product dealings. With Merrill Lynch there was a breakdown in governance and insufficient appreciation of risk at senior levels. These led to poor, or no, management decisions, lack of a firmly defined risk appetite and tolerance for risk relative to liquidity (within the confines of firm strategy), and a lack of checks and balances. The company was also burdened with many manual risk data processes and relied too heavily on statistically computed results.

We will explore these themes, summarized in Figure 1.1, at greater length in the balance of the book. The one-hundred-year floods seem to reoccur not only with eerie regularity, but also with surprising similarity. Fixing these flaws will undoubtedly help stem the financial damage that comes with each new crisis.

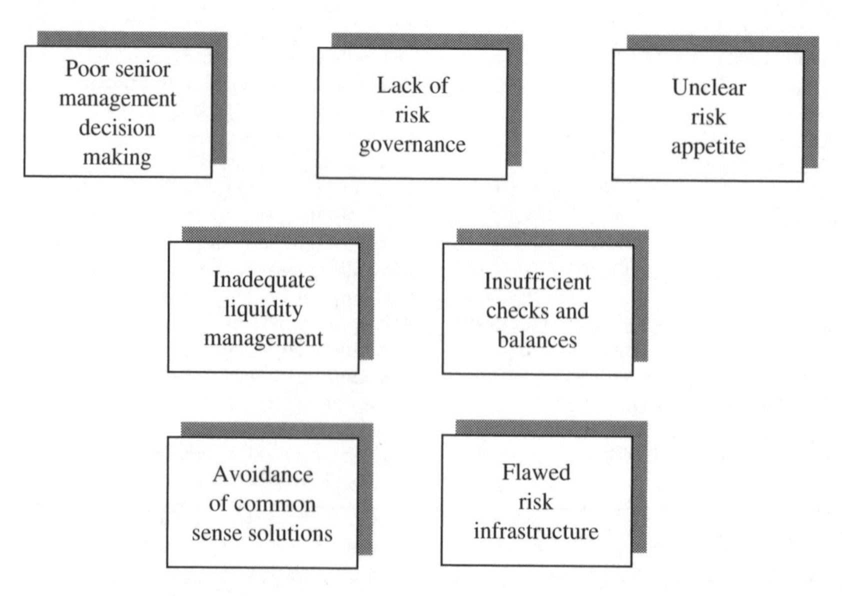

Figure 1.1 Breakdowns in the risk process

2
The Basics: A Common Understanding of the Risks

A financial or corporate institution is exposed to a broad range of risks: risk of its business model being wrong, risk of margin erosion, risk of customers not turning up to buy their products, and so on – these "operating risks", as we refer to them, have a direct and continuous impact on earnings. In the same vein, a company might lose money in its pension fund, fail to hedge its foreign exchange liabilities appropriately, make bad loans, have customers default on receivables or have a trader lose a lot of money – we refer to these as "balance sheet risks", since they are discreet events which in essence affect book value equity immediately and directly. While operating risks are obviously important, the focus of this book is on the universe of balance sheet risks that includes *market risk*, *credit risk*, *liquidity risk*, *model risk*, *suitability risk*, *process risk* and *legal risk*; Figure 2.1 summarizes this "risk universe".

We know that these risks can be damaging if not properly recognized and managed. A firm must therefore spend the time and effort to understand the risks to which it is exposed. Executive management and the various governance bodies, in particular, must know what these risks are, what they mean to the organization, and how and when they might appear, before being able to take action. In so doing it is also important for a firm's executives to remove themselves from what seems to be reality and think of the unthinkable. To help in this task a common understanding of each category of risk is critical in any organization – it allows managers, risk takers and control officers to discuss the issues in common terms and naturally creates greater transparency around the various risk exposures. Risk in itself is not "bad", and need not necessarily be eliminated or avoided at all cost – properly managed risk-taking can benefit some firms by providing attractive returns. Before this can happen, though, decision makers must understand their risks.

2.1 MARKET RISK

Market risk is the risk of loss due to an adverse move in the market value of an asset – a stock, a bond, a loan, foreign exchange or a commodity – or a **derivative** contract linked to these assets. The market value of this contract will depend on many things, including the price of the reference asset, its volatility, prevailing interest rates and time. Intuitively, it makes sense that a change in any of these will cause a corresponding change in the value of the contract – favorable changes generating profits, unfavorable changes losses. Some of the most common types of market risks include directional risk, volatility risk, curve risk, time decay risk, spread risk, basis risk and correlation risk; these are highlighted in Figure 2.2.

Directional risk is the risk of loss due to an adverse move in the direction of the underlying reference asset. Changes in market direction happen because supply and demand forces are constantly at work – bargains struck between buyers and sellers set asset prices. These move both up and down and are used as reference points for valuing many outstanding assets.

Since directional risk appears in most common financial instruments we digress briefly to discuss a few key concepts (and introduce a small amount of unfortunately unavoidable

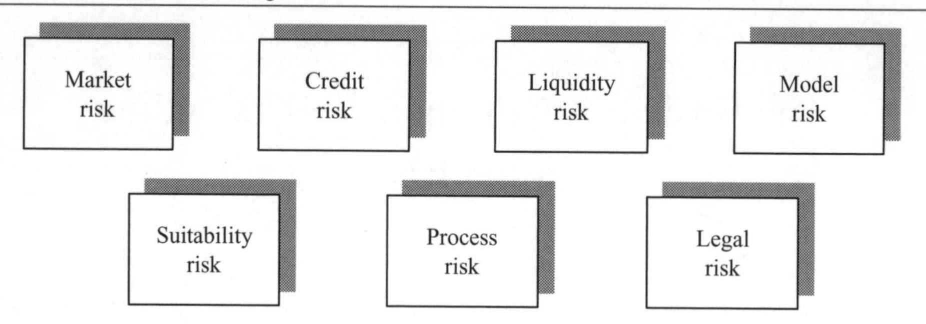

Figure 2.1 Universe of balance sheet risks

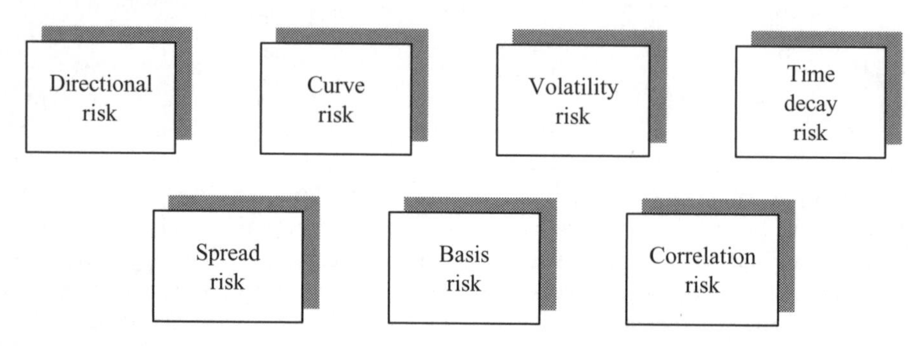

Figure 2.2 Market risks

technical jargon!). Some asset prices move in tandem with the latest bargain struck between buyers and sellers. Others move differently. Assets that are the same as those in the latest bargain price obviously move accordingly – the value of your IBM stock moves up and down with the latest price on the New York Stock Exchange! We refer to these as "cash" or "spot" assets or positions. Financial instruments or contracts that mimic their movement (such as a futures contract or a forward contract) are considered **linear**, i.e. a small increase in the market leads to the same small increase in the value of a long position, while a large increase in the market leads to the same large increase in the value of a **long position**. The opposite is true for a short position: if the price of IBM rises by 1, the contract value falls by 1 and if it falls by 10, the contract value rises by 10.

Contracts that are **non-linear** behave differently: while a small increase in the market leads to the same small increase in the value of a long cash position, a large market increase leads to an even larger increase in the value of the long **call option** position. Now a 10 point market increase could lead to an 11 point contract value increase, a 20 point market increase could lead to a 24 point contract value increase, and so on. The rate at which the contract value changes relative to the reference asset is known as the **delta** and is an important measure of directional risk. Thus, if a contract has a delta of 0.5, a unit change in the market creates a 0.5 change in the contract. The rate at which delta changes is known as the **gamma** and is a reflection of the non-linearity of the contract – the greater the gamma, the greater the non-linearity, the greater the change in contract value for some large market change. The distinction between delta and gamma is important when dealing with directional risk, as large market moves can create ever-increasing gains or losses. This is critical, for example, when a firm sells options (e.g. a **short** gamma position) – very sharp and sudden market moves can create large losses before positions can be re-hedged. For instance, if a firm owns 100 barrels of crude oil at $20 per barrel, the value of the oil position is $2000: if the price falls to $19, a directional move of $1, the value of the oil is $1900 – a directional risk loss of $100; if the price falls $5, the directional risk loss is $500. But if the position is based on options, the $5 fall might create an $800 loss as a result of gamma.

A single large option position (or many small positions with the same strike price and maturity) that is trading very near its **strike price** as expiration draws near is susceptible to a kind of directional risk known as **pin risk** – the risk that a small move above or below the strike will change the value of the position and leave the buyer or seller with an unwanted position that needs to be liquidated. For instance, if a bank sells a call option it might hedge its risk by purchasing shares (e.g. as the liability on the short call increases with a rising stock price, the value of the shares it owns increases in tandem, offsetting the loss if purchased in the right amount). As expiry draws near and the market price trades near the strike price, the bank faces two scenarios: if the option ends just in-the-money, the buyer exercises the call and the bank delivers the shares (as expected). If it ends just out-of-the-money, the bank ends with shares that it will have to sell. If the position is reasonable in size the bank has directional market risk – before it can actually sell the shares it will be exposed to a change in the direction of the stock, which might create unanticipated and unwanted gains or losses. If the position is very large, the bank might actually face broader liquidity risk issues, possibly losing a lot of money as it tries to unload the position in a market that cannot accept the size. We discuss this concept – asset liquidity risk – below, and at greater length in the next chapter.

Curve risk is the risk of loss due to an adverse change in the maturity structure (known as the curve) of a reference asset – an interest rate, security price, volatility level, and so forth. Buyers and sellers reach bargains on financial instruments with varying maturities. A curve defines the structure of these prices (or imputed interest rates, etc.) across these maturities – from one day out to many years. For instance, overnight interest rates might be 4%, six-month rates 4.5%, five-year rates 5.5%, and so on; connecting these individual points creates a curve. Any change in the prices of bargains reached can create parallel shifts or twists in this curve, resulting in a gain or loss in any position that references it. For instance, if traders perceive short-term equity markets will continue to be very turbulent in response to corporate earnings announcements, but medium-term markets will be calmer as the economic picture improves, the equity volatility curve might be "downward sloping" (e.g. high in the short maturities and lower in the medium maturities). If the equity volatility curve twists – perhaps declining in the short-end and rising in the long-end – a firm will gain if it is short the curve (i.e. placed a bet on the volatility curve steepening) and lose if it is long (i.e. placed a bet on the volatility curve inverting further). In the interest rate markets, fiscal and monetary forces – including economic strength, supply of, and demand for, government bonds, and inflation, investment and spending expectations – can influence the shape of the interest rate curve. A curve risk loss in interest rates might occur when an upward parallel curve shift impacts a firm's long 5-year and 30-year Treasury bonds, for example. In the case of a yield curve twist (where the curve moves up or down by different amounts in different maturities), an upward rise in the 5-year rate and a downward move in the 30-year rate create a loss in the 5-year bond and a profit in the 30-year bond.

Volatility risk, *or* **vega**, is the risk of loss due to an adverse movement in volatility prices. Volatility is a measure of turbulence or tranquillity in a particular market – a calm market has low volatility, a turbulent market high volatility. Buyers and sellers place bets on whether they believe markets are going to be turbulent or not. They do so by agreeing on volatility prices and these prices in turn influence the value of other assets. Options use volatility as one of the factors to obtain a price – when volatility is perceived to be low, the **implied volatility** valuation of the option will be lower than when it is perceived to be high. For instance, if a firm sells hedged options that lose $1000 of value for each 1% increase in volatility, it loses $2000 if unstable markets cause volatility to rise by 2%. On the other hand, calm markets dampen volatility, and can produce a gain on this same position. This risk is commonly referred to as vega. In addition to changes in the direction of spot volatility, a firm can also be exposed to changes in the volatility curve (as noted above) as well as changes in **volatility smile** and **volatility skew**. The smile compares implied volatility to an option's strike price (e.g. **out-of-the-money**, **at-the-money** and **in-the-money**) and plots a curve between the points. In some markets out-of-the-money options trade at a higher volatility than at- or in-the-money options, under the assumption that the "disaster scenario" is more common than financial theory normally predicts. Volatility skew measures the difference in volatilities between out-of-the-money puts and calls; in some markets puts trade at a higher volatility than calls, reflecting the fact that buyers and sellers value insurance more highly on the downside than on the upside. Regardless of the specific shape of the smile and skew, a firm runs a risk that it will lose money if these relationships change in an adverse manner (e.g. the smile becomes a "frown", the spread between put and call volatility narrows or widens, and so on).

Time decay risk, sometimes known as **theta** risk, is the risk of loss due to the passage of time. This risk is found primarily in derivatives, which obtain some of their value from time. In general, the more time until the maturity of the contract, the greater its value, and vice versa; time is therefore a "wasting asset" for most derivatives prices. If a firm buys a portfolio of options with time decay risk of $10 000/day, it will lose $10 000 each and every day, assuming all other option inputs (e.g. price, volatility, interest rate) stay the same. A firm might buy options and expose itself to this certain time decay risk because it believes it can make money through trading its long gamma position – what it will lose for certain in time decay it might gain back from being long gamma in what it hopes will be a volatile market.

Spread risk is the risk of loss due to adverse changes between two reference assets that may not have a common link, such as a risk-free asset (e.g. US Treasury bond) and a risky bond (e.g. corporate bond with some probability of default). The spread between the two assets fluctuates all the time based on supply and demand forces, market and liquidity conditions, credit events, and so on. Thus, if a firm owns a corporate bond which it decides to "hedge" with a risk-free US Treasury benchmark, it loses money as the spread widens – either the price of the Treasury rises and its yield falls (while the corporate bond remains constant), or the price of the corporate bond falls and its yield rises (while the Treasury remains constant), or both. The hedge, however, protects the firm from changes in interest rates, which will affect both assets to some degree.

Basis risk, like spread risk, is the risk of loss due to adverse changes between two reference assets. In this case the reference assets are related in some way, but are not perfectly fungible. Some event might push the price of one up and the other down, causing a loss or gain. For instance, if an oil company attempts to hedge a position in Brent crude oil with NY Mercantile Exchange oil futures (based on light sweet crude), it may lose money from the changing basis between Brent and West Texas Intermediate (WTI, the proxy for light sweet crude). While Brent and WTI generally move together (meaning the hedge can remove much of the directional risk mentioned above), changing supply/demand, quality and transportation issues might make one of them more valuable at a particular point in time, creating a basis risk loss or gain.

Correlation risk is the risk of loss due to an adverse move in the correlations, or price relationships, between assets or markets. When looking at the history of financial prices it is clear that assets sometimes trade with, or against, one another; these price relationships, expressed in terms of correlation, are often used as the basis for hedging or investing. Correlation risk is actually contained in asset/asset and asset/hedge relationships (and is a key component of the spread and basis risks described above). An investment manager might look at the historical price movement between two securities and determine there is a high probability that their prices will converge – she may thus buy one asset and sell the other; if the asset prices decouple, the historical correlation between the two breaks down and she loses money.

2.2 CREDIT RISK

Credit risk is the risk of loss due to inability or unwillingness by a counterparty to pay on its financial obligations; this usually leads to a default and losses for those extending credit. Actual credit losses depend on **collateral** and **netting** agreements; in some (but not all instances) collateral taken can be **liquidated** upon default to cover losses, while a netting agreement allows a portfolio of deals to be collapsed into a single payable or receivable. Final credit losses also depend on **recoveries** received after bankruptcy proceedings (e.g. senior, unsecured creditors might receive 30 or 50 cents on the dollar). We might therefore say that gross credit losses are a worst-case scenario that can be offset or reduced by collateral, netting and recoveries. Credit risk, as summarized in Figure 2.3, can appear in the form of direct credit risk, trading credit risk, contingent credit risk, correlated credit risk, settlement risk and sovereign risk.

Direct credit risk is the risk of loss due to counterparty default on a direct, unilateral extension of credit, such as a loan, security, receivable or deposit. While these obligations are not perfectly fungible, they can usually be bought and sold in a secondary market and are considered somewhat marketable. Unsecured direct credit risk always creates exposure for the lender, meaning a default always creates a loss. If a bank makes a loan to a company, which then defaults, the bank loses money; likewise, if the bank purchases marketable securities issued by the company and the company defaults, the bank loses money.

A company (or country) that issues debt or borrows under a bank facility can become severely impaired but still not default (e.g. as was the case in 1998 when Russia defaulted on its rouble debt but did not default on its US dollar-denominated debt); when this happens, the

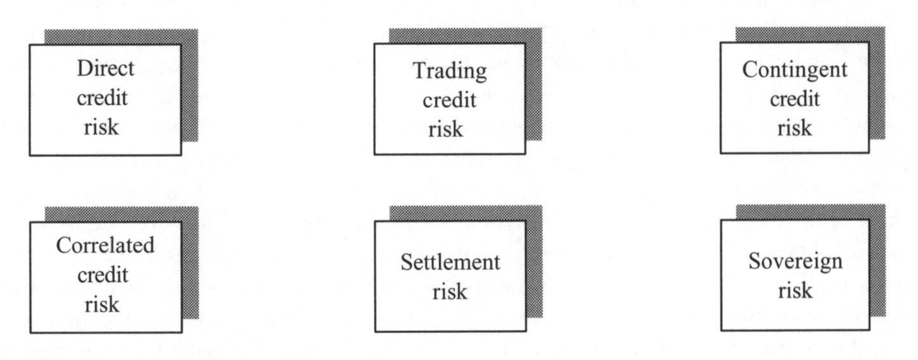

Figure 2.3 Credit risks

market value of the debt is likely to fall dramatically, but remain above default price levels. Losses sustained in these situations can be described either as credit or market risk losses.

Trading credit risk is the risk of loss due to a counterparty defaulting on a bilateral obligation; this risk usually appears in structured products, like derivatives or **repurchase agreement** financings (or "repos" – a repo is a short-term collateralized borrowing, where one firm agrees to sell securities to another firm and simultaneously agrees to repurchase them at a future time; the securities sold act as collateral, the cash proceeds from the sale act as a loan. A **reverse repurchase agreement** ("reverse repo") is the same transaction seen from the perspective of the lender). These obligations do not always expose a firm to risk of loss – depending on whether a contract has been purchased or sold, and how much the contract is worth at the time of default. For example, if a bank sells a company an option, once the option has been paid for it does not have any credit risk since it is not looking to the company for performance – there is no scenario where the company can owe the bank money. In contrast, the company that has bought the option expects the bank to perform and so has credit risk to the bank. However, if the contract is close to expiring and out-of-the-money when the bank defaults, it will not lose any money.

Contingent credit risk is the risk of loss due to counterparty default on a possible future extension of credit. Though many credit-sensitive transactions have credit exposure on trade date, some might not carry any risk until some future point – if at all. For instance, a client might draw down on a revolving credit facility or commercial paper program in the future – or might not! If it draws down, the bank faces additional credit risk, if it does not, then no incremental exposure arises. Though the bank does not know for sure whether the exposure will come into being, we believe it is sensible to be conservative and take account of the "contingency" when considering its overall credit risk exposure. Similar contingent exposures can arise by granting letters of credit or guarantees, or by entering into derivatives that might only become "active" once particular market levels are reached. Once a contingent event has been "crystallized" the credit exposure is treated as any standard direct or trading credit risk.

Correlated credit risk can appear in certain financial transactions and increase the magnitude of potential loss. Correlated exposures exist when counterparty exposure grows precisely as its ability to pay declines, or when the value of collateral taken as security deteriorates in tandem with ability to pay. For instance, if a counterparty sells a put option on its own stock, the value of the put to the buyer increases as the counterparty's stock price falls – a falling stock price might reflect an increasing inability to perform on financial obligations, and could result in a credit risk loss. Correlated risks can also relate to broader portfolios. A firm might extend credit broadly to an entire sector that is very sensitive to particular market variables/conditions, such as energy prices, emerging bond prices or currency rates. An adverse move in the market variable could weaken the entire sector and create credit problems across an entire portfolio. For instance, a bank might actively lend on a repo basis to many leveraged hedge funds, using emerging market bonds as collateral. If the bonds weaken (or even default), the bank's exposure to all hedge funds with the same positions may sour at the same time.

Settlement risk is the risk of loss due to a default after a payment of foreign exchange or delivery of securities has been made to a counterparty, but before an equivalent exchange has been received from the same counterparty. This risk comes from differences in settlement procedures, markets and time zones. For instance, if the foreign exchange desk of a bank delivers Japanese yen in Tokyo before taking receipt of dollars in New York, it has to authorize the yen payment before it can confirm receipt of dollars. If the counterparty defaults after receiving yen, but before paying dollars, the firm faces a settlement risk loss. Similar risk arises when securities are delivered "free" rather than via standard "delivery against cash/receipt against payment" conventions – known as DVP (**delivery versus payment**), which explicitly link the two activities such that delivery cannot occur without payment. Financial institutions carry a significant amount of settlement risk as a result of their securities and foreign exchange activities. It is one of the most difficult to monitor, as it relies on the availability of a technologically intensive, real time, all-encompassing system – something few, if any, firms possess. It unfortunately tends to be placed at the bottom of the priority list of risks to worry about.

Sovereign risk is the risk of loss due to actions taken within a country's financial system. This can occur through exchange controls (e.g. **convertibility risk**, a regulation preventing offshore participants from converting and possibly withdrawing local currency funds), **devaluation** (e.g. devaluation risk, a large financial depreciation in the value of a local currency) or default (e.g. default risk, non-payment on principal/interest of a country's own debt obligations). Sovereign risk is often associated with emerging nations – countries broadly defined to include those that control capital flows and the convertibility of their currency, as well as those that might lack the capacity to pay their debts. If a bank trades the local currency of an emerging country, it might sustain a sovereign risk loss if the country devalues the currency dramatically over a short time period, or if the country's central bank forbids the conversion of the local currency back into convertible currencies indefinitely. For instance, in 1997 the Malaysian government imposed currency controls that prohibited foreign investors from immediately converting Malaysian ringgit assets back into dollars and withdrawing them; though the value of the ringgit did not change much (and thus did not produce foreign exchange losses to foreign owners of ringgit-denominated assets), currency positions could not be hedged or withdrawn for several years.

2.3 LIQUIDITY RISK

Liquidity risk is the risk of loss due to a mismatch between cash inflows and outflows and can arise from an inability to sell a position (**asset liquidity risk**), fund a position (**funding liquidity risk**), or both. Asset sales may be required to meet anticipated outflows, cover unexpected payments or realign/reduce an asset portfolio. If assets are lower quality, complex or less liquid (e.g. non-current issues, those with a more limited investor base or simply very large concentrated positions), or if the sale has to be done quickly under stressed market conditions, an unanticipated loss may ensue. When a firm cannot fund itself through its normal sources as needed, it faces the specter of a funding liquidity risk loss. Inability to tap alternate sources of funding (e.g. commercial paper or medium-term note program, bank credit line/revolver, repurchase agreements) quickly and easily might force a firm to arrange more expensive financing or post collateral. In the extreme, a self-fulfilling liquidity crisis might follow – failure to rollover existing funds or arrange new financing might lead credit providers to withdraw their facilities; upon hearing the news, more lenders might cancel their facilities; and so forth, until the firm is left without any financing options. The nexus of asset and funding liquidity risk, where a firm is simultaneously unable to raise funding and is forced to liquidate assets at "distressed" prices, can quickly lead to very large losses or bankruptcy. Since liquidity exposure is such an important dimension of risk – though one that we feel has not been written about enough – we have dedicated the next chapter to it!

2.4 MODEL RISK

Model risk is the risk of loss arising from the use of inappropriate models and analytic tools to value financial contracts. While some assets can be valued quite precisely using mathematical formulas, other assets (particularly contracts that are complex, illiquid or long-dated) rely on much more sophisticated financial mathematics and assumptions. Errors in the math or assumptions can lead to model risk losses – something that most institutions, at some point, have encountered. For instance, in 1997 Bank of Tokyo Mitsubishi lost a reported $83 million and National Westminster Bank (now part of RBS Group) $144 million from model losses. Various other large banks, such as Chemical (now part of JP Morgan Chase), Bankers Trust (now part of Deutsche Bank) and UBS have similarly declared large model-related losses in the past. Model risk losses can come from a variety of sources: errors in mathematical formulas, simple/unintentional mistakes, flaws in programming or code implementation, or bad behavior/fraud.

Products and transactions that are valued using models instead of market prices are subject to **marked-to-model** risk, or the risk of loss if the actual value of the product or transaction is not realizable as predicted by the model. For instance, if a company runs a long-dated derivative book that cannot be valued using market prices (since the maturities are longer than those actively traded in the market place) it has to mark its positions to model. As the transactions start moving to the liquid part of the market, where prices can be observed, the company can switch to a standard mark-to-market mechanism. When it does, it might find a difference between the two values: if its model is conservative, it might actually earn profits from the switch, and if it is liberal, it could sustain a loss.

2.5 SUITABILITY RISK

Losses can arise from client transaction suitability issues. This **suitability risk** most often occurs when a counterparty claims financial injury as a result of a particular transaction – it may believe the deal was riskier than presented, that it was not accompanied by enough disclosure about the downside, or failed to provide the risk protection sought. The counterparty might disown the transaction or sue for damages. While legal proceedings are not always guaranteed to create large settlements, the specter of loss always exists and should be recognized (this is particularly true since firms that are sued by their clients often choose to settle out of court rather than suffer bad press). For instance, if a bank sells a complex and sophisticated financial derivative and fails to include proper caveats about potential downside losses, there is a possibility that the bank will have to make its client economically “whole” in the event of a dispute. Once again, we feel that suitability risks have not been addressed sufficiently and consider them in more detail in Chapter 4.

2.6 PROCESS RISK

Process risk, a relatively new frontier in the risk management world, is the risk of loss from a failure of internal business and control processes. The scope of process risk (also known as **operational risk**) varies by firm – for our purposes we consider it to include losses from internal control or audit inadequacies (which fail to identify problem areas), internal technology failures, human error, key-man risk, fraud and business interruption/disaster-related events. Process risk affects business as well as risk and control units, and should therefore be looked at on an enterprise-wide basis. This is still new or uncharted territory for most firms and companies are trying to come to grips with ways of identifying and managing these risks. Regulators are equally interested and want financial institutions to apply capital charges to cover these exposures (as they must for market and credit risks).

Small process risk losses are part of the daily operating environment in many large firms, especially those that run high volume businesses – losses from settlement errors, misrouted funds/securities, untimely payments and so on occur frequently; indeed, it is probably true that most large companies lose more than they realize through such operational failures. Bringing these under control, while not simple, can be a good way of improving margins and thus should be a key area of focus for CEOs and CFOs. If the possibility of a large operational loss exists, implementing a robust control process is absolutely necessary. The damaging effects of not doing so are readily apparent. Allfirst, the AIB subsidiary mentioned in Chapter 1, is an example of a dramatic process risk failure: internal fraud, coupled with an inadequate technology platform that could be circumvented to bury trades, created a $691 million loss. Barings stands as another example: internal fraud, lax management supervision, manipulation of programming code, suppressing of risk reports, falsification of settlement instructions and rerouting of trades led to the eventual demise of the bank.

It is unclear just how large process risk losses actually are, since reporting is generally very vague and individual losses can be small in absolute terms (though ultimately large in total!). Also, institutions sustaining process risk losses often prefer to "keep them quiet" rather than announce them publicly – so the true magnitude of the problem is not precisely known. But two estimates give us an indication that the problem is potentially very big: as noted in Chapter 1, one estimate indicates that 110 institutions (including 55 banks) lost $7 billion on process losses in 1998–1999 (with a useful reminder that the "true" amount of losses (i.e. those going unreported) was a multiple of that figure), while another indicates that the fund management industry alone may have sustained as much as $9 billion in process losses over the past decade.[1] Since process risk is a significant, and increasingly important, area of risk management, we discuss it at length in Chapter 5.

2.7 LEGAL RISK

Legal risk is the risk of loss due to failures in the legal process. Legal mechanisms – including confirmations, master netting agreements, collateral and valuation agreements, loan agreements and financial covenants – are part of most financial dealings; they contain important legal provisions that are designed to protect the parties in the event of dispute or default. For instance, a proper collateral agreement perfects a firm's security interest in collateral pledged on a trade; a proper netting agreement (in an appropriate legal jurisdiction that recognizes netting) lets a firm manage its exposures on a net, rather than gross, basis. Failure to negotiate proper documentation or obtain necessary protection in the signed agreements can lead to legal risk losses in the event of default or dispute. If a firm has a portfolio of derivative transactions with a counterparty but fails to negotiate a master swap agreement, in some jurisdictions, in the event of default, a bankruptcy receiver may dismiss all contacts with value to the firm, thereby causing a loss. Legal risk can be exacerbated by different business units within a firm handling their own documentation (applying different standards in the process) and by the existence of very large backlogs in getting documents signed. Since many transactions happen before legal

[1] Estimate of the International Association of Financial Engineers, 2002.

documents are finalized, legal departments at large firms are constantly trying to play catch-up and reduce the risks generated by such backlogs.

It should be clear from the brief discussion above that a firm can face a large universe of risks! These risks can change as markets, products, regulations and competitors change and evolve. As such, defining the nature of risk must be a dynamic process. It is imperative for a firm to continuously review its operations and make sure that it has identified all sources of risk – and that management shares a common understanding of these risks. Formalizing this through regular annual reviews is a good discipline.

3

Liquidity: The Heart of the Matter

In our experience liquidity risk is a critical, but often overlooked, area of risk. Mismanagement of liquidity risk can lead to severe financial losses and, in extreme situations, even bankruptcy. Indeed, loss of liquidity – rather than a loss in risk taking that might spark a liquidity crisis – has ultimately been the reason for most bankruptcies or liquidations in the financial industry. The term liquidity risk has been a lot more prominent since the collapse of LTCM. It seems, however, to be used with different meanings – depending on the context – and needs to be better defined. In this chapter we propose a definition centered on asset and funding liquidity risks – as well as the effects of combined asset/funding problems – and discuss mechanisms for monitoring and controlling such risks. Figure 3.1 highlights these broad categories of liquidity risk.

3.1 ASSET LIQUIDITY RISK

In Chapter 2 we defined asset liquidity risk as the risk of loss due to an inability to realize an expected value on a position when needed. A firm might have to sell assets to meet payments, make an alternative investment in financial instruments or plant and equipment, repay maturing debt, or comply with regulatory or corporate directives. If it cannot then sell an asset at its carrying value, it faces the risk of loss. There are many reasons why a firm might not be able to sell assets, and any of these can be a contributing factor in creating a loss:

- The asset might be so large in relation to the issue or market that it cannot be sold without moving the market.
- The market might be thinly traded, unable to absorb an asset sale of any meaningful size.
- The asset may be so esoteric and complex that it attracts few buyers.
- The asset might not be readily transferable without some legal effort.
- The asset might be subject to restrictions on convertibility, capital withdrawal or regulatory approval.

Every company has to decide the carrying value of its positions. This decision is critical as it leads to the computation of key information – the amount of equity and debt needed to support assets, the book value and income statements of the company, and so on. Additionally, this carrying value has to fit into accepted accounting principles. In the *corporate world*, most assets (such as plant, equipment, buildings, furniture) are investments and therefore carried at cost or the depreciated value. In the *financial world*, many assets are held for resale. If a price is available on an exchange or in the market place, it is carried in the trading books at that price.[1] However, if the size of the position is large or unique in some way (e.g. complex, very long-dated), the price at which it is held may not be the price obtained in the event of a forced sale. Liquidation will therefore crystallize an unanticipated loss. If the loss is large relative to the company's earnings and equity, financial trouble may follow. For instance,

[1] Note that as an exception positions held in investment, rather than trading, accounts can be valued at the lower of cost or market value; however, these must follow strict accounting rules and cannot easily be transferred in or out of such an account.

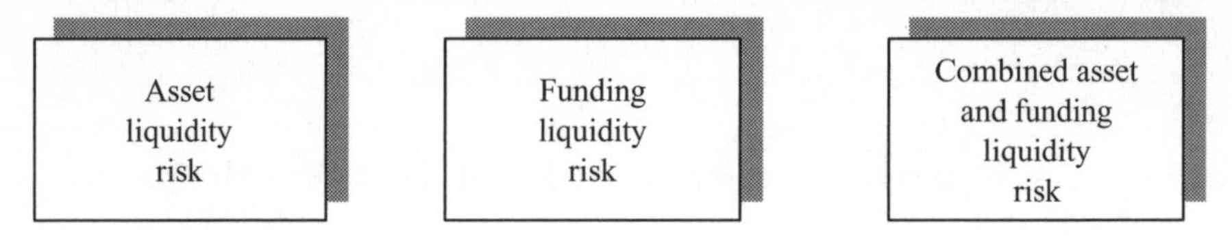

Figure 3.1 Liquidity risks

if a company has $100 million of emerging market bonds – valued at what it believes is a correct price of 100 – and needs to sell them quickly, it might find that prevailing market conditions cannot absorb the block at a price of 100. The best bid might be 95, meaning the company loses $5 million as a result of asset liquidity risk. Since the company is a "forced seller" it has to dispose of these bonds in poor market conditions. If it can sell them at a leisurely pace – maybe $10 million a day over 10 days, it might be able to do so at its carrying value of 100 – minimizing or eliminating the risk of loss. A forced, or distressed, seller is thus more likely to sell at a loss. The less liquid the assets for sale, the greater the loss.

Asset liquidity risk is also relevant when looking at credit risk and it cannot be casually dismissed if credit exposure to a counterparty is supported by a lien or collateral. Though collateral taken to secure a credit exposure is usually of sufficient quality to cover the obligation, there are times when a firm accepts riskier securities. Again, the assumed value of a security may be lower in the event of a forced sale for exactly the same reasons cited above. If this happens the collateral may be insufficient to cover the full value of the loan, thus creating an unsecured credit exposure. Say a bank takes $50 million of A-rated corporate bonds as collateral to support an equal amount of counterparty exposure. If the value of the bonds falls below $50 million and the counterparty fails to deliver any additional collateral, the bank will be forced to protect its position by terminating the deal and selling the bonds. Poor market conditions might yield proceeds of only $45 million, which is insufficient to cover the counterparty exposure. On the remaining $5 million the bank can only rely on whatever other assets are available at the counterparty – the credit is therefore unsecured. Liquidity risk therefore affects prices of assets on and off the balance sheet, but also potential credit exposure for transactions supported by liens or collateral.

Not every firm faces the same amount of asset liquidity risk for the same portfolio of assets. A firm that has valued its assets correctly and has the luxury of being able to hold all assets until maturity faces minimal asset liquidity risk. However, since very few companies enjoy such flexibility in their operations, asset liquidity risk should always be considered, identified and managed.

3.2 FUNDING LIQUIDITY RISK

Funding liquidity risk is the risk of loss that comes from an inability to fund assets, payments and other obligations when required. A firm typically uses some form of debt – payables, short-term notes, repurchase agreements, commercial paper, deposits, long-term bonds, convertible securities, bank loans – to finance its operations; any disruption in the funding program can lead to funding risk losses. More specifically, this kind of risk can arise from:

- Inability to rollover, or renew, maturing financing when required;
- Inability to access new funding when needed.

Say a firm uses short-term debt to finance its operations. To keep funding its assets or make anticipated payments it might rely on regular rollovers of its short-term debt. If it cannot do so – maybe depositors are withdrawing funds to put to work in other assets, lenders generally are pulling away from the short-term market, or the company is perceived as bad risk – it will be forced to find alternate, typically more expensive, funds. Likewise, a firm might not always be able to obtain incremental funding when needed. If it faces unexpected payments (e.g. payments to suppliers, margin calls, and so forth) and has fully tapped its existing financing sources it must look to other instruments or markets to cover the shortfall. Again, its only alternative might be to pay for very expensive borrowing, at greater cost. For example, if a company with fully drawn commercial paper and bank facilities needs to make a $100 million emergency payment, it might have to turn to the term loan market, paying an incremental spread of 50 basis points over its normal borrowing cost; this translates into an economic loss of $500 000.

Funding facilities are sometimes granted in "committed" form, where the borrower pays the lender a higher rate (e.g. a per annum fee) to ensure the lender does not withdraw the facility. Withdrawal is usually only possible if a **material adverse change** (MAC) occurs – e.g. a major market dislocation, difficulties with the borrower's own financial condition, and so on. Unfortunately, a borrower often needs to access emergency funds precisely when something bad is happening – at that point the lender may well invoke its rights under the MAC and cancel the facility. In extreme events, committed facilities may not really be committed at all! Borrowers are also often fearful of testing a **committed funding** facility; refusal by the lender to fund (e.g. by playing the MAC card) might spook other lenders, cause them to pull their lines and precipitate a broader liquidity crisis. "Escape-proof" committed facilities (without MACs or with very precise MAC language covering specific events) are probably the only way of ensuring that lenders are on the hook to fund when needed.

As with asset liquidity risk, not every firm faces equal funding liquidity risk. Firms that have comprehensive and committed funding programs with enough of a buffer to cover unexpected requirements may never be in a position of losing money through funding operations. However, since it is difficult to know this for certain a firm should always recognize, and prepare for, a funding-related crisis and possible losses.

3.3 ASSET AND FUNDING LIQUIDITY RISK

Asset and funding liquidity risks come together to form the nexus of a firm's liquidity operations. Some banks already attempt to consider and manage these risks together, but we feel that even more firms should be doing so as the consequences of not doing this can be significant. Asset liquidity risk losses can occur without a corresponding funding loss (e.g. losses generated by marks that do not properly reflect the risk characteristics of the asset), just as funding losses can also occur without associated asset liquidation losses (e.g. borrowing at a higher cost or pledging assets as collateral). However, asset and funding liquidity risk are intricately linked – if incremental or rollover funding cannot be secured, and the only recourse is to sell assets (quite probably on a distressed basis), then a larger loss may result. Indeed, the nexus of asset and funding liquidity risk can create truly devastating losses, as we learned from the LTCM case described in Chapter 1. There are many other examples – Askin Capital, hedge funds that invested in Russian rouble bonds in 1997/1998, and so forth. In 1994 Askin Capital, a hedge fund that invested heavily in esoteric mortgage-backed securities, watched its portfolio erode as the Federal Reserve tightened interest rates. As rates rose Askin's illiquid bonds, which were used as collateral against funding, declined sharply in value. Wall Street firms revalued the collateral, discovered shortfalls, and made margin calls. Since the assets were esoteric, the market for them was illiquid. The Askin portfolio sustained very large losses as collateral was liquidated in a hurry. The fund was ultimately unable to realize enough value on its assets to repay the loans that had become due and was forced into bankruptcy; various banks that had lent to Askin on an unsecured basis, or had assumed that collateral taken would be sufficient to cover loans, suffered credit losses. Investors in the Askin funds also lost their money. In a similar light many US hedge funds, and the banks that lent to them, lost considerable sums in 1998 when the Russian government devalued the rouble and defaulted on its rouble-denominated Treasury securities (so-called GKOs and OFZs). Funds that had purchased GKOs and OFZs and then pledged them as collateral for more loans (for the purchase of even more rouble securities!) were unable to meet the margin calls from banks once the government defaulted. GKOs that had traded near 100 were suddenly worth 10 – meaning that any asset disposal to cover bank loans left the hedge funds woefully short of what they needed to make good on the loans. Numerous funds were forced into bankruptcy and many large US and international banks lost a lot of money on the loans they had granted. Figure 3.2 portrays the potential effects of asset and funding liquidity risk.

The combination of asset and funding liquidity risk must also be considered when there are no borrowings. For instance, a mutual fund (that is not permitted to borrow or pledge securities)

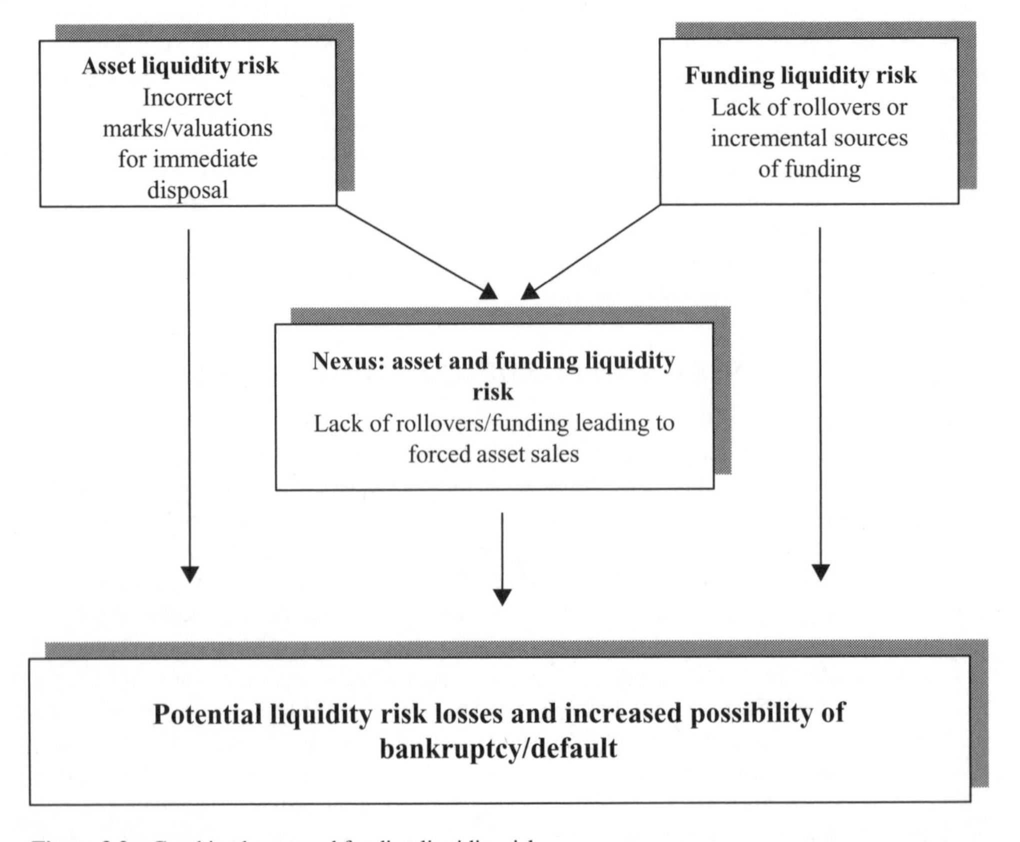

Figure 3.2 Combined asset and funding liquidity risks

runs the risk that all holders sell their shares back to the fund at the same time. Since the fund holds only limited cash for such redemptions it has to sell assets. However, it may only hold 20 very large positions in liquid stocks and find it difficult to sell these at the prices that make up its announced net asset value (NAV). As it starts selling, the NAV will start to collapse – favoring the investors who redeemed their shares first. The remaining holders of the mutual fund are, in essence, mutually insuring each other for the value of the assets in the fund at the prices posted by the manager/fund administrator. The fund is, in short, a mutual insurance company. Investors are effectively writing daily put options on the portfolio of stocks at the prevailing marks and selling them to all other investors. An investor exiting the fund exercises a normally valueless at-the-money put – if too many investors are doing the same thing at the same time, these puts may no longer be valueless!

3.4 LEVERAGE ARBITRAGE

Leverage arbitrage occurs when a company takes advantage of a "disconnect" between its perceived credit rating in the market place and reality. This is worth touching upon as it normally incents bad financial behavior and can create very large asset/funding liquidity losses. It can occur, for example, when the marketplace (and perhaps even the credit rating agencies) assesses a company based on *reputation* instead of *fundamentals*. The company is motivated to use its stronger than deserved ability (and credit rating) to borrow a large amount of cheaper funds than it would normally be afforded (most likely in the short-term market), and invest in longer term, higher yielding, less liquid assets. These assets will not do justice to the rating or the perceived quality of the outstanding debt. In the process, the company typically ends up taking significant liquidity risk, funding maturity mismatch and credit spread risk. Who can blame them? Funding BB-rated assets at AAA-rated financing rates, on a highly leveraged basis, generates a handsome spread! Profitability thus generated will often get misperceived as being driven by great management skills, thus perpetuating the disconnect in perception of the true value of the debt.

Investors and analysts too often forget to analyze how much of a company's results are driven by leverage and forget to compare these to the performance of a market portfolio of similar assets and liabilities. Such analysis will provide the true picture of the "value added" being brought by management. As long as rating agencies choose not to penalize this behavior through a lower credit rating, and bank credit departments remain influenced by reputation rather than fundamentals, this game will continue. When analysts, lenders or investors wake up to the fact that these activities are often no different from those found in leveraged and speculative hedge funds (that can only typically borrow on a secured basis), the liquidity arbitrage disappears and earnings collapse. If leverage is very significant and the investments are particularly illiquid, worse things could happen!

Many Japanese corporations in the 1980s were enticed into this means of generating earnings. Banks were willing to lend companies money based on relationships rather than fundamentals, and the companies used the borrowed money to fund investments that were not core to their operating strategies. Much of this was in real estate and equity markets, which at that time were booming. Some companies ended up making more than 100% of their profits from such investment activities! As the equity and real-estate markets collapsed and banks got tougher on credit risk, the whole house of cards collapsed. In the US, for example, highly rated GE Capital borrows heavily on a short-term basis and often invests in a range of illiquid assets. It is unclear how much of this borrowing is dependent on "support" from the rest of GE's industrial activities. In 2002 GE Capital was the focus of ire by investment firm PIMCO, which questioned the firm's business model, excessive leverage and overreliance on short-term borrowing. After publicly critiquing GE Capital's use of leverage arbitrage, investors pushed the stock down and forced GE to replace a significant portion of its short-term funding with longer term debt.

Leverage arbitrage can only be contained by a ratings downgrade, a pullback by lenders or robust return on capital allocation rules enforced either by management or regulators. It is not surprising any firms earning money primarily through leverage arbitrage are usually either unregulated or lack a strong return on capital allocation process (or do not even have one!). If a good capital allocation process exists, then the amount of capital that will be required to support the activities described above will soon compress the arbitrage – corporate profit hurdle rates will not be met as the amount of capital needed to support these risky activities will rightly be too large. Banks that are strictly regulated cannot typically get away with this type of leverage arbitrage – the combination of shareholder return hurdles and regulatory capital allocation would typically cause the arbitrage to disappear!

3.5 MONITORING LIQUIDITY RISK

Since liquidity risk can be damaging it has to be understood, measured, monitored and managed. Unfortunately, there is no simple way to measure liquidity risk – in our view the best that can usually be done is to refer to certain proxies that will indicate the presence, and direction, of liquidity risks.

First, from an overall perspective a firm needs to take account of its legal structure – this allows it to understand whether liquidity will be available when needed or whether it will get trapped. Assets in one part of the organization may not be readily or cheaply accessible by another part in times of need; likewise, a financing facility granted to one subsidiary may not be available for drawdown by another subsidiary. A company might be able to raise funds in one subsidiary but not channel them to a subsidiary where they are actually needed. Though the entire company may be liquid and solvent on a consolidated basis, such restrictions could actually cause it to default! Capital that exists to support the operations of one legal entity often cannot be repatriated or moved to another part, and should not be considered part of an emergency liquidity plan (even if allowed, there might be high tax costs associated with the transfer). Enterprise-wide knowledge of legal entity structure, and associated assets, liability, capital, financing facilities, commitments (along with a "forward view" of operations) and tax/regulatory restrictions is crucial to proper liquidity management.

A firm must also be aware of **double leverage** thresholds that could impair its credit standing or breach regulatory rules. For example, if a company borrows directly through its holding company and must tap the debt markets through its operating company for additional funding (e.g. in the event of an unexpected need), it has to make sure its consolidated borrowing (e.g. leverage at the operating and holding company levels) does not run foul of credit rating triggers or regulatory restrictions; excess double leverage can raise borrowing costs, hamper access to liquidity or lead to a rating downgrade. Any of these can exacerbate the liquidity crunch, and lead to a broader liquidity spiral.

Second, from an asset liquidity perspective a firm must monitor its:

- Asset maturity profile,
- Portfolio credit quality mix,
- Aged assets,
- Concentrated risk positions.

By tracking *asset maturity* a firm knows when assets will be converted into cash or be written down to zero – allowing reinvestment, repayment of maturing debt or a lowering of equity. A financial trading firm or investment company features a fairly high percentage of short-term assets, while an industrial company has more long-term fixed assets. If the financial firm's asset maturity profile starts to lengthen, it may be more susceptible to increased liquidity risk (the same would be true for the industrial company, though its proportion of assets in the liquid sector is much smaller to begin with). The mix of *credit quality* in the portfolio also needs to be monitored closely; it should always contain a relatively large proportion of high-quality assets that can be converted into cash with no (or minimal) discount in value. This is especially important in a deteriorating credit cycle, when the credit quality of the assets in the portfolio starts to decline, to the point where they are far less liquid and cannot be realized without taking a loss. Monitoring the size and movement of **aged assets** – those that have been on the books for several months but are assumed to be available for sale – can also be a good liquidity indicator. This proxy is applicable primarily to trading companies, which should feature regular turnover of assets as a normal part of the business. If asset turnover slows and more of the balance sheet shifts into an "aged" category (e.g. 90, 120 or 180+ days), asset liquidity risk is likely to be on the rise. A large amount of aged assets also often indicates a problem with valuation of these positions. Traders are very quick to point out when a position is undervalued, but rarely do the reverse. A position that is overvalued is unlikely to be attractive to others in the market place and will sit on the books. Monitoring *concentrated positions* can also help identify problems. As noted earlier, large positions are generally less liquid than smaller ones; in the extreme, a large position held on a firm's books may take days, or even weeks or months, to sell at, or near, the carrying value. Watching the size and number of concentrated positions can serve as another "early warning" indicator. Balance sheet, off-balance sheet and credit exposures should be monitored in such a fashion – asset liquidity is just as relevant in derivatives or credit risk as it is in cash instruments.

Funding liquidity risk can be monitored by looking at:

- Liability maturity profile,
- Funding source concentration,
- Commitment percentages,
- Contingent triggers.

Knowing the *maturity of liabilities* is essential in understanding what needs to be refinanced, when and at what relative rates, and whether refunding will coincide with cash from assets coming due.[2] For instance, if a firm has 75% of its liabilities maturing over a three-month window, it may not have confidence in its ability to refinance everything. Accordingly, it has to compare the liability profile with maturing assets, match off any maturing assets with expiring liabilities and identify other assets that will have to be sold to meet the liability refunding. Monitoring *funding source concentration* is vital, and creating a diversified program of funding that crosses lenders, markets, products and maturities is advisable. Concentrations can lead to an increased incidence of funding-related losses, as the disappearance of a significant banking source might force the firm to seek more expensive alternatives (or turn to asset sales). It is also important to monitor the percentage of lenders willing to extend funding on a truly

[2] Financial institutions commonly compute a "funding gap" by comparing interest rate-sensitive assets and liabilities that are maturing or "repricing" over particular intervals, e.g. every six or 12 months. This helps them capture any gaps that might exist and indicates how they will be impacted if rates rise or fall during a given repricing period.

committed basis (e.g. "escape-proof"); if the percentage starts to decline, the firm's funding liquidity risk may be on the rise as it could lose access to lines precisely when it needs to tap them. This becomes especially evident when downgrades are afoot. For instance, over the past few years a number of large CP issuers – including Xerox, Kmart, Daimler Chrysler, PG&E and Lehman Brothers, among others – have been temporarily or permanently shut out of the CP market as a result of credit downgrades. This forces such companies to quickly find alternatives – precisely when market perception of them is negative. Facilities with **contingent triggers** should also be kept to a minimum (or triggers should have such a remote chance of being set off that they cannot realistically be a factor). Certain bank facilities contain language that allows cancellation (or forced repayment) if a firm is downgraded below certain levels, its stock falls below a prespecified price, or financial ratios are breached (e.g. leverage, liquidity, earnings). Knowing when these triggers might come into play, and how they can affect funding access, is an important part of liquidity management.

A firm cannot overlook the forward structure of on- and off-balance sheet obligations at various time horizons; this provides an indication of gaps that may exist, additional commitments that might need funding, or assets that might have to be sold. Use of derivatives, securitization, special purpose vehicles and other off-balance sheet mechanisms has exploded in recent years. Failure by the accounting profession to keep pace with these changes means that there is often a disconnect between a firm's stated balance sheet and what is really going on – as revealed in the corporate accounting scandals unearthed in 2001 and 2002. Heavy reliance on off-balance sheet activities can reduce current funding needs but might create enormous liabilities in the future. These may be too large for the company to manage and honor. Only very detailed analysis of financial footnotes may reveal the extent of this risk, if at all. It is clear that the standard balance sheet and earnings reports do not provide much insight to future "IOUs", and estimating the forward balance sheet is not easy – sometimes it has to be based on assumptions about future events that are very uncertain (e.g. it is impossible to know six or 12 months ahead of time whether a particular client will exercise an option or draw down on a revolving credit facility), so some "guesstimate" has to be made. Though imprecise, in our view some future estimate of what the balance sheet might look like is a useful and necessary step in helping manage liquidity and credit risk.

The measurement of asset and funding liquidity should not be confined solely to these proxies, but can be supplemented by others. We have found the tools presented here to be the easiest to measure and promulgate throughout an organization. Figure 3.3 summarizes important liquidity monitoring tools.

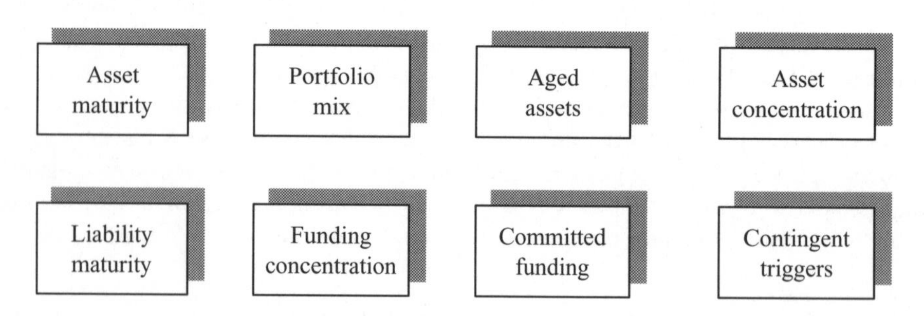

Figure 3.3 Liquidity monitoring tools

3.6 INFLUENCING BEHAVIOR TO ALTER LIQUIDITY PROFILES

We have found certain mechanisms useful in elevating the issue of liquidity within a company in an attempt to limit exposures. These include:

- Balance sheet targets,
- Concentration limits,
- Aged/illiquid inventory limits,
- Adequate "haircuts",
- Diversified funding.

We briefly describe these mechanisms below and consider them more fully in Chapter 7, where we incorporate them into a liquidity risk framework that enables risks to be limited and monitored continuously. Other techniques can, of course, be considered as the attention paid to liquidity risk brings about greater sophistication over time.

3.6.1 Balance sheet targets

Managing asset liquidity risk means preserving the most liquid profile possible, while still functioning within the broad guidelines of a firm's strategy. Industrial and capital-intensive companies that invest heavily in fixed plant and equipment do not typically have to remain as liquid as trading/financial companies, since valuations of their assets are typically not as volatile; indeed, an overly liquid industrial company is probably not maximizing asset efficiency or meeting its return targets. Its liquid assets should, however, be truly liquid – e.g. cash, short-term, high-quality investments and short-term receivables – so that obligations/contingencies/capital redistribution can be met with ease. Depending on industry type, a company might elect to hold no more than 20% of its total assets in liquid form, the balance being held in capital assets. With the recent corporate scandals and breakdown of valuations in the telecommunications industry, however, some boards may wish to be very prudent. In contrast, trading and financial companies must remain as liquid as possible in their operations; though they may be "match funded" (e.g. matching the maturities of assets and liabilities as closely as possible), they run the risk that funding can be withdrawn (e.g. retail depositors may withdraw money, interbank lenders may pull back lines, the repo market may dry up). While a lending institution will feature a certain amount of illiquidity in its loan book (e.g. long-term, non-transferable credit facilities), its remaining assets should be liquid. Though a tradeoff between less liquid/higher returning assets and more liquid/lower returning assets has to be considered, a firm should manage its operations within such predefined balance sheet targets.

3.6.2 Concentration limits

The management of asset liquidity can also be strengthened by setting concentration limits. As noted earlier, large concentrated risk positions may be, or can become, illiquid and should be controlled through specific limits. A firm may wish to impose concentration limits based on asset type, rating and maturity – these can serve as a proxy for liquidity: higher rated assets are generally more liquid than lower rated ones, simple securities are typically more liquid than esoteric ones, and so forth.

3.6.3 Aged/illiquid inventory penalties

A firm may also consider imposing financial penalties that are directly related to a business' target liquidity profile. This helps ensure discipline in minimizing "problem" positions that are too difficult to sell, and avoids the gradual build up of an illiquid balance sheet. For instance, a firm might apply an internal monthly financial charge on any position on the balance sheet for more than 90 or 180 days and apply increasing penalties until aged positions are reduced below some predefined amount; when positions are sold, the sums taken as penalties can be returned. Here some allowance must be made for the target liquidity profile of the business. A business that deals in less liquid products might be given a somewhat larger threshold than one that deals in very generic, liquid products. Thereafter, of course, the two should be treated the same way. Thus, a bank's syndicated loan book – which must negotiate the sale and documentation of each loan in a manually intensive fashion with considerable lead time – might be permitted an aged position limit of $50 million, after which penalties accrue; the bank's US Treasury bond trading book, in contrast, might be given an aged position limit of $0 – since the product is liquid and prices are transparent, there should be no reason for the firm to hold aged Treasury bond trading positions (unless, of course, the positions are held as long-term hedges against other exposures).

To properly implement the process, a firm's financial controllers must be sufficiently experienced and knowledgeable to ensure that market prices on all aged positions are accurately represented, and that markdowns occur until clearing levels are discovered. Again, in our experience a trader is quick to tell of a position that is marked conservatively (e.g. underestimating profitability), but rarely the contrary! As positions stay on the books for a prolonged period of time, the probability that they are marked at the wrong price increases; a penalty system can thus also be a useful way of minimizing these bad marks.

3.6.4 Adequate haircuts

As a general operating rule, we have found that collateral taken to secure credit exposures or securities that form part of a broad reverse repurchase agreement operation (e.g. secured lending book) should be as liquid as possible. Even with liquid, high-quality securities (e.g. US Treasuries), but especially when a firm cannot get liquid securities, it has to make sure it takes an appropriate haircut or discount – sufficient to cover possible credit exposures in the event of forced liquidation. For example, if a firm extends a $10 million reverse repo loan secured by $11 million of US Treasuries it should have a big enough cushion to cover itself in the event the borrower fails to repay the loan (especially since the securities are valued daily and collateral calls are made as needed). However, if the $10 million loan is secured by $11 million of high-yield bonds, it might not have enough collateral to cover the loan in the event of default. The high-yield bonds are likely to be far less liquid, and a forced sale to cover the exposure might generate proceeds of only $7 or $8 million, creating an open exposure and potential credit loss. Properly "haircutting" any collateral taken as security is an important way of controlling liquidity-driven losses; this can be done by defining haircuts by broad asset class and specific security. These haircuts should be controlled in a very stringent manner by the credit department rather than the trading desks – so as not to have the inmates running the asylum! It is worth noting that "lesser quality" assets taken as collateral should also be counted against relevant concentration limits on the firms' own positions. We have often noticed that lesser quality assets tend to be financed by counterparties that carry a high degree of exposure to such assets. The counterparty and credit exposures therefore tend to be closely correlated with the value of similar positions owned by the lender.

3.6.5 Diversified funding

To manage its funding liquidity risks, a firm can specifically limit the amount of financing that it derives from any particular market or lending source. This forces the creation of a funding program that draws from different markets, lenders, instruments and maturities – in committed form and with a minimum of contingent triggers, whenever possible – and with enough buffer to meet unexpected payments.

It is worth stressing, once again, that liquidity risks can precipitate broader financial problems at a firm. While a large market or credit risk loss will obviously be disturbing to stakeholders, a significant liquidity problem can be deadly. Appropriate sensitivity to this fact, at all levels of the firm, is absolutely critical.

3.7 TEN USEFUL LIQUIDITY RISK QUESTIONS

To summarize it is useful to ask, and follow up on, the following questions about liquidity:

1. Has the firm experienced any asset or funding liquidity risk losses and what were the lessons/remedies?
2. Does the firm have mechanisms and policies in place to control the liquidity profile of its assets and liabilities?
3. How are illiquid assets valued, and are those responsible for valuations properly qualified?
4. For assets available for resale, does the firm place limits/penalties on concentrations or aged inventory?
5. Are adequate haircuts applied to collateral and who monitors these? Do any other collateral restrictions exist?
6. Does the firm have a comprehensive funding program that includes multiple lenders, terms, maturities, products and markets?
7. Do the firm's "committed" facilities contain any "escape language" (e.g. broad MACs, contingent triggers)?
8. Has the firm ever tested its bank facilities to ensure smooth functioning?
9. How does the firm limit and monitor the liquidity of its off-balance sheet assets and liabilities and its forward commitments?
10. Are proper capital allocation rules applied to assets and liabilities in order to encourage "rational behavior"?

4

Suitability: Coping with Customers

In thinking about the way customers or counterparties can affect the risk profile of an institution most people focus primarily on credit risk. Credit analysis is still taught as a discipline of understanding financial accounts, estimating cash flows, determining leverage and interest coverage, and so forth. While important, this analysis is often static, and may not be enough to truly understand the dynamic nature of credit risk and the complexity of credit and business relationships. The explosion of creativity in financial engineering that started in the mid-1980s has made the analysis of credit risk a lot more difficult. Increasingly, traditional credit portfolios are becoming malleable through the use of credit derivatives, special purpose vehicles and securitization technology. As a result, credit exposures can be assumed or defeased through many mechanisms that can dramatically alter risk profiles. Collateralized exposures are an equally important part of the risk portfolio. Accordingly, the analysis of credit risk has become very complex and the once distinct credit and market risk disciplines are gradually converging. Unfortunately, risk, accounting and regulatory disclosure standards have not adjusted to this new environment and now deserve to be an important topic of focus and debate.

The legal dimensions of dealing with clients, such as suitability and authority, have also changed. To date, very little has been written on the subject of unsuitable transactions, despite the fact they have been at the center of some of the largest financial disputes, damaged reputations, penalties and settlements over the past years. We do not have to look very far to find evidence of damage caused by legal risk – to financial institutions, their clients, or both. It is worth noting that these risks impact retail, as well as institutional, clients. While prudence demands that all clients be handled with care, individual investors, with less financial resources, can ill afford losses created by excessively risky or complicated financial dealings and must therefore be given even greater attention.

Ultimately, in a dispute, it is often the financial institution that pays out – either because the courts declare they have done something wrong or because they try to protect their reputations. They may also be trying to salvage their client relationships so that they can win future business – in their eyes it might be better to "make the client whole" on trades that have gone sour if it means the client will be back for more business in the future. In the late 1980s, for instance, a number of UK local authorities, including Hammersmith and Fulham, were on the wrong end of derivative transactions and accumulated major losses. They argued that they should not be held responsible for honoring them as they were acting out of their permitted scope; many banks lost money following a judgement in support of this claim. In 1999 Merrill Lynch paid the Kingdom of Belgium more than $100 million in settlement of leveraged currency options that at one point had created $1.2 billion of losses for the country. The Kingdom alleged that the potential downside of the transactions had not been fully disclosed by the bank. Many other examples abound. We will consider four in detail – Orange County, Procter and Gamble, Sumitomo Corporation and Prudential Securities – to help illustrate some of these legal risk issues. We then consider some of the key issues related to the management of client suitability risk.

4.1 SUITABILITY CASES

4.1.1 Orange County

Orange County, Southern California, operated an investment pool that invested proceeds on behalf of county organizations. Over a period of several years the fund posted very strong returns; by late 1993 the fund, under the guidance of county fund manager, Robert Citron, had grown to $7.5 billion in size, and was attracting more funds than it knew what to do with. Betting that interest rates would continue to drop, Citron had built up very large interest rate positions primarily through repurchase agreements (e.g. buying securities and pledging them as collateral for more loans, using those loans to buy more securities, pledging those securities for more loans, and so on) and the purchase of leveraged **inverse floaters** (floating rate notes which pay an above-market coupon that increases the more interest rates decline and vice versa). The $7.5 billion was thus ultimately leveraged to $20.5 billion. When the Federal Reserve began raising rates in February 1994, the fund suffered large losses. By the end of 1994 – after rates had risen by 300 basis points – the portfolio had lost $1.6 billion. The liquidity profile of the fund was such that it ended up with insufficient cash to pay member participants. As a result the county declared bankruptcy. The portfolio was liquidated and a spate of lawsuits commenced against those who had actively dealt with the fund, including Merrill Lynch, Bear Stearns and Nomura Securities. Some parts of the case centered on whether Citron, as investment manager, knew what he was doing and if he was actually authorized to enter into these transactions – or whether he was being hustled by fast-talking Wall Street salesmen and acting outside the county's investment guidelines. Though the courts eventually determined that Citron knew what he was doing, it remained unclear whether he was acting within scope – several of the lawsuits emerging from the case were settled out of court before final judgement was rendered (e.g. Merrill Lynch pleaded "no contest" and agreed to pay $437 million as a settlement, perhaps to avoid damaging its other important client relationships in Orange County and in other counties and states across the US). This incident demonstrates the importance of understanding the financial goals and capabilities of the client – what we call the "know your customer" rule. It also highlights the importance of finding out if the client is operating within the scope of its authorities and has the financial wherewithal to support large risk exposures; this is especially true when government or non-profit institutions are involved.

4.1.2 Procter and Gamble

In early 1993 Procter and Gamble (P&G) purchased derivatives from US bank Bankers Trust (BT, which has since been acquired by Deutsche Bank). P&G was apparently motivated to use interest rate derivatives to help lower its funding costs. In November 1993 the company bought the first of several leveraged derivatives from BT; these deals had complex payout formulas that required P&G to pay BT increasing amounts as interest rates rose and receive flows from BT (and thus lower its effective financing costs) as interest rates remained constant or declined. These payout arrangements were essentially interest options embedded in **swap** contracts. The company initially benefitted, as interest rates remained stable. In early 1994, however, as the Federal Reserve started hiking rates, P&G's swaps started losing money (in fact, the inaugural November 1993 transaction required the company to pay 450 basis points over its commercial paper cost of funds, equal to an incremental $40 million!). By April 1994, when P&G arranged for BT to "lock in" rates on all of its leveraged deals, it had accumulated $195 million in additional financing costs. The company subsequently took a $157 million pre-tax charge on the transactions and filed a lawsuit against BT for failing to disclose important information related to the deals (such as how to compute the payout profile of the leveraged swaps under various scenarios), misrepresenting the risk of the transactions and breaching the fiduciary/advisory relationship. The court case was accompanied by the disclosure of embarrassing material from the BT trading floor tapes, which reflected "aggressive" sales practices and attitudes by select BT employees. The case was settled out of court prior to judgement, with P&G agreeing to pay BT only $35 million of the $195 million due under the derivative contracts. As above, a financial provider must be aware of the financial sophistication of its customer, its motivation for entering into particular types of transactions and whether these are truly suitable. It also highlights the importance of running hypothetical stress scenarios that demonstrate the financial gain or loss that a client could sustain if the unthinkable actually happens (e.g. a 300 basis point move in interest rates in 12 months).

4.1.3 Sumitomo Corporation

Sumitomo Corporation, a large player in the global metals market, built a considerable trading capability in the early 1980s under head trader Yasuo Hamanaka. Hamanaka became so successful at trading in the copper market that Sumitomo gained a reputation as one of the savviest and most powerful copper dealers in the world. In fact, as Hamanaka's influence grew, he became known as "Mr 5%" for routinely being able to control 5% of the global copper market (trading primarily through the London Metal Exchange (LME), the world's largest forum for listed copper trading). By all accounts, Hamanaka actually posted strong profits for the company between 1991 and 1995; thereafter, he appears to have posted profits only by manipulating the market and hiding losing trades. Hamanaka's apparent success allowed him to remain in his trading position for many years (a process that is contrary to the personnel rotation schemes practiced by most Japanese firms). Thus, over a period of years he built a team of copper traders around him and gained control over all front- and back-office duties.

Global copper prices finally weakened in early 1996, as years of copper oversupply overwhelmed demand. At that point Hamanaka, who had successfully manipulated copper prices for at least six years (and perhaps as long as 10 years), had a very large long position in both actual physical copper as well as derivative contracts based on the price of copper. As his attempts to drive market prices became more obvious internal company auditors, as well as US and UK regulators, began investigating his activities. Hamanaka was soon "promoted" out of the copper trading department. Hedge funds and other speculators, recognizing that Hamanaka's "promotion" meant irregularities, quickly drove the price of copper down (pushing it from $2700 to $2000/ton in just four weeks!). As the internal investigation unfolded, it became apparent that by controlling trading and back-office processes (including various unauthorized and unreported accounts) and manipulating prices on the LME, Hamanaka was able to post fictional profits. He was also aided, wittingly or unwittingly, by several large international banks, which supplied Sumitomo with generous credit lines to meet LME margins. Sumitomo initially declared $1.8 billion of losses from illegal trading – equal to approximately 10% of its equity – and eventually upped the figure to $2.5 billion. In 1999 the company decided to sue JP Morgan Chase, Merrill Lynch, UBS and Credit Lyonnais for $1.7 billion, claiming they knew, or should have known, about Hamanaka's illegal trades. Several banks pleaded "no contest" and settled the matter out of court (including Merrill Lynch, which paid $275 million and JP Morgan Chase, which paid $125 million). This example illustrates the need for financial providers to ensure that their clients are duly authorized to deal, and that the most senior managers within the client organization sanction any potential financial engineering transactions. It also points out the need for managers at financial providers to review the activities of their own salespeople (who obviously get paid for the business they bring in); while not foolproof, it can help ensure that everything being done with a client is prudent and "above board".

4.1.4 Prudential Securities

As noted above, suitability issues can also affect retail customers who may, knowingly or unknowingly, invest in securities that are inappropriate in terms of potential risk. Prudential Securities, a subsidiary of US insurer Prudential Insurance, paid a heavy price for not exercising proper care in selling $8 billion worth of risky limited partnerships. From the early 1980s to 1990s Prudential's salesforce sold its retail clients units (e.g. shares) in approximately 700 limited partnerships that invested in a range of assets, from residential and commercial properties to energy projects. Most of the units were illiquid and speculative, with large amounts of credit and market risk. As one after another of these partnerships soured, irate clients took legal actions against Prudential on various grounds: lack of proper disclosure, misrepresentation of risks/returns and liquidity, and misvaluation of investments. The firm was investigated on criminal grounds and found guilty of fraud and negligence (though it escaped a criminal indictment). Prudential Insurance was ordered to establish a client restitution fund that eventually topped $1 billion, and restructured its securities subsidiary with new management and controls. This example illustrates the need for financial organizations to ensure that products aimed at individual investors are truly appropriate (with prudent amounts of risk) and accompanied by full and accurate disclosure of the potential downside that might be caused by poor performance, credit, market or liquidity events. It also highlights the need for the strictest possible financial reporting controls so that investors receive regular, and proper, valuations.

Many other disputes between clients and financial providers have arisen over the past few years; Table 4.1 summarizes some of these incidents.

Table 4.1 Client/financial provider disputes

Financial provider	Dispute
Prudential Securities	Risky limited partnerships targeted at retail investors
Bankers Trust	Derivatives with Gibson Greetings, Air Products and Chemicals, Sandoz, Jefferson Smurfit, various Asian clients
Deutsche Bank	Swaps with South East Asian companies (Malaysia, Thailand)
JP Morgan	Swaps with Korean companies
Merrill Lynch	Options with Kingdom of Belgium
Various international banks	Credit lines for Sumitomo Corporation's LME derivatives
Various international banks	Repurchase agreements and other leveraged instruments with Orange County
Various UK and international banks	Swaps with UK local authorities

4.2 KNOWING YOUR CUSTOMER

As these examples illustrate, client and legal problems can lead not only to financial pain but also reputational problems. These disputes have a nasty habit of being ventilated in the public domain, thereby potentially damaging perception and financial standing – whether or not there is fault. It is often, therefore, the reputational aspects of the conflict that are the driving force for management. Those sustaining such damage are not always able to survive – witness BT (ultimately subsumed by Deutsche Bank after a series of client derivative problems irreparably damaged public confidence in the bank) and Andersen (broken apart after the Enron collapse led to client departures and a criminal indictment).

A strong and disciplined approach to dealing with clients is therefore a prerequisite to a well-managed company. A central part of the process must center on a firm's client risk philosophy. This should clearly delineate the types of clients the firm intends to target, how much and what type of risk it is willing to assume in the process. Dealing with a client base should not be a matter of random prospecting, but should be backed by strong research about:

- The nature of the client base,
- The value added that can be brought to that client base,
- A client's rationale for being willing to entertain an approach,
- Detailed knowledge of a client's operating strategies and its level of financial sophistication.

These points, which we summarize in Figure 4.1, can be collectively thought of as the **"know your customer" rule**. This rather simple, but often overlooked, rule requires management to focus resources on predetermined customer segments and places the burden of "knowing one's client" on the shoulders of relationship managers, bankers or originators of transactions and their respective managers. They must be intimately familiar with the client, its financial sophistication motivations and needs, and also be in regular contact to ensure that important information (e.g. credit-related, strategic focus, management changes) is forthcoming. This rule is also important from a legal perspective. In our experience it is not uncommon for a salesperson to believe the firm is dealing with a particular client, only to discover after a credit-sensitive transaction has been agreed to that the actual counterparty is a small, offshore subsidiary of the parent company – absent a parent guarantee or collateral, the firm may now have ill-advised credit exposure on its books. Thus, if a firm pursues a strategy to focus its resources narrowly on corporate institutions, it should not be dealing with highly leveraged funds or emerging market governments; the control requirements needed to monitor and manage such client relationships are very different. Likewise, if the firm intends to market to, and deal with, a very large number of clients in diverse sectors, it must ensure that it has sufficient internal and market resources to conduct such operations effectively. We propose later in this chapter a mechanism for vetting transactions and dealing with specific types of clients and products that are more susceptible to reputational and financial pain.

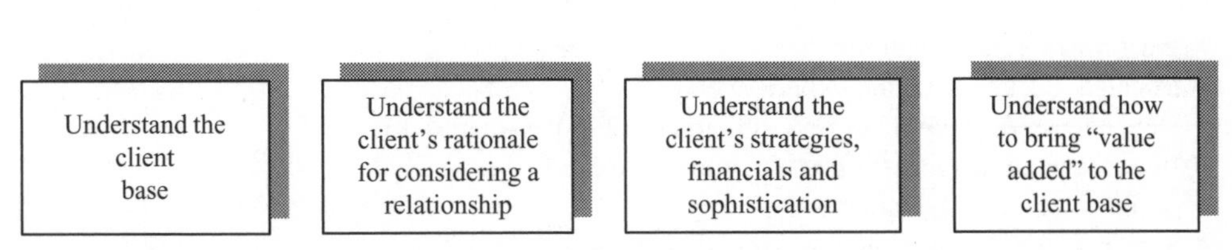

Figure 4.1 "Know your customer" rule

The extension of credit (or the establishment of a non-credit financial relationship) is based, in the first instance, on the financial strength of the client. A client that is financially strong and demonstrates a clear "capacity" to make good on its obligations becomes a candidate for unsecured credit exposure and a broad financial relationship. A client that has strong financial resources but is primarily set up to manage funds using leverage and pledging its assets or a client that does not feature the necessary financial strength may, or may not, be worthy of a financial relationship. Though posting collateral can mitigate some of the obvious credit risk exposures that might exist, other issues – related to reputation and motivation – can arise and may skew these credit decisions. For instance, a client that posts collateral to enter into a derivative transaction to hedge exposure may be considered acceptable, while one that uses the derivative transaction to mislead regulators or confuse investors and auditors is certainly unacceptable – regardless of the collateral posted. Understanding these subtleties is vital! We cover the non-credit aspects of the business decision in Section 4.3.

A credit officer narrowly making a decision about whether to extend credit risk to a counterparty (or even deal with a counterparty on a non-credit risk basis) typically relies on tools such as official company filings (e.g. annual reports, **10Ks** and **10Qs** in the US, and so on), company meetings, equity or rating agency analyst reports, press reports and general hearsay; one would assume that the first two are the most informative and accurate. We review detailed client risk considerations by splitting the counterparty universe into several categories:

- Funds,
- Governments and charitable organizations,
- Other corporate counterparties, including financial intermediaries.

4.2.1 Funds

Most dealing with funds is based on collateral being pledged. It should not be concluded, however, that any fund willing to post appropriate collateral automatically becomes a good counterparty. There are at least three other elements that are critical to consider:

- Is the fund the sort of organization that fits the client strategy?
- Who else is doing business with the fund (and how)?
- What legal issues surround the perfection of interest in the pledged collateral?

Mutual funds and unit trusts disclose reasonably detailed historical information (though rather infrequently); however, dealings with this community are not typically risk-intensive as they are mostly prohibited from borrowing and using derivatives. The credit focus is really on leveraged funds. We can conceive of splitting this universe into three categories of potential clients: the "top notch", the "acceptable" and the "do not deal with". This categorization is very subjective but can be determined by the corporate risk group by analyzing:

- Performance track record;
- Manager background and experience;
- Dependence on a single or few individuals (e.g. key-man risk);
- Investment strategy, infrastructure and controls;
- Sophistication of risk analysis;
- Size and stability of capital and investor base;
- Historical dealings and experience with the fund, and so on.

A combination of performance results analysis, market activity review, regular on-site visits and telephonic contact is needed to reach conclusions. Credit-sensitive business with funds in the "top-notch" category can conceivably be conducted on fairly aggressive terms, whilst dealings with the "acceptables" should be based purely on standard haircut policy, with no exceptions. Those in the "do not deal with" category are best avoided. We believe that it is vital to distinguish between funds in such a manner and conduct business accordingly. It is also important that such a categorization be reviewed frequently. Funds typically have a return experience that follows a "bell curve": when they start out they are "learning the ropes"; then they start performing (if they have all the necessary ingredients); eventually, however, success catches up with them and they revert toward an average performance. As a result, we might argue that ceteris paribus, the life of a fund can have more and less risky periods! Daily behavior of the fund, as observed by salespeople, risk professionals and operational staff, can also serve as an important source of credit information. In-depth and real-time knowledge of the activities of a fund is almost non-existent unless a firm happens to be the sole prime broker – simultaneously the banker and custodian of the investments. This, however, is very rare. Funds, and especially leveraged funds, do not disclose much information about their dealings with other financial intermediaries for fear that it will be used against them. Again, the decision of whether or not to deal with the client, and on what terms, is very subjective. It is a massive game of poker. It must not be forgotten that LTCM was a "top notch" category client for almost everyone on Wall Street the day before rumors of its demise started circulating!

While a client's financial strength is perhaps the most important factor in determining whether obligations will be repaid, its "willingness" to pay must also be considered. "Capacity" relates to a client's *financial strength*, while "willingness" – a much more subjective concept – relates to its *desire to pay*. As noted in the Orange County and P&G examples above, a very strong client that has the financial resources to pay its obligations (e.g. a governmental institution or well-funded corporation) may choose not to do so for any number of reasons – it may believe it has been treated unfairly by the banker (e.g. it has been "ripped off"), that the risk protection it sought failed to provide the benefits desired, that too much risk was embedded in a trade, that the valuations were wrong, and so on. Though it is difficult to know in advance whether or not a client will willingly honor its obligations (regardless of financial capacity), a firm must be alert to the possibility that transactions that have a great deal of risk, are very complicated or unusual, have a greater likelihood of being challenged by an unhappy client (typically in a loss position!). It is also true that the larger the potential loss the larger the potentiality of an impropriety claim, even if the financial agreements are straightforward. Thus, it is critical to choose the types of clients to deal with and the different types of products that can be marketed. It is also important to make sure that senior officials within the client organization are truly on top of financial transactions and potential liabilities before, and during, the life of a financial arrangement.

4.2.2 Governments and charities

Governments, and government-related organizations, should be dealt with only after very careful consideration. Governments, being ultimately political as opposed to economic organisms, have a habit of doing abrupt "u-turns" as political winds change or political gain is being sought. They also find it easy to lay claim to the argument of the weak (Mrs Jones – the poor tax payer) versus the "strong and wicked" (the large bank or corporation), which fuels the press in many countries. It is not surprising that there is a long history of certain government entities disowning loss-making transactions by claiming that the right people were not informed or authorized, that they were dealing outside of their legal scope (e.g. **ultra vires**) or did not understand the risk of the transaction(s) – in short, an "unwillingness" to pay, regardless of financial capacity. Examples such as the UK local authorities swap defaults, the Orange County bankruptcy and the Kingdom of Belgium currency losses mentioned earlier serve as important reminders. These events can very quickly become very public and embarrassing – much to the dislike of financial intermediaries and regulators. Non-profit organizations (e.g. religious foundations and pension funds) similarly have easy recourse to the public domain and should only be considered for business after very careful consideration. For these organizations regulatory oversight should be well understood but not relied upon as a simple means for concluding that official oversight is condoning their dealings.

4.2.3 Other corporations and financial intermediaries

For all other organizations, including corporations and financial intermediaries, it is increasingly true that the accounting profession does not provide us with the whole picture, as acutely highlighted in the Enron bankruptcy. The reputation of the accounting industry and its ability to provide objective and informed analysis of, and opinion on, a company's true financial health have been temporarily – and perhaps permanently – impaired. Long gone also are the days when a well-established name would require less scrutiny. Analysis starts with measures of soundness of business fundamentals, diversification of sources of income, quality and stability of management and the shareholder base, competitive environment, and so on. From there it moves to the financial statements. When it comes to the balance sheet, earnings and cash flow statements, disclosure rules, analyst reports and rating agency reviews often do not provide sufficient information to be able to see through the "financial conjuring" that goes on. In particular, not enough attention is paid to off-balance sheet activities and forward commitments. Yet these are both critical for an adequate analysis to be performed. For instance, with the focus on the Enron debacle, the press has picked up on the fact that many of the offshore off-balance sheet vehicles were not properly disclosed in the required filings (and those that were disclosed were done so in the most cursory way, buried deep in the footnotes of the statements). Lack of knowledge regarding forward commitments can, likewise, lead to misunderstanding about future liabilities and liquidity constraints as well as earnings.

It is worth noting that retail clients are not typically granted unsecured credit exposures as they lack the financial strength to support such obligations. Accordingly, credit analysis does not assume the same importance as it does with institutional clients. However, although secured lending against assets in client securities accounts is reasonably standard practice, financial institutions must still take care to know their clients, make sure that products/transactions are suitable and that disclosure of potential risks is thorough.

It is important for a firm to rely on its own analysis and judgement when it comes to making credit decisions. Though external equity and debt analysts provide certain services, they have different motivations and have proven, on many occasions, to have "missed the boat" when it comes to critical downgrading decisions. For example, Merrill Lynch's debt analyst issued a buy report on Russian rouble-denominated debt 10 days before the default! Such analysts are unfortunately also influenced by their own particular circumstances, as we have all discovered in the debacle involving the "independence" of research on Wall Street.

Against this backdrop, it is safe to say that over the past 20 years the role of the credit officer and the skill set required of a great credit officer have radically changed.

4.3 THE CREDIT DECISION: BUSINESS CONSIDERATIONS

Within each client category the need for information is constantly being balanced by business practicalities. Often salespeople claim that the client will end a business relationship if a particular question is asked or too much information is requested. Once through that barrier a firm is often told by the client that other credit providers do not ask such questions – the implicit statement being that asking questions will lead to a loss of business to more "cooperative" firms. Our feeling is that too few legitimate questions are being asked for the short-term fear of losing business. Clients certainly are able to take advantage of this. Part of the client risk philosophy has to be a clear understanding of where management stands on this issue and dilemma. Our advice is that a firm must always be prepared to forsake business if it cannot get the information it requires, regardless of who the client is, but this needs to be clearly explained. This stance can sometimes prove frustrating for marketers, originators and clients. While in the short run it may not maximize earnings, we strongly believe that it will in the long run. No single dollar, transaction or relationship is worth jeopardizing a great reputation for!

4.4 DEALING WITH CLIENT SUITABILITY

A colleague once noted that dealing with customers carries an asymmetric outcome: "There are no unsuitable transactions, only large losses! If they make money clients are happy, if they lose money they will take you to court." Whilst clearly a fairly jaded view of the world, it is true that there is risk to dealing with customers, even if no credit is extended. BT ostensibly learned this lesson the hard way in its dealings with P&G, Gibson Greetings, Sandoz, Air Products, Jefferson Smurfit, Federal Paper Board, and other counterparties. JP Morgan learned similar lessons in 1998 when five of its Korean corporate and financial clients lost $757 million on derivatives – the bank had to set aside over $500 million to cover subsequent write-offs. Deutsche Bank, Nomura Securities, Merrill Lynch, and many others have also had to pay out on client trades. But they were, are, and will not be alone.

As noted earlier, there is an undeniable responsibility for the financial intermediary to follow the "know your customer" rule – to ensure not only that the customer is well aware of, appropriately empowered and capable of understanding what is being undertaken, but also that the proposed transaction is suitable for the client. This is commonly referred to as the "suitability" test. The reality of the financial industry is such that there is always going to be an aggressive salesperson a little "joystick happy" when close to a transaction, or a client that is totally in control of the circumstances but claiming ignorance *ex post facto* when things do not work out. So how does a firm combat this and ensure that only suitable business is conducted? The only way to catch the transaction that ought not to have been entered into is to force a transaction review process ahead of time. To do so for every transaction is obviously not practical, nor is it necessary. Instead, it is best to choose certain types of transactions that are prone to problems and hope that this catches the majority of them. A firm could, for example, choose to review all transactions with:

- Tax or accounting motivations;
- Special purpose vehicles;
- High gearing (where the customer could quite easily lose a large amount of money);
- Large upfront payment(s) or unusual cash flows, and so on.

In short, transactions that are risky, "non-standard", or which attempt to manage (or legally circumvent) regulatory, tax or accounting issues are good candidates for review.

It is also important to focus on client categories that are more likely to need scrutiny and submit them to the same review process. These might include counterparties that are more prone to disputing transactions, those that are less "market savvy" or those who enter into transactions as "insiders". Again, care should be taken when considering transactions with:

- Governments (or government-related institutions) which, being more subject to the vagaries of prevailing political winds, have at times disowned (loss-making) transactions.
- Charitable, educational, pension or tax-exempt organizations.
- Customers exhibiting unusual behavior, such as requiring upfront payments that represent a large proportion of their normal operating earnings.
- Customers that enter into derivative transactions for purposes other than hedging well-defined exposures (e.g. foreign exchange receivables/payables or bond issuance); this is especially true when the transaction involves the corporation's own stock (e.g. Enron).
- Note that as a general rule very risky or complex transactions with retail customers should be placed "off limits". Any exception to this (e.g. offering leveraged structured notes to individual investors) should be reviewed to consider any special requirements related to appropriateness, disclosure, valuations, and so forth.

An internal committee comprised of senior representatives from relevant corporate functions (finance, risk, audit and legal), as well as senior business representatives unconnected to the transaction, should review any potential deal that has these characteristics. The inclusion of business people is vital as it places a "peer review" burden on the transaction that should enhance the self-governance nature of the process. This further helps to neutralize part of the natural tension that exists between the business advocate and the corporate control functions. It is also useful to place a member of the external auditor team on the committee in order to obtain a "neutral" opinion. Meetings must be "non-bureaucratic" and easy to call at 24 hours' notice so as not to be viewed as a burden – and therefore a hurdle that needs to be circumvented. Attendance by senior-level personnel should be mandatory and detailed minutes should be kept for the record. In order to determine the efficacy of the process, the status of transactions approved in the past should be reviewed on a periodic basis. A firm should always seek the opinion of counsel (internal or external) regarding a given counterparty's ability to execute specific transactions; time and effort spent on legal due diligence, particularly for large transactions or extensive relationships, can be well worth it!

In our experience the mere act of forming such a committee stops many of the more opportunistic and outrageous transactions from even appearing. However, this process, even when it works well, is not failsafe. There will always be transactions that – with hindsight – should not have been done. When they do go wrong, having a rigorous process to point to will certainly help in the defense. Part of the process should, of course, include a "post mortem" on transactions that go wrong – this allows a firm to enhance existing, or establish new, relationship and transaction criteria in order to avoid future problems.

4.5 TOWARD BETTER DISCLOSURE

We have already referred to problems of insufficient disclosure – this relates equally to non-profit organizations, government entities, funds and other financial and corporate institutions. Disclosure for corporations and non-profit organizations, as well as disclosure in many countries not subscribing to **Generally Accepted Accounting Principles** (GAAP), is also problematical. Though US GAAP is taken by many to be "the standard", it is certainly not the only valid one: there are many other acceptable ways of considering and treating the same kind of financial information. For instance, **International Accounting Standards** (IAS, to which many non-US companies adhere) is an equally valid standard – though one that often treats financial accounts differently than US GAAP. Consider just a few simple differences between IAS and US GAAP (but ones that can dramatically skew the presentation of financial accounts!):

- Under IAS intangible assets, investment property, plant and equipment, can be revalued periodically above or below historical cost; under GAAP this practice is strictly forbidden.
- Under IAS **special purpose vehicles** have to be consolidated into parent accounts when the substance of the relationship reflects "control"; under GAAP consolidation is based on "risks and rewards" (e.g. who bears the risk and earns the profits) rather than control.
- Under IAS intangible assets that are acquired have to be capitalized and amortized over a period of less than 20 years, but they can be revalued; under GAAP they have to be capitalized and amortized over their "useful life" (which can be indefinite), but they can never be revalued.
- Under IAS inventories have to be valued at the lower of cost or net replacement value on a "first in–first out" or "average" method; under GAAP they are valued on a "last in–first out" basis.
- Under IAS impaired assets are written down to the higher of net selling price or discounted cash flow value; under GAAP they are written down to undiscounted cash flow value.
- Under IAS unrealized gains/losses in investments available for sale can be recognized through the income statement or the equity account; under GAAP they must be recognized through the equity account.
- Under IAS convertible bonds are classified on a "split basis" between the debt and equity accounts; under GAAP they are treated strictly as debt.
- Under IAS gains/losses on instruments used to hedge forecast transactions are included in the cost of the asset/liability being hedged; under GAAP no gains/losses are included.
- Under IAS two years of historical accounts are required (though interim reporting is not mandatory); under GAAP three years of historical accounts are required (except for the balance sheet) and quarterly reporting is mandatory for domestic SEC registrants.
- Under IAS no mandatory operating and financial review is required; under GAAP a management discussion focused on liquidity, capital and operations must be prepared.

Clearly, understanding the disclosure differences generated by different accounting standards is a key part of the analysis process.

For many funds the relevant information is actually not difficult for them to assemble or compute; it is the same information that traders ought to be looking at on a daily, and even hourly, basis. However, the stated excuse for not making it available is often the result of legitimate concerns that competing trading desks could use the information. Whilst we buy this, it is being overplayed. It is possible to set up strong, legally binding, segregation of information within an organization – so-called **Chinese walls**. It is also possible to engage a third party to filter the information to protect some of the detail, and yet not reduce its usefulness to the creditor. The events described in Chapter 1, in which certain organizations made use of inside information against LTCM, do not exactly prove our point. We do, however, believe that the market place or regulators will, over time, force greater disclosure. We sincerely hope that such regulation and disclosure rules will actually be useful to investors.

There is a large void to be filled by accounting and regulatory agencies in both financial accounting and risk disclosure. The former has certainly been highlighted by the collapse of Enron (to wit, major companies such as GE, Williams Companies, JP Morgan Chase and others have since supplied more detailed financial analyses), however, not much attention has been paid to the latter. For accounting disclosure there is an urgent need to better segregate earning changes from operating results and those arising from revised financial assumptions (e.g. pension liability discount rates); there is a need to add to the "point in time" balance sheet and earnings statements a **forward balance sheet** and earnings statement which details material future and off-balance sheet commitments; there is also a need to enhance transparency in all organizations primarily by getting rid of management accounts and the ability for management to smooth earnings. The financials that everyone sees internally ought to be the same ones shown to shareholders. This keeps things simpler, transparent and honest. In addition to improved GAAP and IAS there is an urgent need for the accounting and regulatory community to dictate useful standards of risk disclosure for financial and non-financial corporations, funds, not-for-profit organizations and governments – which could be referred to as the Generally Agreed Risk Disclosures (GARD). These would provide detailed position disclosure, risk and liquidity measurements, and counterparty exposures; setting such standards would take time to perfect but would certainly fill a very large void. The initiative for this will not willingly come from market practitioners – for obvious reasons!

Dealing with clients is complex. Firms must construct and follow a very disciplined approach using all available tools – risk philosophy, policies, "know your client" rule, due diligence, client or transaction vetting committees, independent credit/risk assessment, and so on – to reinforce their client management process and protect their franchise. To get a full picture of an ever-sophisticated client's financial set-up, especially given the creativity of financial markets and the current state of the accounting community, is asking too much. Without more of the necessary information but with the need to generate earnings, many decisions are being made with too many unknowns. We are back to playing financial poker.

4.6 TEN USEFUL SUITABILITY RISK QUESTIONS

In wrapping up it is always useful to ask, and follow up on, the following questions about suitability:

1. Has the business experienced any client suitability problems and what were the lessons/remedies?
2. Has management clearly defined its target client base and is it adhering to that list?
3. How does management treat clients that are not on its target list?
4. Does the firm's credit policy state clearly which clients it will extend credit to and on what terms?
5. Does the firm have a process that ensures transactors/originators "know their clients" – their capabilities, needs, financial standing and authorizations?
6. How does the firm filter transactions for client suitability and does the process include representatives with enough experience and independence to make decisions?
7. What special procedures does the firm have for dealing with government, non-profit and charitable organizations?

8. Do transactors/originators provide clients with sufficient information about potential transactions risks/downside scenarios and regular valuation updates?
9. Does the credit risk group have the experience and stature to conduct comprehensive credit analysis and client follow-up?
10. If credit officers/originators are unable to obtain from a client the financial information necessary to pursue business, does management terminate a business relationship?

5
Process Risks: The Next Frontier

5.1 DEFINING PROCESS RISK

Process risk is the term that we use to encompass all risks that do not fit into the market, credit, liquidity, model, legal or client buckets. It is often called "operational risk", probably because operational errors or fraud – such as payment of funds or delivery of securities to the wrong counterparty – have received the most attention. It is, however, precisely because the understanding of these risks should not be limited to operational errors that we chose the expression "process risk". A more precise definition is therefore all risks of failure in the process after decisions on market, credit, liquidity, legal and client risks have been made. In this chapter we will analyze and categorize the breakdowns in the process that can take place. In the next chapter we consider measurement of process risk, and in Chapter 9 we propose how best to create incentives to mitigate it. This area of risk management is very important and has historically cost firms lots of money, most certainly more than most of us know; as we have indicated earlier, it is very difficult to know precisely how much money these risks cost individual companies or entire industries, but all available estimates suggest the amounts are very large – perhaps several billions each year. It has also recently become of keen interest to financial regulators (as mentioned in Chapter 2, regulators are imposing process risk capital charges for financial institutions).

5.2 CATEGORIZING PROCESS RISK

For the smooth running of an institution the entire basic infrastructure has to be functioning. People need access to the building, the lights, and phones, computers and sources of data have to be in working order, and so on. After a transaction has been agreed to, it needs to be uploaded into the computer systems from which documentary evidence of the transaction feeds into the risk, financial, operational and regulatory compliance infrastructure of the organization. Customers can then be sent details of their dealings, legal documents can be drawn up, monies and securities exchanged, financial records updated, liens created or re-evaluated, risk data analyzed, and so on. A lot can go wrong in this long chain! If it does, luck has it that it usually results in a loss. As with other categories of risk reviewed in earlier chapters, it is important to know where your strengths and weaknesses lie. We find that the most logical categorization of various ways in which things can go wrong follows the chronological order in which business is done. We therefore propose segregating process risks into various categories, including **disaster recovery risk**, **business recovery risk**, **people risk**, **front-office error risk**, **operations error risk**, **software error risk**, **authorization risk**, **structured product risk**, **documentation follow-up risk**, **collateral risk** and **regulatory compliance risk**. This is, of course, just one way of classifying and considering process risks – firms may choose to include some, all or more categories. Since process risk is so "all-encompassing" – touching

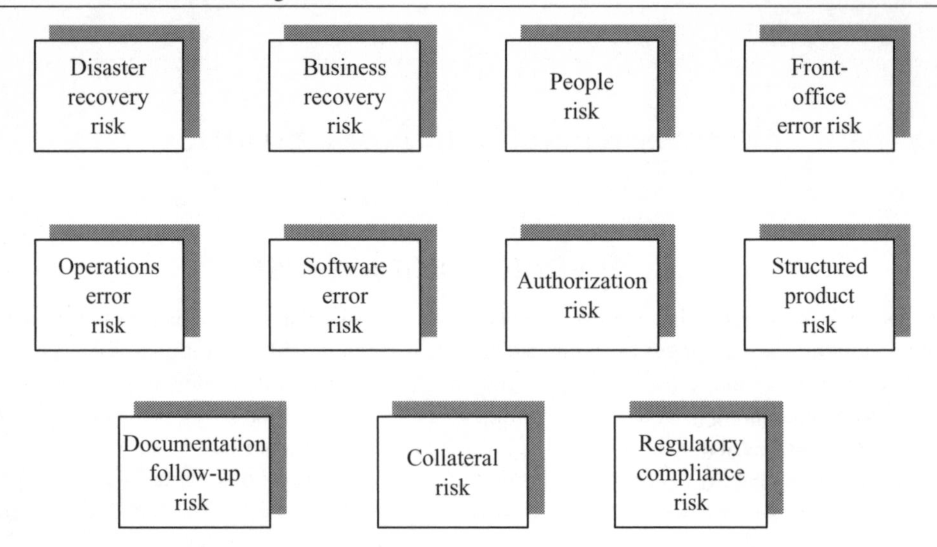

Figure 5.1 Process risks

on aspects of business flow that are broad and often unique – it is important for each firm to define and categorize its own risks.

Figure 5.1 summarizes the main process risks.

5.3 DISASTER RECOVERY RISK

People need to work in a familiar environment. Disaster recovery can be defined as the process that needs to be followed when a company loses access to this working environment – head office, one or several floors of a large building, or a smaller branch office. The term "working environment" also needs to be defined broadly. For instance, the building may be accessible but none of the computers might be working as a result of loss of electricity, fire, sprinkler systems getting activated, etc. Disaster recovery is different from dealing with a temporary interruption of business, which we address in Section 5.4.

Conversion to the euro, followed by preparations for "Y2K", heightened awareness of the need for robust planning for alternative working premises and infrastructure. Thankfully, though there were small "hiccups", no large-scale activation of these plans was required. By contrast, the events of September 11, 2001 in New York required considerable disaster recovery action. The luckier organizations simply lost access to their premises temporarily, the less fortunate ones lost access to their premises for a prolonged period of time, others lost permanent access and some, tragically, most of their personnel. All of these events provide very fertile ground for examining what can go wrong and what can be done to overcome such problems.

On the morning of September 11 personnel had been evacuated from the Merrill Lynch headquarters campus (adjacent to the World Trade Center Towers). These buildings housed executive management and investment banking personnel, the key debt and equity trading floors, as well as most of the supporting technology, finance, risk, research and middle-office groups. The core operations functions were located in Jersey City (across the river from downtown Manhattan). Merrill Lynch's data centers were split between a location further up on the west side of Manhattan and Staten Island. These two data centers served to back each other up in the event of one going down. Two new buildings were at the point of coming on line – one in Jersey City and another close to Princeton. Merrill Lynch had also recently acquired a specialist in over-the-counter stock trading which had a trading floor located one train stop north of Jersey City.

The advent of Y2K had forced the organization to galvanize itself around a real event and much work had gone into producing lists of contacts, home and mobile telephone numbers, communication chains, inventory of technology programs, and so on. However, severe cost-cutting in 2001 had led to the disaster recovery planning budgets in the institutional businesses being halved. Partly as a result of this, on September 10 Merrill Lynch's institutional business did not have an actionable disaster recovery plan to cope with what was about to happen. In its defense not many organizations had plans that were designed to accommodate the eventuality of two planes destroying the Twin Towers – thereby causing the whole of lower Manhattan to be inaccessible for several weeks and much of its infrastructure to be severely impaired.

On September 12 the operations group (responsible for processing, clearing and settling trades), being based in New Jersey, was essentially intact and ready for work. The equity division ended up squatting in the premises of the newly acquired over-the-counter specialist. The debt division moved into the new building in Jersey City with technology, finance and corporate risk management personnel, whilst investment bankers ended up mainly working from home or the Princeton area. Even though people could be physically accommodated somehow, the primary challenge was to make them operational. This required rebuilding of large portions of the communications and technology infrastructure within and between the various Merrill premises and, more importantly, between these premises and the outside world. The firm was now at the mercy of a handful of telecommunications and computer/telephonic hardware providers – who were not without problems of their own – and the people who could make this hardware operational.

In addition to restoring the ability for people to operate and communicate there was a need for traders, operational, finance and risk personnel to know their positions. Some businesses ran truly global infrastructures and were able to immediately switch to databases and personnel based in London or Asia. Most businesses, however, were running very fragmented technology. Each business in the institutional division possessed its own software programs in support of its activities, and there were very few standards imposed across the entire division. Firm-wide transparency to positions and client dealings across the division were very manually intensive to construct.

Critical trading floor technology hardware and software in New York was located under each trading floor. With the appropriate communications technology it would have been possible to run this technology remotely from the data centers – however, the head-office building subsequently temporarily reached temperatures of over 140°F and all computers had to be shut down. In such an event one would usually turn to back-up tapes to reconstruct the positions. Tapes backing up daily or weekly positions were being created. However, they were being kept under the trading floor, not removed and stored away from the premises as is common practice. Groups of personnel, led by the vice chairman of the company, were sent in under special authorization from the "Ground Zero" rescue effort to recover thousands of tapes. Once retained it was discovered that for some businesses the discipline of creating back-up tapes was weak and the information was over three months old!

Merrill Lynch thus ended up dependent on people working 24 hours a day, sieving through thousands of tapes. It took a full two weeks before all positions were retrieved and the financial records could be re-established. In the meantime markets were very volatile and the firm was going into quarter-end reporting of earnings. Having learned the lessons of 1998, management had fortunately instituted a new funding policy that lowered the firm's dependency on the commercial paper market (and enabled it to fund itself for one year without needing to access the debt markets). Therefore, even if news of these difficulties had spread, Merrill Lynch's liquidity profile was very secure.

Lehman Brothers, Bank of New York and countless others went through their own versions of this trauma. It would be equally interesting to study the specifics of each experience. To gain some first-hand lessons on disaster recovery, we can consider what went wrong and what went right with the Merrill Lynch trauma.

What went wrong?

- The underlying premise for disaster recovery did not match the incident.
- Recovery plans were not actionable.
- The communications infrastructure plans were not appropriate for the event.
- Dependency on a few key suppliers and service providers was not well understood.
- Back-up data tapes were not being stored off the premises.
- Technology was very fragmented, with few firm-wide standards.

What went right?

- Businesses were spread out – in particular, the operations functions and main data centers were not located with the debt and equity businesses, and therefore not affected.
- The equity business possessed a "similar operating environment" in a separate location.
- Merrill Lynch had surplus real estate in a condition to be quickly usable.
- Merrill Lynch had "muscle" with the authorities and suppliers to be able to get help fast.
- Merrill Lynch thankfully did not lose substantial numbers of critical personnel in the incident.
- The quality of personnel was excellent: people were creative and worked very hard.
- The company's liquidity profile was very secure.

Since it is not possible to plan for all disasters, how does one choose which to plan for? And how does one create disaster recovery rules that can easily be applied by some units but not others?

We feel that a firm should develop a handful of "common sense" loss control steps that provide a core level of protection for any disaster situation. It is very important that these steps be "actionable" rather than theoretical so that they protect and add value as soon as a crisis strikes. It is pointless to create a theoretical disaster recovery framework that is so complicated and involved that no one can follow it when needed! Examples of these loss control steps would include[1]:

- Diversifying businesses geographically.
- Splitting front- and back-office functions into different physical locations.
- Segregating data center(s) from the main operating locations.
- Copying sensitive and relevant electronic information to offsite data centers (every day, without fail!).
- Archiving original documents offsite.
- Replicating business origination and trading facilities offsite (on a smaller, but still useful, scale).

---

[1] Note that many of these can also be applied to smaller scale business interruptions, as described in the next section.

- Creating *simple* instructions (with a deliberate emphasis on simple) on where key personnel should go, and whom they should contact, in the event of a disaster.
- Working with, being aware of and testing supplier disaster recovery plans. This would include communications, payments, security, safe custody and so forth, and may necessitate diversification of suppliers.

Ultimately, it is up to executive management and the board, working closely with its regulators, to decide what type of disaster the company is trying to protect against. It is critical that each firm then prepares itself for such an eventuality by conducting quarterly *real-time tests* of the control steps mentioned above (e.g. testing daily data back-up and retrieval procedures, migrating business, risk and finance personnel to offsite trading locations, having them conduct "mock trades", and so forth). We strongly believe that there is a need to divulge the premise for this planning and for management to publicly sign off that it has funded and regularly tested the necessary working plans. Hopefully, since the unfortunate events of September 11, everyone is taking disaster recovery plans more seriously!

Disaster recovery risks can be broad-based, such as those based on September 11-type scenarios, or institution-specific. When disaster strikes many institutions at the same time, the possibility of systemic interruptions is heightened and the chance of much larger financial losses is far greater. When institution-specific, problems can still be serious but should be more contained – and much less destructive from a system-wide perspective. The market, however, may be less forgiving to that single organization in a single-institution event.

5.4 BUSINESS RECOVERY RISK

Business recovery is the action taken when a business is temporarily interrupted. For example, internal computer networks may "go down", market prices may not be available at market open, and so on. This is distinct from the disaster recovery mentioned above in that the interruption is known to be temporary and very specific. (There have, for example, been instances in which brokers executing customer orders have been unable to fulfill their regulatory obligation in the US to provide *best execution* because of computers "being down".)

Unlike disaster recovery, for which there is an acknowledgment that there will be disruption which detailed planning is attempting to minimize, here the specificity of the cause and temporary nature of the problem (a few minutes to half a day) necessitate detailed planning of a contingency that can be immediately activated to allow business to continue in a seamless manner – without impairing client and firm activity. Most of these interruptions are also too temporary to require activation of the more lengthy process of disaster recovery planning – however, disaster recovery remains an ultimate "backstop" solution which needs to be actionable at any time.

Business recovery issues tend to involve detailed technology, communication hardware and software planning. It is usually best to prioritize businesses in order of importance to the organization and run various scenarios of what could possibly cause each business to be interrupted on a temporary basis: loss of exchange or supplier connections, loss of telephone connections, loss of power, loss of computer networks, and so forth. A detailed plan of action should be prepared for each of these and promulgated throughout divisions of the organization likely to be affected. We have traditionally found a stronger user "buy-in" for such preparations as they are closer to the everyday reality that people can relate to. Again, it is critical that each firm provides transparency and sign-off on the types of scenarios that have been envisaged, planned and regularly tested.

5.5 PEOPLE RISK

With a robust working environment, investors need the right personnel *in situ*, well organized and led by good leaders with strong business capabilities. Occasionally an institution becomes overly dependent on one person or a few people for a critical part of its business. We refer to this as **key-person risk**. We have invariably found that at most stages of development, any institution possesses a few people without whom profitability, business strategy, a smooth operating environment or the willingness of the rest of the organization to follow enthusiastically is severely impaired. It is interesting to note that these may not all be people at the top of the tree. It is also interesting to note that sometimes the impact of their departure can take many years to observe.

Why should we concern ourselves with this? Simply a very profitable business dependent on one absolutely critical person is less valuable than the same business conducted by several people. The impact of that person leaving is greater in the first case and the probability of everyone leaving at the same time is lower in the second case. It is important that an organization understand its criteria for the value of an employee: the person who is a great politician, the person's best friend, the person who is the most vocal, the person that some person sitting in a human resources "ivory tower" puts on a list, the person who is truly adding value (over and above the value of the position that they occupy), and so on.

A great trader with a lengthy track record of profitability, true value-added ideas and great risk-management discipline is a rarity. We have historically found that not enough organizations know how to differentiate between the "value of the seat" and the "value of the trader". In other words, a trader who makes a lot of money occupying the seat which sees the most flow in a specific market is worth less than the trader making the same amount of money in the same product on a consistent basis in a seat with only half that flow. In some cases it is the seat that entitles most of the money to be made! This is especially true for organizations that have a strong recognizable franchise and goodwill: clients may be dealing with the organization at large rather than an individual in particular. Mistaken judgement of who is really adding value will lead to a misappropriation of the risk of an employee leaving and a misallocation of resources.

An increasing body of work on "neural networks" within an organization is pointing to the fact that there are people, not always in the most obvious hierarchical positions and not always the most vocal, who are critical to the smooth and efficient operation of an organization: the person who marks and checks the collateral every night, the person who has been in the organization for a long time and is the "go to" person to get things done, the person who is the local opinion leader, and so forth. Very often these people perform more important roles on a daily basis than many in lofty senior positions. Yet these people often go undetected and can be a far greater loss when they decide to depart. Ultimately, however, great human resources management is about understanding which people are truly adding value and nurturing their interest in the company via great leadership, communication, training, empowerment, promotion and remuneration.

People risk can also manifest itself in the people who are present rather than the people who depart. For instance, mismanagement or general lack of supervision by those higher up in the chain can lead to breakdowns in business or control process and increase the likelihood of errors and losses. In fact, mismanagement appears to be a factor in virtually every large loss experienced by financial institutions. We consider management issues at greater length in Chapter 13.

5.6 FRONT-OFFICE ERROR RISK

As customers convey orders and salespeople/traders place orders, communication can sometimes get tangled up. Although this does not happen often it is part of where the process can break down: a customer says "sell" and the clerk enters "buy"; the price of an order was 99.05 and the salesperson entered 99.15; and so on. Such errors are typically "money losers" for the institution, either because they are assumed by it as a *mea culpa*, or because they result in a customer dispute. We also suspect instances in which orders placed by customers end up being placed by the broker shortly thereafter in the error account if the market moved the wrong way. These are not strictly errors, but as brokers' remuneration often does not take account of losses in error accounts they may have an incentive to accommodate customers in such a manner.

This area of process risk is very hard to monitor and receives little focus. Yet in many organizations, particularly those dealing with high volume/small size retail flows, it can end up being quite costly. Several possible solutions come to mind. In the short term a firm should ensure appropriate management and supervision are in place, and that people are well trained and held strictly accountable for any mistakes or violations. In the longer term, a firm should attempt to use as much "straight-through processing" technology as possible – technology that does not require human intervention and which can automatically detect front-office trade errors ("out trades", cancellations, revisions, and so on).

5.7 OPERATIONS ERROR RISK

Operational errors, possibly the most commonly associated with process risk, include mistakes such as late payment or delivery of securities (leading to payment of a late charge or non-receipt of interest), money being sent to the wrong counterparty, **fails to deliver** not being monitored, securities being sent to a fraudulent account, accounts not being established or reconciled properly, and so on. With hundreds of billions of dollars of money and securities changing hands on a daily basis, it is easy to see how a few can go wrong – when they do, the cost can be quite high.

To combat this problem we feel that there needs to be action on four fronts:

- First, the front office and operations groups need to work hand in hand. The critical separation of duty between the two naturally needs to be stringently maintained. If, however, this leads to the groups not even knowing the names or faces of their respective counterparts, there will be no sense of professionalism or care – only jobs.
- Second, there needs to be a high quality of personnel, training, leadership and sense of purpose in the operations areas, without excessive turnover in personnel.
- Third, there needs to be rigorous and timely financial explanation of financial results and reconcilliation of inventory and collateral accounts; many of these errors will thus come to light, allowing solutions to be developed.
- Fourth, there needs to be diligent and timely review of personal trading accounts. Unusual activity or cash movements, which are many multiples of a person's annual salary, usually point to there being something worth investigating!

5.8 SOFTWARE ERROR RISK

Financial engineers produce the formulas for the computation of the value of a financial risk. These are then entered into the computer systems by a programmer; very often these are separate people with separate skill sets. Sometimes disaster can ensue. Bankers Trust had the "Andy Krieger" affair in 1989 where the computation of some cross-currency forward values was programmed wrongly, Kidder Peabody experienced the "Joe Jett" affair in which the stripping of coupons from US Treasury securities in the computer system allowed for misvaluations, and so forth. These events are closely related to the topic of model risk touched upon in Chapter 2. Standard models for the computation of forward curves, options and other financial variables should be imposed by a model group resident in the independent risk management function. This group should maintain a readily available library of software code for each model that it has authorized.

Software programming errors can end up costing a lot of money. We would argue that although many of these boil down to programming errors, half or more of the fault lies with the traders and accounting personnel who, if competent, ought to be able to observe that the computer-generated results do not agree with their intuitive or risk-imputed results. Any trader or accountant who relies on computers to be more than sophisticated multi-tasked calculators is asking for trouble!

5.9 AUTHORIZATION RISK

With both traders and operations personnel handling hundreds of millions, and sometimes billions, of dollars on a daily basis it is vital to have a very disciplined approach to the hierarchy of authorization: who can handle what product, up to how much and what sign-off is required for products or amounts in excess of the authorized amount. These rules need to be very clearly defined and reviewed on a regular basis with new and existing personnel. They also need to be inculcated into the software applications that ultimately perform the actual movement of the cash or securities. In commercial banking institutions, this type of discipline is more readily apparent, where authorizations for dealing, approving transactions and credit lines, and so on are more deeply ingrained. In a securities trading environment, where the pace is often more frenzied and reactive, the discipline is far less rigorous.

5.10 STRUCTURED PRODUCT RISK

There is more risk of error throughout the life of a complex transaction involving many component trades ("legs") than there is in the purchase of a security with delivery versus payment settlement. Once a complex transaction has been undertaken there is a distinct tendency for the "producer" to move on to the next transaction and leave the follow-up to someone else. Yet, after such a transaction has been completed the confirmation has to be drafted, checked and sent out. It must accurately represent the terms of the agreement. There has to be assurance that the counterparty is authorized to enter into the agreement, understands and agrees to the written terms, counter-signs and returns the confirmation. The formal legal document must then follow. The transaction (and all the various legs) have to be entered into the financial and risk systems of the firm, ensuring again that they accurately reflect the liability that has been created. Operations personnel have to comprehend the transaction. Payment and delivery instructions have to be established for monies and securities that are to exchange hands. Collateral, and maybe trust or pledge agreements, have to be put in place. Internal and external accountants have to be able to independently value all legs of the transaction, and it has to be understood by risk personnel. This has to go on until the transaction matures – which could be in three months, 15 years or longer.

Solutions exist to cope with this risk. The more coordinated the "follow-up" the less room for error; the more divorced the "follow-up" is from the dealmakers the greater the chance for errors. Coordination must thus be stressed. The more involved in the process the "follow-uppers" feel, the fewer errors there will be. The more the "follow-uppers" are qualified to understand the complexity of the transactions, and the more trained they are, the fewer errors there will be.

We feel it is important that transactors be held accountable for ensuring ongoing follow-up of any deal-related items; while they obviously should not lead the charge in negotiating legal documentation (which is the work of the lawyers) they need to be available, cooperative and feel accountable for following the transaction throughout its life.

5.11 DOCUMENTATION FOLLOW-UP RISK

Some businesses require manually generated confirmations and final documentation. Even though the documents may be sent out promptly, it may take a long while for them to be returned in signed form. Some transactions have been known to mature before documents have been formally signed by both parties – hardly a legal comfort! Any dispute in the interim would rely solely on the short version confirmation of the transaction and perhaps taped telephone conversations. This is bound to carry greater risk. A status report of legal documentation follow-up must be produced for each business, and every item on that report must be tracked down and resolved.

5.12 COLLATERAL RISK

Transactions backed by collateral, or linked to collateral, require ongoing management of the collateral, how its price changes over time, how its form (e.g. stock splits), ownership (e.g. name of the company) and liquidity change over time, and so on. In large organizations this is a very specialized function dealing with hundreds of different collateral agreements that are often documented in different legal jurisdictions. Different degrees of automation are used and sometimes price feeds are automatically taken from outside services. In such instances it is critical to spot-check prices. Less liquid instruments often get repriced more infrequently and may not accurately reflect current market valuations! Again common sense must prevail. The operational group that is responsible for obtaining, monitoring, adjusting and releasing collateral should develop, and adhere to, procedures related to valuation, frequency of review, and so on; it should also circulate a list of concentrated, less liquid and less creditworthy collateral positions to the risk and business groups – ongoing awareness of such sensitive collateral positions can focus attention on potential problems before they occur.

5.13 TRAINING AND REGULATORY COMPLIANCE RISK

A firm has to make sure that all of its business personnel are appropriately trained to perform their duties and that they comply with governing regulations and licensing. This means making sure that all personnel possess the appropriate skills and regulatory qualifications empowering them to undertake their jobs. As their jobs change over time training and qualifications may need to be updated – a regular check is thus vital. Similarly, a regular review of employee securities and cash transactions is a vital way of checking on possible fraud or insider trading activities. A firm should not put itself in a position where it runs foul of regulators over simple things like proper adherence to securities rules and regulations. The regulatory impact of these violations, once in the public domain, can be very damaging.

5.14 CONTROLLING PROCESS RISKS

Since process risks touch on so many aspects of a firm's operations, managing these risks demands efforts on various fronts, including:

- Creating a disaster recovery plan and testing it regularly.
- Developing business interruption plans and testing them regularly.
- Obtaining property/casualty insurance coverage (including permanent replacement and business interruption covers) to indemnify against financial losses and an inability to conduct business.
- Adopting appropriate operational control and documentation policies.
- Instituting relevant technology and infrastructure to track and monitor errors, reduce the possibility of manual/human mistakes, and aid in processing/reconciliation of business flows (e.g. trades, collateral, legal documents).
- Auditing transaction flow processes on a regular basis to locate weaknesses.
- Creating management teams with proper leadership that appropriately disseminate knowledge and information.
- Reviewing pricing models/software independently and making sure changes occur in an auditable and secure technical environment.

We shall discuss some of these aspects of process risk control in greater detail in subsequent chapters.

5.15 TEN USEFUL PROCESS RISK QUESTIONS

In wrapping up it is useful to ask, and follow up on, the following process risk questions for any business:

1. Has the business experienced any historical process risk-related problems or losses and what were the lessons/remedies implemented?
2. Does the firm have appropriate internal and external disaster recovery and business resumption plans (e.g. are functions split geographically, have remote business locations been established, are data centers segregated, is sensitive data copied every day, do suppliers have adequate plans of their own)? Are these recovery plans successfully tested regularly?
3. Does technology supporting the business easily provide accurate and timely visibility and transparency to data consistent with firm standards?
4. If it is a business that requires complex support, what is the coordination between front office and support functions like (e.g. are the people good, trustworthy and qualified, is management strong and empowered, and is the documentation follow-up done on a timely basis)?
5. Does the business operate in new, complex or less developed markets and, if so, what precautions have been taken against this?
6. Is profitability and control critically dependent on one or very few people and, if so, are these people well known to senior management?
7. Have all the models being used for valuations been vetted by the model control group?
8. Is a structure of transaction authorization in place and well monitored?
9. Is the business in regulatory compliance with segregation of duties, personnel qualification and personal trading rules?
10. What are the results of the recent internal audit reports?

6

Measurement: Quantifying the Risks

When a firm realizes that it is running risks like those described in the previous chapters, it must know approximately how much money it is putting at risk. To get to this it must start by measuring its exposures. It needs to perform this analysis for the small changes that occur in the market place almost every day as well as the "one-hundred-year floods". This measurement process is key to crystallizing risk appetite for the firm, managing daily exposures and providing a common language of risk data (we will discuss these topics in the next chapter).

A great deal has been written about risk measurement, and we are in no way trying to compete with that extensive body of work – we would certainly not be doing the topic justice by trying to present a detailed treatise in one chapter alone! Instead, we try to provide a simple "layman's guide" on various measures and how they might be used to quantify different risks. For our purposes we divide measures into the mathematical – measures that involve heavy-duty math and statistics – and the **subjective** – measures that rely on experience and intuition. We think it is very important to point out that most measures are ultimately based on simplifying assumptions designed to make computation practical. Unfortunately, these simplifications can actually over- or understate risks. When this happens it is usually not that the formulas are wrong, just that they are being misinterpreted. Quantification, like many other aspects of risk management, is an art!

6.1 MATHEMATICAL MEASURES

A host of mathematical measures can be used to quantify risks, including those based on:

- Statistics,
- Analytics,
- Scenarios,
- Value-at-risk (VAR),
- Maximum loss.

Statistical measures are computed using assumed patterns of occurrences of events and are meant to describe what might happen in the future, thereby giving an estimate of the risk a firm might face at different points in time. These measures rely on assumptions about the shape of the distribution of occurrences. For instance, if prices move in an orderly manner without major jumps up or down, the graph of the number of times a price movement from current levels is observed is shaped like a normal distribution (e.g. standard "bell curve"). If jumps to the upside occur more often, the distribution is skewed to the right (lognormal distribution). If we observe many instances of large movements in prices the distribution is said to have "fat tails" (e.g. a larger portion at the extreme part of the distribution, indicating the greater possibility of larger movements). Knowing the distribution, we can apply "statistical confidence levels" – the level of statistical certainty desired, such as 95% or 99%, and obtain an estimate of the result to a particular level of accuracy. In general, the higher the confidence level, the higher the resulting exposure. Thus, a statistical measure of credit exposure on a five-year interest rate swap might indicate a maximum risk of $1 million with 95% certainty or a maximum of $1.5 million with 99% certainty.

Some exposures can be measured using very well-known financial mathematics – which we term **analytics** – that do not make assumptions about what might happen in the future, they simply indicate how much will be gained or lost on a position (e.g. delta, gamma, vega, theta, as discussed in Chapter 2). If the size of the position is known, a specific financial formula can be applied and a result obtained. Thus, an analytic formula might indicate that a $1 million bond position will gain or lose $10 000 for every 10 basis point move in five-year interest rates; unlike statistical measurements, it attempts no prediction at how likely the occurrence of a 10 basis point move will be.

Scenarios attempt to indicate what might happen to a position under different market circumstances by answering a series of "what if" questions, i.e. given a position, what will happen if the equity market falls by 5%, what will happen if the yield curve rises by 50 basis points, what will happen if all BB counterparties in a certain country default, and so forth. Scenarios can, and should, cover very probable events (e.g. high frequency, small loss) as well as disaster events (e.g. the "hundred-year floods" that generate very large losses). Since scenarios are expressed in profit and loss terms, they give risk managers and business managers instant information about the economic impact of exposure. For example, a manager applying scenarios will know that the 50 basis point shift in the yield curve will gain or lose $1 million, or that the BB defaults will cost $10 million – there is no need for interpreting complicated risk information. We have found that scenarios are a simple and useful way of considering risk and use them as one of the key elements of the risk framework discussed in the next chapter.

Since the mid-1990s **value-at-risk** (VAR), a statistically based process, has become an "industry standard" way of looking at portfolios of financial risks (the process started with market risk portfolios and has since been applied to credit risk portfolios). In its simplest form, market VAR takes the firm's market risks and estimates how much they might lose over a given time period (e.g. the period it takes to sell or flatten the risk, often called the liquidation or holding period). Creating a VAR process is complicated, but centers on applying to a portfolio of risks the following:

(A) The volatility of the underlying asset (e.g. equity or bond price, currency rate);
(B) A matrix of correlations (e.g. the historical price relationships between equities, interest rates, currencies, credit spreads, and so on);
(C) A liquidation period (e.g. one day, one week, one month or however long a firm thinks it will take to unwind or neutralize its risk);
(D) A statistical confidence level (e.g. 95% or 99%).

The end result is a VAR portfolio estimate that reflects how much a firm will lose across its businesses. For instance, if a firm has a one-day, 99% VAR of $50 million, then 99 days out of 100 it should not expect to lose more than $50 million. Unfortunately, VAR does not tell us anything about how big the loss might be on the 100th day. In addition, it is based on historical correlations (which can break down particularly in times of market stress, just when it matters!) and statistical assumptions (which may or may not be true). As such, it has to be interpreted and used with caution. It is worth noting that VAR can really only be used for portfolios that are revalued (marked-to-market) every day; since those valued as the lower of cost or market are not actually remarked every day, the VAR measure is not relevant (this essentially means most non-financial corporations cannot generally use VAR to measure risks).

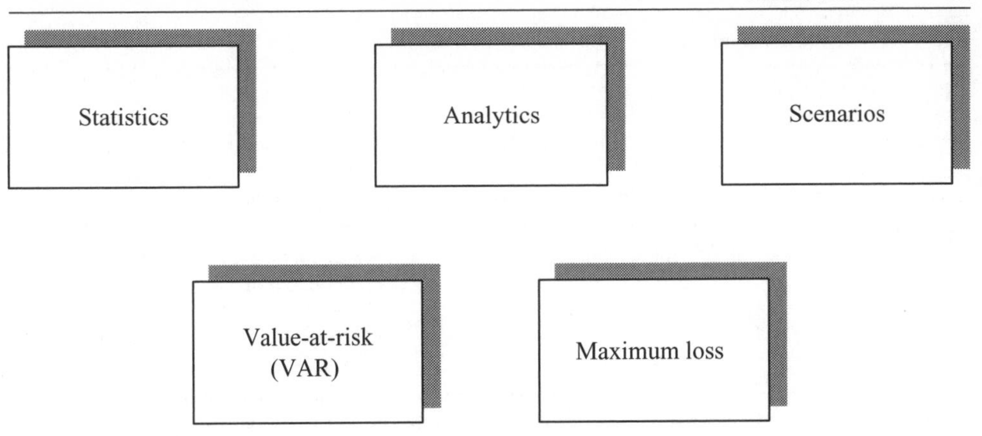

Figure 6.1 Commonly used mathematical measurement techniques

A related measure that we have found to be useful, if conservative, is **maximum loss**. Maximum loss expresses how much a firm might lose across a portfolio of risks by ignoring the "beneficial" effects of correlation (i.e. not all bad things that can happen to a portfolio will usually happen at the same time) and by using the worst occurrences (rather than the 99th or 95th worst); since these two factors usually reduce anticipated risk in a portfolio, maximum loss yields a greater loss number than VAR. The measure takes the maximum loss generated by a series of scenario shocks for each risk class (e.g. currency volatility risk, directional interest rate risk) and adds them together to get a division-wide or firm-wide loss amount. By adding these variables together a firm is not making any assumptions about correlations – it just assumes that the worst that has happened actually happens. Since maximum loss is a conservative measure we feel that it comes closer to really capturing the hundred-year flood disaster scenario for which most other commonly used measures provide little insight – though even the maximum loss measure can never guarantee the absolute worst case is captured. We discuss its use in greater detail in Chapter 7.

Figure 6.1 summarizes commonly used mathematical risk measurement techniques.

6.2 SUBJECTIVE MEASURES

There are times when mathematical measures cannot be used to quantify risk exposures. This might happen when formulas fail to adequately describe what might happen under different market events or when not enough is known about the behavior of the asset, market or process. If a firm cannot measure a risk "neatly" it should not try and convince itself that it can. In our view it is far better to apply a subjective approach – using experience and intuition to develop an estimate of what could happen. For instance, a bank might realize that when transaction volume hits particular thresholds additional process risk arises from system stress, human errors on confirmations, and so on – it might therefore estimate its exposure based on this experience rather than a formula or distribution. Subjective measures can also be applied to areas such as legal risk, client suitability risk or process risk, which do not easily lend themselves to financial modeling. Indeed, these are areas where human actions and behavior can greatly affect whether any exposure will exist and how the exposure will be treated. Subjective measures can also be used to override mathematical measures. For instance, a firm may compute credit risk

Table 6.1 Summary of measures

Measure	Pros	Cons
Statistical	• Useful for estimating risk exposures that vary over time • Can be applied to a range of credit and market risks	• Relies on assumptions about asset price behavior and distributions which might not always be accurate
Analytic	• Simple to implement and interpret	• Cannot be applied to all risk exposure computations (e.g. cross-risk portfolios) • Cannot be used to estimate future exposures
Scenario	• Provides risk information on a range of outcomes • Makes no assumptions about probabilities • Expressed in understandable terms (e.g. P&L) • Applicable to a range of credit, market and liquidity risks • Useful for single transactions as well as portfolios	• Difficult to implement
VAR	• Allows aggregation across risk portfolios	• Relies on assumptions about volatility, correlations, confidence levels and liquidation horizons • Fails to indicate what can happen in extreme cases • Difficult to implement • Only applicable to mark-to-market portfolios
Maximum loss	• Provides a conservative aggregation methodology across portfolios and risk classes	• Very conservative as it ignores correlations and confidence levels • Only applicable to mark-to-market portfolios
Subjective	• Can be used when no suitable quantification approach exists or to override quantitative results	• Purely judgemental and thus open to criticism

through statistical formulas for all of its counterparties, but may want to discard the results when dealing with sub-investment grade counterparties and apply a more stringent – and subjective – rule.

Each one of the measurement approaches we have described has its pros and cons. We summarize these in Table 6.1.

6.3 MEASURING DIFFERENT RISKS

In Chapter 2 we introduced a classification for the various types of risks a firm might face. Having suggested different tools that can be used for measuring risks above, let us analyze which measurement tools may suit each category of risk best.

6.3.1 Market risks

The market risk of individual transactions (or small portfolios) can be calculated through statistics, analytics and scenarios. We consider simple examples of each:

- Under a *statistical* approach a firm might estimate its exposure to a large sterling interest rate swap by examining the statistical distribution of rates underlying the derivative and creating an interest rate curve which it can evolve over time; it might conclude that sterling interest rates are distributed lognormally, and can then compute the value of the trade on that basis.
- Under an *analytic* approach a firm might calculate the risk parameters of derivatives (e.g. delta, gamma, theta and vega) through option pricing models. For instance, if the delta of an equity option is 0.5, then a unit change in the price of the equity will cause the value of the option to change by 0.5, or 50%, of that amount. So if a firm has an option worth $1 million when the stock is at $10 it will be worth $1.5 million when the stock is at $11. Similar computations can be performed for gamma, vega and theta.
- Under a *scenario* approach a firm might examine the impact of a range of market moves on a deal. For instance, if it has a yen/dollar currency option it can run scenarios based on changes in the spot yen/dollar rate and yen/dollar volatility: by strengthening the dollar by 1% and 3% against the yen the scenarios might indicate losses of $100 000 and $500 000, respectively, and by increasing the volatility of the position by 1% and 5% the position might gain by $250 000 and $1 million, respectively.

Risk in broader portfolios – covering business units, divisions or the entire firm – can be determined through VAR, maximum loss and scenarios. Again, we consider examples of each:

- If a firm is trying to figure out its total exposure to European equities and European bonds, it can run a *VAR* process. If its one-day VAR is $5 million, it knows that its equity and bond market risks will not be expected to lose more than $5 million 99 days out of 100 (given assumptions on correlations, holding period and distributions).
- Computing the *maximum loss* for these portfolios involves an incremental step: abandoning the confidence level by taking the worst possible situation (effectively the 100% confidence level) and eliminating the beneficial effects of correlations by aggregating the results across equities and bonds; in this case the resulting figure might be $8 million rather than the $5 million estimated through VAR.
- The *scenario* approach described above for a single transaction can also be extended to cover portfolios. Continuing with the same example, the firm might run portfolio scenarios for European equities (say 1% and 5% moves in the direction of equities and 1% and 10% changes in volatility) and European bonds (perhaps 10, 50 and 100 basis point parallel shifts in the curve, 10 and 25 basis point twists in the curve for each maturity bucket, and 1% and 5% changes in interest rate volatility). The results reveal the sensitivity of the equity and interest rate portfolios to a range of moves, without making any assumptions about probabilities of occurrence.

Scenario analysis can provide valuable information on the ongoing riskiness of businesses. In our view it should become a routine process within any firm; a regular regimen of scenario analysis sensitizes decision makers about the risk profile of the firm in a way that is easily understood (e.g. the P&L effects of particular market moves). To make it useful we have found that it is best to run scenarios "grounded in reality" – based on events that have actually happened – rather than simply trying to create "disaster moves" that no one believes can happen.

Table 6.2 Market risk measurement approaches

Type of exposure	Measurement choices
• Single transactions • Very small portfolios	• Analytics • Statistics • Scenarios
• Large portfolios	• Analytics • Statistics • Scenarios • VAR • Maximum loss

For instance, a firm might select from among the various hundred-year floods we described in Chapter 1 (e.g. 1987 crash, 1998 Russian/hedge fund crisis, 2001/2002 tech stock meltdown), determine the movement of all important risk variables that occurred during the crisis, and use that as the scenario "template" to apply to its positions every month or quarter. Thus, when senior executives are presented with an analysis that says if the 1987 stock market crash were to happen again today the firm would lose \$100 million, it has some basis in reality. It is also important to focus on the *change* in the scenario results from period to period, rather than just the absolute results. While it might be informative for senior managers to know that they could lose \$100 million in a repeat of the 1987 crash, it is actually more important for them to realize that when the same scenario was run the prior month (or quarter) the figure was only \$75 million – meaning the overall riskiness of the firm is on the rise. What caused this increase is something worthy of much focus!

Market risk measurement approaches are summarized in Table 6.2.

6.3.2 Credit risks

With credit risk, losses occur if the counterparty defaults, or if the collateral supporting the credit extension is insufficient and the counterparty defaults; this applies to a single counterparty transaction as well as multiple trades with a single counterparty. Losses can also occur if there is a failure in the settlement process or if a sovereign action takes place.

Direct credit risk, trading credit risk and contingent credit risk – three of the broad classes of credit exposure we defined in Chapter 2 – can be estimated through statistics or analytics. We consider simple examples of each:

- *Statistics* can be used for trading credit risk transactions with value (and therefore risk) that fluctuates over time, like derivatives and repos/reverses. Since a counterparty might default in the future, a firm wants to estimate what it might lose on that future day – a statistical process can provide some indication of what this amount will be. Thus, if a bank enters into a 10-year swap with a company, the value of the swap will change as time passes. A statistical process might indicate that in four years the swap will have reached a maximum possible loss value of \$10 million – if default occurs at that point, the bank will sustain a loss which the statistical assumptions say will be no greater than \$10 million some percentage of the time (e.g. 95% or 99%). If default occurs before or after that time, the amount lost will be smaller. (Note that the net amount the bank will lose depends ultimately on what it recovers after bankruptcy proceedings. As a senior, unsecured creditor it might get back 25–40 cents on the dollar, which would reduce the final loss amount; any credit measurement must thus take account of possible recoveries.)

- *Analytics* can be used to measure direct credit risks arising from transactions with values that do not fluctuate over time (or move only in very small ranges) – such as loans, marketable securities and deposits. For example, a bank might be willing to lend $25 million to a BBB counterparty through a term loan. If the counterparty defaults, the bank, as a senior unsecured creditor, will lose $25 million before recoveries (and a smaller amount after recoveries). Contingent credit risks that might appear at some future time can similarly be measured through analytic formulas. In this case a firm has a choice: it can measure the maximum possible contingent credit exposure that can appear at any time (e.g. a $100 million bank line that might not be drawn today, but three or six months hence) but measure the full $100 million as a risk today, or measure some nominal exposure (e.g. the credit derivative premium value of the option today) and add in the amount of the facility only as (or if) it is drawn. We favor the more conservative treatment of contingent risks by counting undrawn facilities/exposures as if they were fully drawn.
- *Statistics* can also be used to measure collateralized transactions, but here understanding the nature of the collateral is important: enough high-quality collateral can defease most of the credit exposure, while poor-quality collateral, or collateral that is highly correlated to the performance ability of the counterparty, might not add much benefit. For example, if a firm has $10 million of derivative credit exposure to a BB company backed by $11 million of US Treasuries (marked weekly, with additional calls made when the value dips to $10 million), a statistical measure might suggest only a small amount of credit exposure – perhaps less than $1 million – as the performance of the collateral and the counterparty are uncorrelated and with the appropriate documentation the firm can liquidate the US Treasuries quickly and efficiently in the event the counterparty defaults. A small residual exposure to the BB credit remains as the underlying derivative exposure might move further in-the-money while the Treasuries are being liquidated – leaving the firm with the possibility of being unsecured. If the security on the $10 million credit line is based on $11 million of high-yield bonds, the statistical measure would suggest a much higher amount of exposure to the BB credit. We can imagine two scenarios. First, the high-yield bonds default at the same time the BB counterparty becomes impaired (e.g. highly correlated), meaning the BB credit exposure is unsecured and the firm sustains a loss; in this case the measurement might indicate exposure to the BB credit near $10 million. Second, the high-yield bonds continue to perform, but in trying to sell them quickly to cover the exposure of the defaulting BB credit full value is not realized – e.g. perhaps only $7 million is obtained for a $10 million exposure (this goes back to the asset liquidation we discussed in Chapter 3). In this case the measurement might suggest exposure to the BB credit of $3 million.
- *Analytics* can be used to measure settlement risks (based on notional amounts that might be subject to settlement/delivery problems). For instance, foreign exchange deliveries of $500 million mean $500 million at risk, even if only for a short period of time. Sovereign risk exposures can be considered through analytic or statistical formulas. If trading credit risks are involved, e.g. a derivative with a sovereign, or with a local counterparty in a local currency that might be subject to exchange controls, then the quantification exercise is precisely equal to what we have discussed above. If direct credit risks are involved, e.g. a loan to a sovereign, then the analytic approach we have mentioned is valid.

Table 6.3 Credit risk measurement approaches

Type of exposure	Measurement choices
• Single transactions (private, sovereign, settlement)	• Analytics • Statistics
• Portfolios (single or multiple counterparty)	• Statistics • Scenarios • VAR

Exposure to portfolios of counterparties can be measured through statistical processes as well as scenarios:

- A firm can use *statistics* for single transactions to quantify an entire portfolio of deals with a counterparty. For instance, if a bank has 10 swaps with a company it might use statistical methods to compute the risk of each transaction. Then, using the same statistics (and allowing for netting of trades if a master netting agreement exists), it can obtain a portfolio measure.
- A firm might also use *scenarios* to quantify the effects of different variables on single or multiple portfolios. For instance, it might want to quantify its risk to all BBB counterparties, or to all counterparties in a particular industry segment or country and thus run scenarios where all counterparties default, or where underlying markets move by specific amounts and cause an increase or decrease in credit exposure. These scenarios provide a macro assessment of the state of the firm's overall credit exposures.
- A firm can use a credit *VAR* measure to compute its credit risk exposure across portfolios of counterparties; as with market VAR, this requires some assumptions (in this case related to correlations and counterparty default distributions which migrate over time). The end result is a portfolio credit loss across all counterparties adjusted to some statistical confidence level.

Credit risk measurement approaches are summarized in Table 6.3.

6.3.3 Liquidity risks

Liquidity risk can be measured through analytic formulas and scenarios. Let us consider some examples:

- The focus of liquidity risk is on balance sheet and off-balance sheet items that might require funding or disposal. Measuring these risks – such as maximum gap mismatch (e.g. gap between assets and liabilities, per maturity bucket), maximum aged inventory or future funding commitments – can be done through *analytic* formulas based on absolute dollar amounts. For instance, a firm measuring aged inventory might add up all bond positions over 180 days and all non-AAA-rated positions over a certain dollar amount to get one estimate of asset illiquidity. A similar exercise might be performed for mismatches: if $100 million of short-term liabilities are coming due in the next 30 days the firm might see what assets are available over the next month to help repay the liabilities. If only $50 million are coming due (and another $50 million are not coming due for three months), the firm faces a $50 million liability mismatch that it will have to manage through alternate funding sources or non-current asset sales.

- *Scenario* measures can also be useful. For instance, for the same $50 million gap just described, a firm might want to estimate how much it will cost to borrow that incremental $50 million at rates that are 10, 50 and 100 basis points above its normal funding costs – this gives an indication of the economic loss it will sustain in covering the gap. Alternatively, it might run scenarios that focus on covering the $50 million gap through asset disposals – e.g. selling particular assets at 5%, 10% and 25% below their carrying values; these might represent "fire sale" scenarios if the incremental funding cannot be arranged.

6.3.4 Process risks

Some elements of process risk measurement can be accomplished – at least theoretically – on the basis of *statistics*. By taking a large number of actual operational risk losses a statistical distribution of occurrences can be created; it can be "enhanced" by incorporating some of the very large process risk failures observed in the market (e.g. Barings, Allfirst) to make sure the tails of the distribution are appropriately "fat". In order for this exercise to be truly effective, comprehensive data collection is an absolute must; unfortunately, this is not an easy task! We feel that applying statistical techniques to process risk is not necessarily the wisest choice given the limited experience and data, as well as the strong likelihood that a lot of losses are not usually known about. As experience deepens and firms collect and analyze more of their process risk loss data, a move to mathematical solutions might be a good idea – until then, a *subjective* approach is probably more realistic. For instance, if a firm is trying to measure its risk exposure to unsigned confirmations it might first tabulate all outstanding transactions without signed confirms. It might then apply a rule related to trades it feels are "at risk" – perhaps those with sub-investment grade counterparties, those with counterparties located in emerging nations, those with hedge funds or offshore fund managers, and so forth. These "at risk" designations might actually have come from prior bad experience. Taking these two factors together (unsigned confirmations and "at risk" counterparties) allows it to produce an estimate of possible risk exposures.

6.3.5 Legal, suitability and reputational risks

Measuring exposure on legal and client suitability risks is similarly best done by applying *subjective* rules based on judgement and experience – rather than trying to "over-engineer" the problem by developing mathematical metrics. For instance, if a bank wants to estimate its possible exposure to client suitability risk from certain derivative transactions, it can review its client portfolio on a trade-by-trade basis and determine which, if any, trades might be challenged by unhappy clients at some future time. For instance, it might begin by flagging all trades done with government institutions, charitable organizations and corporates, and then filter them by trades that have the potential of generating payouts of up to $25 million. This gives a list of transactions that might possibly cause problems, and can be used as a subjective estimate of suitability risk. In the same light, a firm interested in capturing possible legal risk coming from poor documentation of derivatives might review its master netting agreements (which allow credit exposure to be considered on a net, rather than a gross, basis) and find which ones contain legal language that does not provide the right kind of protection or are governed by legal jurisdictions that might interpret clauses differently. There is obviously no way to apply formulas or equations to this kind of legal documentation risk, as each agreement has to be reviewed and considered individually.

Table 6.4 Summary of risk category measures

Risk class	Best measures
• Market risks (single deals, small portfolios)	• Statistics • Analytics • Scenarios
• Market risks (large portfolios)	• Scenarios • VAR • Maximum loss
• Credit risks (default risk for single deals)	• Statistics (for private or sovereign trading credit risk transactions that vary with time) • Analytics (for direct credit risk and settlement risk transactions that are static)
• Credit risks (single and multiple counterparty portfolios)	• Scenarios • VAR • Statistics
• Liquidity risks	• Analytics • Scenarios
• Process risks	• Subjective measures
• Legal risks	• Subjective measures
• Suitability risks	• Subjective measures

Table 6.4 summarizes broadly different kinds of risk measures that can be used for each different risk class.

We think it is important to emphasize once again that risk measures – while useful and necessary – are never perfect. Each has limitations, and these limitations often become brutally evident when markets are difficult – that is when some of the underlying assumptions fail to perform as expected (e.g. correlations break down, statistical distributions do not properly represent reality, and so forth). And that, of course, is just when a firm really needs to know what its exposures are! Companies therefore need to be sensitive to the limitations of risk measures and use them carefully.

Part II
Developing a Holistic Approach to Risk Management

7
The Risk Management Process: Building the Foundation

In Part I we introduced the fundamental "building blocks" needed to understand risk. In Part II we bring these, and other, concepts together to create a holistic risk discipline for the organization. In our experience developing and managing an entire risk process should follow logical staging and sequencing – this helps to ensure that risk-taking activities are *synchronized* with a firm's strategy and capabilities and that they are appropriately *supported* and *controlled*. A logical thought process would be as follows:

(1) In order to delineate what kind, and how much, risk to take, a firm first defines its *risk philosophy* and *risk tolerance*.

Risk philosophy is based on:

- Corporate goals,
- Focus of desired risk activities,
- Shareholder expectations.

Risk tolerance is based on:

- The amount a firm is willing to lose,
- The financial resources it has available,
- The amount it is getting paid to take risk (risk/return).

These together lead to the creation of a *risk mandate* – effectively the firm's risk operating guidelines. We discuss the risk philosophy, tolerance and mandate in Chapter 8.

(2) Once it has defined its mandate, executives and directors must then agree to, and abide by, *risk principles* – these principles should surround the entire risk process, be promulgated throughout the firm and followed religiously. Governing risk principles include:

- Clear risk appetite,
- Efficient risk allocation,
- Efficient and independent control functions,
- Thorough business reviews,
- Focus on the top 10 risks,
- Solid risk infrastructure,
- Zero tolerance for violations,
- No surprises!

Risk principles are covered in Chapter 9.

(3) Proper *governance and accountability* must accompany any risk process if it is to be effective. Those deemed to be accountable for the firm's risk and risk process *must* be held accountable. This accountability must in turn have a hierarchy to it and, in our view, be shared by both internal *and* external parties:

- Internal parties include the board of directors, CEO, CFO, head of risk management and the corporate risk group, business managers and internal auditors.
- External parties include regulators, external auditors, rating agency analysts, equity analysts and shareholders.

We consider governance and accountability in Chapter 10.

(4) To crystallize the economic impact of the risk mandate, and to create an ongoing management tool, a firm must next develop a framework of risk limits; this financial *risk framework* helps a firm monitor and cap balance sheet exposures, flag violations and elevate concentrations of risk to the appropriate level of the organization. The limits contained in the framework must be a direct reflection of the tolerance levels identified in the mandate. Quantifying framework exposures can be done through one of several *risk measurement tools*, including those we have discussed in Chapter 6.

We elaborate on the risk framework in Chapter 11.

(5) To manage its exposures on an ongoing basis – that is, to ensure that exposures remain within the mandate and that risk principles are being followed – a firm must then implement a series of *automated management* and *manual management processes*.

Automated management processes include:

- Risk framework implementation,
- Exceptions rules,
- Organized risk taking,
- Capital rules,
- Accounting rules,
- Earnings rules,
- Process rules,
- Client rules,
- Scenario planning.

Manual management processes center on:

- Professional skills,
- Human resource management,
- Motivation/incentives,
- Knowledge,
- Communication,
- Spot checks.

We discuss these automated and manual management techniques in Chapters 12 and 13.

(6) The risk process must ultimately be supported by robust *risk infrastructure*; this permits proper identification, quantification, tracking, management and reporting of risk exposures. Risk infrastructure is based on effective:

- Policies,
- Framework limits,
- Reporting mechanisms,
- Data,
- Technology.

We consider infrastructure issues in Chapter 14.

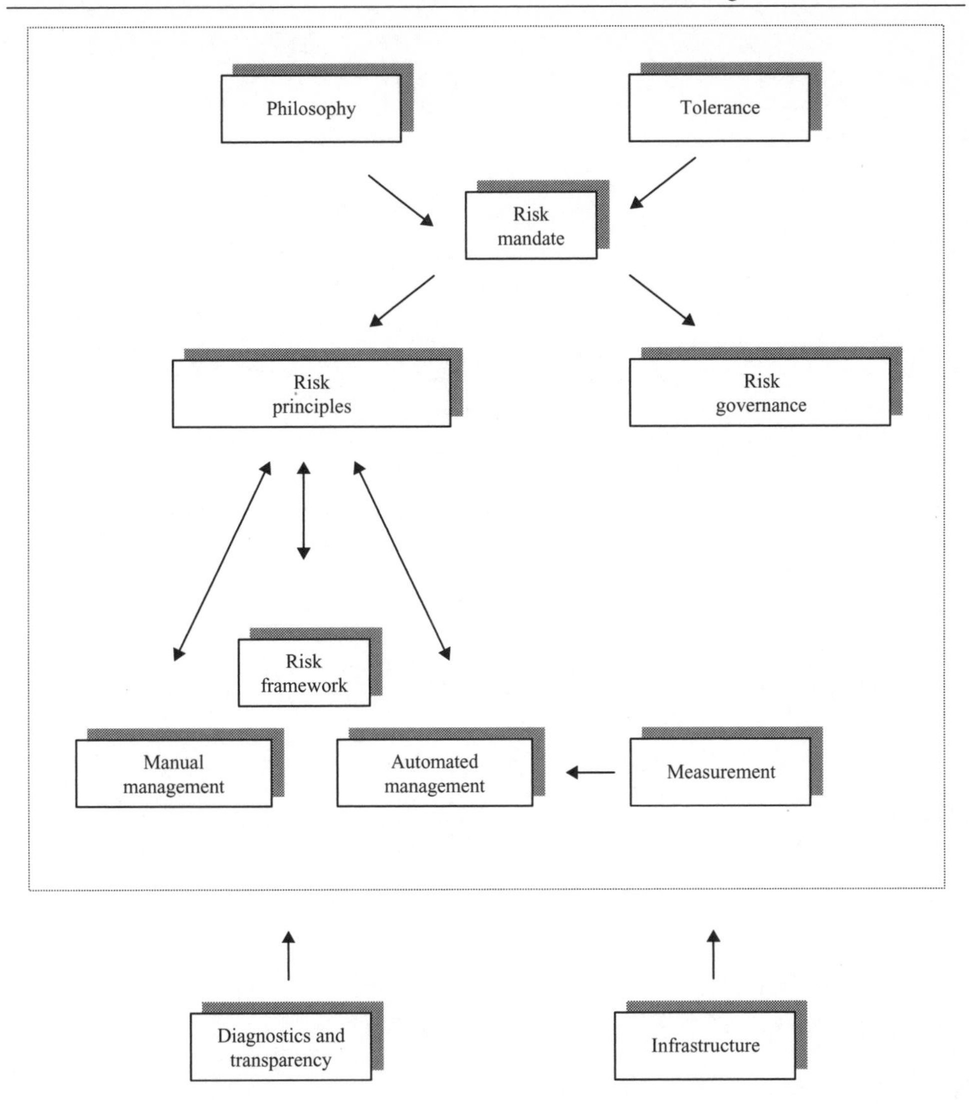

Figure 7.1 A holistic approach to risk management: market, credit, model, liquidity, suitability, legal and process risks

(7) Finally, to make sure the entire risk process is always working as it should, and to ensure adequate transparency in risk operations, a regular regimen of *diagnostics* has to be put in place. This lets a company know if things are not working properly and how they can be fixed. It also lets different constituents know what they should be watching out for.

We discuss diagnostics and transparency in Chapter 15.

We feel that proper implementation of these components is not difficult to achieve and leads to the creation of a practical, holistic and robust risk process as summarized in Figure 7.1. If followed diligentlly, we feel that such a process can help a firm avoid many of the mistakes and problems described in Chapter 1.

8
The Financial Risk Mandate: Developing a Philosophy and Loss Tolerance

In our experience defining an appetite for risk, and then managing to that appetite, is the single most important action a risk-taking firm can undertake. It sets the tone and posture toward the management of risk and, if implemented correctly, limits potential losses. As usual, this is often easier said than done.

The discipline begins by defining the operating risk parameters of the firm. A firm has to consider how risk relates to the rest of its activities (e.g. are particular risks important, not important, irrelevant, integral to strategy, performance and valuation), the intended focus of risk activities (e.g. will risks be taken proactively, or as a by-product of other operating activities, as a specialized "niche" player or as "all things to all people", will a particular product or market focus be emphasized), and the internal and external perception of the firm's risk business (e.g. do regulators, lenders and shareholders know what risk the firm is taking, believe it is empowered to do so, and so on). Defining these factors leads to the development of a **risk philosophy**. Every firm also needs to understand how much money it is willing to lose through such risk activities, whether it has the resources for this and whether it is being properly paid for taking such risks. These allow the expression of a **risk tolerance** for the organization. We consider each in greater detail below. A philosophy and tolerance together give rise to a **risk mandate** – the firm's risk operating parameters. To be useful, the board of directors should sanction the mandate and executive management should approve and implement it – this is vital as it ensures that everyone understands the risk-related "rules of the game". If large, unacceptable losses occur within the risk mandate, directors and executives cannot blame others – they have to accept responsibility. If the losses are not within the scope of the mandate, directors and executives are still responsible, as it is up to them to ensure that violations of controls or flaws in the process are identified and dealt with immediately. The mandate should be fluid rather than rigid – revisited regularly and updated when necessary. In the same way that companies often publicly express earnings growth targets, we believe the risk mandate should similarly be publicly announced. Figure 8.1 summarizes the suggested make-up of the risk mandate.

8.1 RISK PHILOSOPHY

A risk philosophy is based on:

- Understanding how risk relates to a firm's goals;
- Deciding which risks to focus on;
- Making sure that the firm and its stakeholders have a consistent view of the risks being taken.

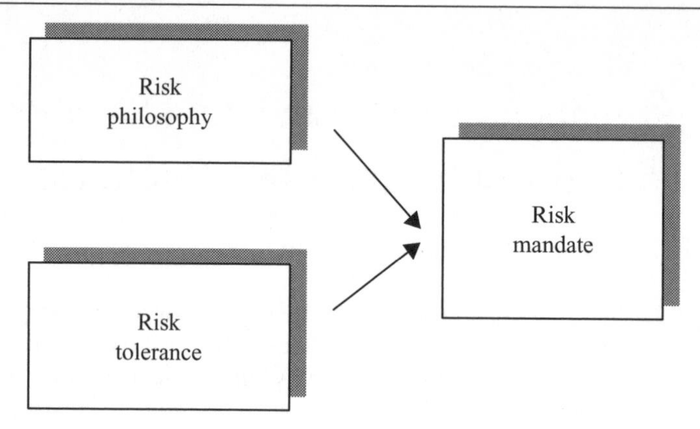

Figure 8.1 The risk mandate

8.1.1 Financial risk and corporate goals

Before doing anything else, a firm needs to understand what risk means to its business operations – essentially knowing if risks complement, enhance or harm its activities, and whether they form a significant part of revenue generation. A typical bank, for instance, is in business to take risk and generates revenues based on extending risk; risky activities are consistent with its overall goals, so its philosophy should encourage initiatives related to the prudent management of risk exposures. An industrial firm, in contrast, generates more earnings from industrial production and might only want risks that are a by-product of its core business lines (e.g. commodity risks, product risk, and so on) instead of those coming from financial sources. If risk exposures are not consistent with its goals then they should be realigned, eliminated or dealt with cautiously. So, for example, the oil company that focuses on managing its commodity exposures should not actively position equity or interest rate derivatives, as this would be contrary to its corporate imperatives and not part of its core expertise – in short, not part of its risk philosophy. Where it has no choice but to take risks that are not part of core competency (e.g. the management of a pension fund), it should only do so with expert advice and under very conservative accounting policies.

8.1.2 Focus of "balance sheet" risk activities

Focusing sharply on contemplated risk activities is critical in developing a risk philosophy. A firm seeking risk must consider whether it should do so actively or passively, if it should be proprietary or client-focused, in which markets and products it wishes to be active, and so on. Some firms might favor proprietary trading, while others might wish to emphasize client-driven risk businesses. Some might want to keep risk activities closer to home and their area of expertise, while others might be willing to take risk in different local markets and products. Establishing this focus is important as each approach features unique characteristics that will impact risk tolerance. Identifying which risks are then being run, per the classifications summarized in Chapter 2, is very important. This allows a company to consider whether it will be taking credit and market risks (willingly or as a corporate by-product), if it will be exposed to model or client suitability risks, whether it will encounter liquidity, process or legal risks, and so on. In our experience, firms that focus on taking risk where they have a comparative advantage, rather than those trying to be "all things to all people", are often the most successful.

8.1.3 Stakeholder expectations

Knowing what shareholders expect of a firm is an important – though often overlooked – ingredient of the process. Internal parties (business managers, control managers and employees) and external parties (debt and equity investors, bank creditors, regulators, rating agency analysts) may think a company is in business to take certain risks and have an interest in ensuring that corporate actions coincide with these expectations. Management alone cannot unilaterally decide to assume or reduce risks – actions that they take have to be consistent with what others believe or have been informed the company is, or is capable of, doing and empowered to do. When views diverge managers need to resolve the issue quickly – there should be no surprises about the nature of a firm's risk-related business. Regulators, for instance, do not like to see an institution losing money in markets or products that it was not authorized to deal in or from activities that are far broader in scope than they believed were being undertaken. Shareholders also buy a company's stock based, among other things, on a belief that a particular level of risk is, or is not, being taken; companies that do not take much risk appeal to a certain class of investors, while those that take a great deal of risk appeal to others. A company taking risk that is not seen by shareholders as part of strategy, and that subsequently loses money, will pay a heavy price through a lower stock multiple. One that runs significant proprietary risk may have lots of earnings volatility, but the fact that its activities are consistent with its philosophy, and well known to investors, may not translate into a lower multiple. Within the financial community some firms are associated with large proprietary risk taking (e.g. Salomon Brothers (before its acquisition by Citibank), Goldman Sachs). Large and systemic risk-related losses at these firms might disappoint investors, but would not be unexpected and should not necessarily be reflected in a lower multiple. Other firms are not considered big risk takers (e.g. Merrill Lynch and Smith Barney in the early 1990s) and large risk losses are more likely to result in lower valuations.

Figure 8.2 summarizes the suggested make-up of the risk philosophy.

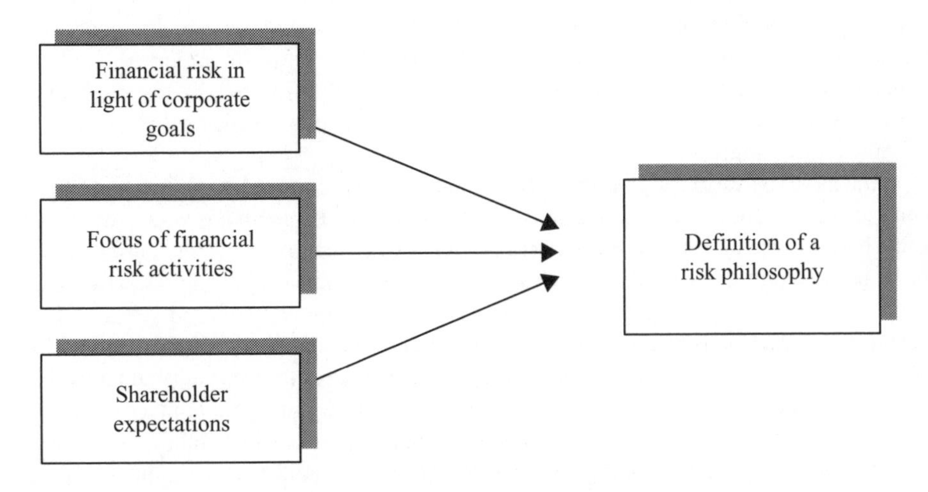

Figure 8.2 Definition of a risk philosophy

8.2 RISK TOLERANCE

After creating a risk philosophy, a firm must crystallize a risk tolerance level by determining:

- How much it is willing to lose as a result of its stated risk activities;
- Whether it has enough resources to handle such losses;
- Whether it is getting paid enough to take risk.

8.2.1 How much is the firm willing to lose?

A firm might decide that it is willing to risk losing no more than $100 million per quarter in its risk-taking activities. It might arrive at this figure by looking at its businesses, determining the nature and stability of its operating matrix and how much each of its units can earn from risk-related activities, the kinds of risks each will run, and link this to how much it will let each one lose, *in extremis*, whilst still remaining an attractive business. It might then aggregate individual maximum losses to reflect a firm-wide total. It will also need to review external expectations: will lenders, rating agencies, regulators and investors be comfortable if the firm loses this amount? Thus, this maximum loss cannot be set in a vacuum – it has to be an iterative process based on communication inside and outside the company. It also has to make sure that it will not, under a variety of disaster scenarios, lose more than that amount. This, unfortunately, is not an easy task, as markets do not behave in a predictable or orderly way. If a firm could be 100% certain that it would never lose more than a stated amount, risk management would be much easier – and returns on risk much lower! Nonetheless, each firm must attempt to crystallize this maximum loss.

8.2.2 What resources are available?

While a firm might conceptually be willing to lose a certain maximum sum on its risk activities (e.g. the $100 million every quarter), it must have the resources to support both these activities and potential losses. Not only does it need the right human resources (e.g. risk-taking skills) and infrastructure (e.g. process efficiency, technology, data, policies), it must also have enough earnings and capital to take such risk. In a typical bank, risk activities are a major source of revenues and most capital will be devoted to the risk-taking effort. In an industrial company financial risk taking might be a less important (and desirable!) source of revenues and thus receive less capital allocation. The amount of financial capital available for risk has to be earmarked accordingly.

Capital has to be attributed to a firm's credit, market, liquidity, model, process and legal risks to protect against unexpected losses. According to financial theory, that is what part of a firm's capital base is to be used for. While current earnings, or reserves drawn from current earnings, can be used to protect against low severity, higher probability losses, capital exists to guard the firm against low probability, high severity situations – the one-hundred-year floods. Risk appetite therefore has to be a function of the amount of capital erosion a firm can withstand before it runs into trouble: risk can create losses and losses eat into earnings and may deplete capital. Capital erosion therefore creates an "outer boundary" on the amount a firm should be willing to lose. If too much capital is depleted through risk losses, financial ratios will weaken and pressure from regulators, rating agencies, investors and creditors will mount. Severe losses might then jeopardize the ongoing survival of the firm. Trading and financial businesses rely heavily on public confidence. Loss of confidence, often expressed by withdrawal of liquidity lines, can very quickly shut a company down.

However, in practice, assuming there is sufficient capital, most managers benchmark risk appetite to current earnings – earnings simultaneously drive and constrain risk taking. If a business generates good earnings, it becomes more willing to underwrite risk activities (and the accompanying potential losses). These earnings will also cap potential risk-related losses well before any real erosion in capital is considered. The common view must be that once earnings have been depleted and capital starts to erode, the punishment from shareholders will already be too severe for management to be able to withstand!

8.2.3 Is the firm getting paid to take risk?

It is not enough to know that a firm is willing to lose a certain amount of money in risky businesses or that it has enough earnings and capital to handle the losses – it also has to know whether it is getting paid enough to take the risk. The term "being paid enough" needs to be addressed in two manners:

- Is the company providing an attractive return on shareholder capital?
- Is the market providing an attractive valuation on such "balance sheet" risk-related earnings?

8.2.3.1 Return on capital

The goal of any profit-motivated corporation is to maximize earnings by increasing revenues, lowering expenses, or both. Increasing revenues can be accomplished by pursuing new or higher margin business; this can often mean higher risk business. But is higher risk business always more profitable than lower risk business once the possibility of losses is taken into account? In order to determine whether the new or incremental margin being earned for that higher level of risk is justified, a firm has to compare the returns earned from different risk businesses on an equal footing – in other words, it needs to "risk adjust" its returns. This applies to operating, as well as balance sheet, risks.

Narrowly focusing on "balance sheet" risk, a bank might have an opportunity to enter into one of two transactions with an A-rated counterparty: a five-year cross-currency derivative that will earn $1 million and a 180-day US Treasury repo financing that will earn $100 000. On the surface, the derivative looks more attractive – who would not rather earn $1 million instead of $100 000? However, in measuring the exposures on the two trades, the firm might discover that the derivative is much riskier – longer term and more volatile – and therefore requires a capital allocation of $5 million. The financing, with lower risk exposure, only requires $200 000 of capital. The risk-adjusted return on the derivative is thus 20%, while the return on the financing is 50% – the financing now looks like the better trade, and the firm would do well to pursue that transaction. Indeed, if it can replicate the same trade with other A-rated counterparties (e.g. same risk and profitability parameters), the firm will earn $2.5 million on $5 million of allocated capital, instead of the $1 million from the derivative! In allocating scarce capital it is therefore essential to look at both components of the equation – the return *and* the risk – and direct resources accordingly.

In order to figure out if enough is being earned on any business line, a firm must create a capital allocation methodology and promulgate its return on capital goal or, more specifically, its **risk-adjusted return on capital** goal. Risk-adjusted return on capital tells a firm how much it earns for every dollar of capital allocated to a transaction or business, having adjusted for relative risks. Again, we believe that this methodology needs to be valid for both financial and operating risks. If returns are not sufficient, there is little point in pursuing the activity. Inadequate returns on risk essentially mean an underpricing of risk – which, if perpetuated broadly, will ultimately lead to deeper financial problems. If the returns are not adequate, a firm should have a much lower tolerance for risk. Equally, if proper returns are available, a firm should feel more comfortable taking risk. If an incremental unit of risk generates an acceptable return, then additional exposure can be a good thing – although there is, as we note below, a limit to this.

In our view the risk capital allocation process should be an automated part of risk management. Firms should be in the habit of automatically directing their capital to opportunities with the highest possible risk-adjusted returns. A sound risk-based capital allocation methodology and risk-adjusted return hurdles will influence such behavior. There are, of course, limits: a firm cannot increase risk infinitely, regardless of the margin being earned. It has to be sensitive to concentrated risk exposures – which, as we have already noted, can lead to liquidity problems – and must adhere to capital constraints and restrictions imposed internally or by regulators (e.g. US bank regulators impose capital-driven single lending limits on the amount of credit exposure that can be extended to any one counterparty). Simply pursuing the highest risk-adjusted returns without constraint means a firm will reach a point where it has too much risk, regardless of what it is being paid! Thus, the *primary driver* needs to be the risk appetite defined by the firm – which will cap the amount of risk exposure to any market, counterparty or source of liquidity – and the *secondary driver* needs to be the risk-adjusted return that can be earned; a firm must first decide how much risk to take and *then* make sure the risk-adjusted returns are optimal and sufficient. This will help avoid risk concentration problems that might appear. We can summarize the sequence through the flowchart contained in Figure 8.3.

This discussion leads us to a related, and absolutely vital, point: in order for this approach to work properly, a firm must have a very high degree of financial transparency throughout the organization. There is a tendency in large organizations to focus on "management accounting". The set of management accounts then created will often differ from "shareholder accounts" and can lead to double counting, fictions about performance, and so forth. The only accounts that are relevant in a properly functioning risk/return process are the very accounts produced for shareholders – no internal "smoke and mirrors", just a straightforward view of the numbers. Failure to adhere to this basic rule will lead to bad risk and risk/return decisions and perpetuate the misallocation of resources.

8.2.3.2 Return on earnings

Not all earnings are created equal. Not all earnings should therefore be valued equally. It might not be enough for a company to simply get paid what it perceives is an appropriate return for taking financial risk; it must also take account of the returns that ultimately maximize the firm's market valuation. Those coming from non-risk sources might be viewed as "better" than those coming from risk activities. Even those coming from financial risk sources might be of varying quality and regarded differently: for instance, returns generated from risk taken in the liquid cash equity markets might be regarded as "better" than earnings coming from illiquid high-yield bonds or long-dated derivatives. Pure financial trading firms (e.g. hedge funds) so far do not seem to command multiples that allow them to trade far above book value. There is therefore little to suggest that pure financial risk taking, without stable and complementary client/origination activities, does anything to improve a company's stock

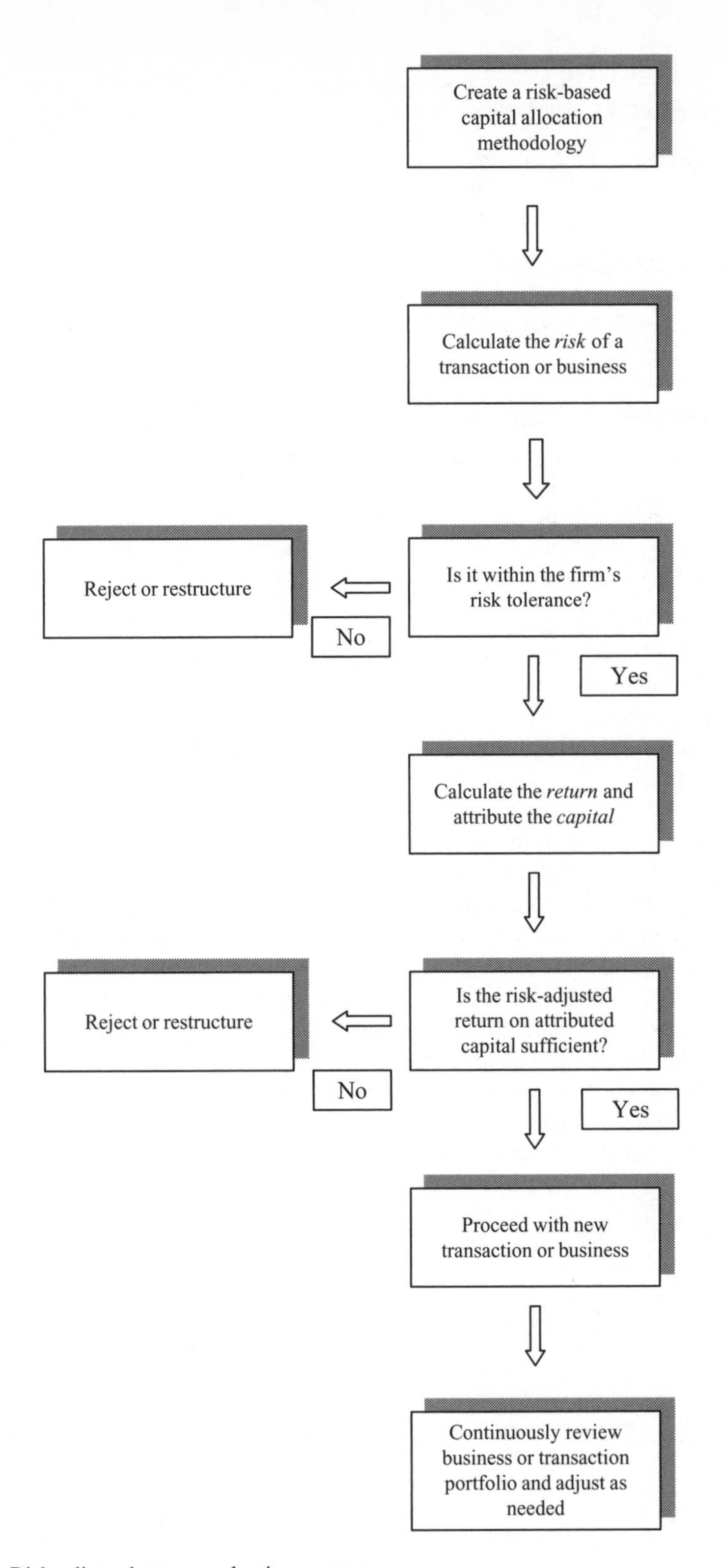

Figure 8.3 Risk-adjusted return evaluation process

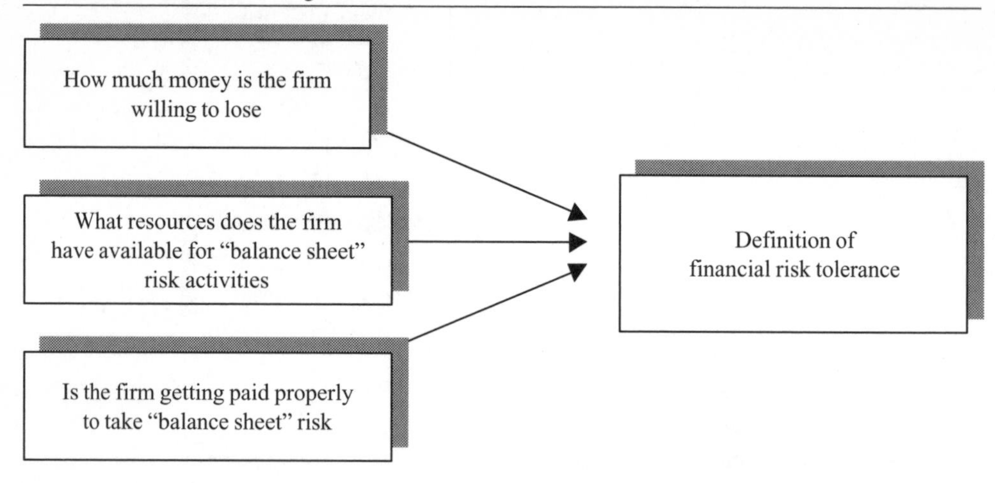

Figure 8.4 Definition of a risk tolerance

market valuation. If this is true, then a public company should not simply take risk for the sake of generating what might be a volatile return. The market will ultimately penalize the company. Each company must therefore always analyze its risk-taking activities within the context of market valuation multiples for such activities. Figure 8.4 summarizes the suggested make-up of a risk tolerance.

Having defined its risk philosophy and risk tolerance, a company can seek approval for its financial risk mandate from the board and proceed to promulgate this information both internally and externally. Information about the mandate should be shared with internal and external stakeholders – this completes the circle and aligns expectations with reality. Awareness and disclosure minimize the chance of negative surprises. Internal constituents will then understand the nature and amount of risk the firm is taking, the specific markets, assets and counterparties it is willing to be exposed to, and the amount of money it could lose under particular stress scenarios. Similar, though perhaps not as detailed, information should be given to external stakeholders. Confidential information regarding the risk mandate can be shared with regulatory authorities, credit rating agencies and select bank credit providers (particularly those supplying committed facilities). Communication must be an ongoing process and interested parties should be informed as changes in the risk mandate occur.

9 Risk Principles: Creating a Code of Conduct

A risk process can only be robust when it is based on a strong and well-articulated risk discipline that permeates the entire organization. We believe the eight cardinal risk principles encapsulated in Figure 9.1 allow such a discipline to develop.

Everyone in the company must understand, believe and follow these principles. Most of these should be self-explanatory, but for completeness let us review each one in turn.

9.1 PRINCIPLE 1: CLEAR RISK APPETITE

Whether risk taking is by default, or design, it is an integral part of a company's existence and cannot be ignored. Risk can enhance or reduce margins and cause monies to be made or lost. One would assume that the larger and more stable the capital and earnings of a company the greater the ability to sustain losses. Therefore the strategy, financial resources and earnings power of a company will have an important bearing on risk taking. Each company's approach to "balance sheet" risk needs to be clearly defined, especially in light of an appetite for potential losses. Once defined, the risk mandate – which encompasses philosophy and tolerance, as defined in the previous chapter – needs to be followed diligently and disseminated throughout the organization.

9.2 PRINCIPLE 2: EFFICIENT RISK ALLOCATION

Capital is a limited resource and so is the capital available for risk activities. It therefore has to be allocated efficiently toward the highest risk-adjusted return opportunities, while remaining within the parameters of the risk mandate. Returns also have to equal or exceed corporate guidelines in order to provide shareholders with attractive rewards on capital usage.

9.3 PRINCIPLE 3: EFFICIENT AND INDEPENDENT CONTROL FUNCTIONS

There seems to be unanimous agreement of the need for an internal risk management function. Organizations have, however, historically vacillated on where it belongs:

- Within a profit center with "dotted" reporting lines to an independent corporate function;
- Independent and away from the business unit, but with no real power of enforcement;
- Empowered and independent from, yet close to, the business unit.

We believe that only the third model delivers added value to shareholders. The risk function needs to be independent and strong in its ability to veto transactions, but cannot turn itself into the "no risk" management group! There have also been a few exercises in turning the risk

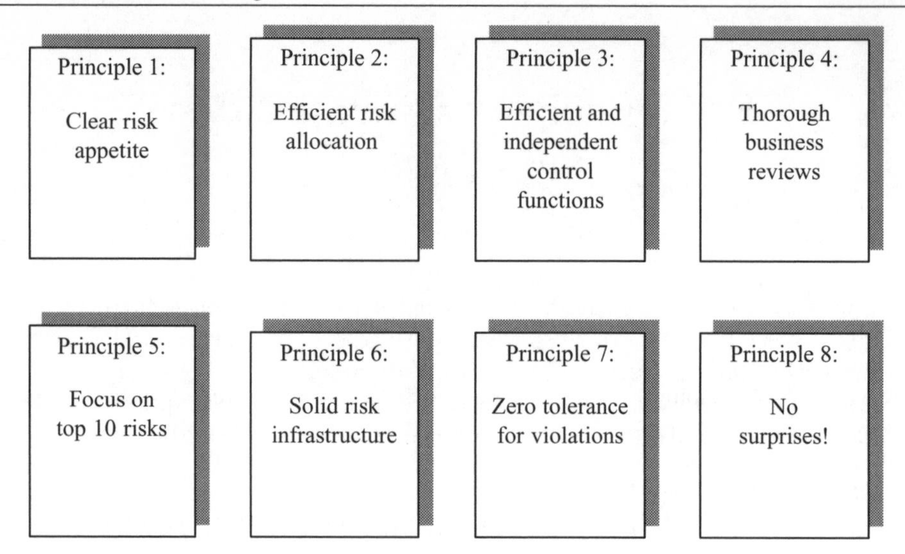

Figure 9.1 Risk principles

oversight groups themselves into profit centers – these have all failed. In so doing all risk has a price, and if the price is right you end up carrying the exposure. Since no institution has unlimited resources there is always going to be some point at which there is no price – whatever the return. Someone therefore needs to set limits and this cannot be done by a "conflicted" profit center. Not surprisingly, large concentrations of risk have typically been the demise of such exercises.

Most accounting functions are independent of business activities within a company. We question, however, whether they see themselves as a very important link in the risk management chain and whether they are truly held accountable accordingly. Without an accurate valuation of positions, in-depth analysis of earnings based on risk taken, strong and effective capital allocation models, and so forth, it becomes very difficult for the risk groups and management to be effective. An accounting function that is independent, qualified and accountable for its role in risk management is, therefore, a fundamental building block. The treasury function for most organizations is also a critical link in the risk management chain.

9.4 PRINCIPLE 4: THOROUGH BUSINESS REVIEWS

Throughout our careers we have found that frequent business reviews are a very healthy discipline. We have always been amazed that these tend to occur mainly when there are losses, or when there has been an embarrassing event. Regular reviews of each business must occur throughout the business cycle and include a review of risk exposures and returns. These reviews should not be "kangaroo courts" or "witch hunts", but non-bureaucratic peer reviews by like-minded, interested business people. A forum that requires a unit to prepare and present their business, risks and returns from risk activities forces strong accountability, focus and debate. The transparency thus created helps to surface issues and disagreements. It is key that the people running these reviews ensure the prompt escalation of major findings, issues and disagreements.

9.5 PRINCIPLE 5: FOCUS ON TOP 10 RISKS

We believe that at every level of the organization any person or body involved in risk should always be aware of, and be able to defend, its top 10 risks. These need to be very specific – not bland so as to obfuscate accountability! Senior management and board members should always be aware of, and accountable for, the firm's top 10 risks and their expected returns. They should always be able to defend these, and explain the outcome of the last top 10 list. As we move down within the organization the degree of specificity increases – but not the accountability or discipline! Those who are primarily responsible for knowing and managing the risks on a daily basis (e.g. trader and risk or credit manager) should be intimately familiar with relevant details. For instance, if a derivative book has a significant exposure to equity volatility, the trader should not simply indicate that the book is short equity volatility and will lose $5 million for a particular market move; nor should the risk manager accept this as sufficient. They both must know the real nature of the volatility risk, how it arose, where it is marked/valued, how it can be hedged or reduced if needed, what reserves exist against the position, what "exit strategy" exists, how sensitive it is to all market parameters (e.g. not just an absolute change in volatility, but a change in the term structure of volatility, the skew, the volatility of volatility), and so forth. Intimate knowledge reflects intimate understanding, and a very good appreciation of how the risk can be controlled and used effectively to generate returns. Enforcing this principle creates focus on what these risks actually are, what they can do to the firm, and how they can be managed. It also stimulates greater transparency on the topic of risk within an organization and places it squarely in the very healthy debate regarding profits and losses relative to risk taken. As a result, everyone starts to participate in the risk management process – and, as far as we are concerned, the more the merrier!

9.6 PRINCIPLE 6: SOLID RISK INFRASTRUCTURE

Risk personnel seem to be in a perpetual battle to ensure that they are analyzing accurate and complete risk information. This is an uphill struggle in most organizations for two main reasons: firstly, business units are seldom held accountable for delivering risk information in a timely, accurate and complete manner to a centralized data repository based on firm-wide standards; and secondly, products are being invented at such a rapid pace that the technology often lags behind.

Without a solid risk infrastructure – by which we mean flexible technology, accurate risk data and proper risk reporting – the risk process breaks down. When this happens the chance of process-related losses, as detailed in Chapter 5, is heightened enormously (e.g. losses from front-office error, operations error, structured product risk). In such cases we believe businesses should have their risk severely curtailed. The rule requiring each and every business unit to utilize a proper risk system that can accommodate all products and produce timely and complete data and associated risk reports should be sacrosanct. No product should be traded unless it can live up to these risk infrastructure requirements. We also believe that data used to populate parallel processes, such as P&L or settlements, should come from the same source. There is little point in trying to explain the impact of risk positions on P&L if the risk and accounting databases are not synchronized!

9.7 PRINCIPLE 7: ZERO TOLERANCE FOR VIOLATIONS

Simply put, violations of risk-related rules should result in reprimand or firing for cause. Too often there is an excuse – the market moved against the position, the trader is too big of a producer, the client needed a price, and on, and on, and on! We are big believers that for each violation there should be a disciplinary review process that is known to be very tough. Such discipline is vital if people are to respect how dangerous risk running astray can become.

9.8 PRINCIPLE 8: NO SURPRISES!

Losses are clearly less pleasurable than profits. However, from a risk management perspective the important test is whether the profits or losses fall within expectations. Something is clearly wrong if you lose more chips than you have at the blackjack table. And something is equally wrong if you are given winnings from a table that you were not aware you were playing on! In the same light, both profits and losses are the logical outcome of prior risk positions and established risk processes. It is therefore very important for a firm to know what it is doing before the fact, and that the outcome falls within expectations. A trader who loses a lot of money with the full knowledge and acceptance of what she is doing (by herself and her superiors) is better than a trader who makes a lot of money unexpectedly. Equally, a firm that is completely blind-sided by a loss coming from an operational process it did not know was ineffective is worse off than one that loses money based on a process that it knows is weak and in need of repair. Surprises have more to do with not knowing what is going on prior to the event than with the outcome itself; they are exemplary of poor risk management and must be avoided.

With a risk mandate and risk principles in hand, a firm is ready to consider governance issues – making sure those that are responsible for enforcing risk practices based on the mandate and principles are truly doing so! We treat this topic in the next chapter.

10 Financial Governance: Assigning Accountability for Risk

10.1 CREATING A CULTURE OF ACCOUNTABILITY

A risk process demands accountability. There is no doubt in our minds that the ultimate accountability for managing the risk profile of a company rests with the CEO and the board of directors (or equivalent body). A company should only run risk as an integral part of its stated strategy and consistent with its financial resources. The CEO and board are responsible and accountable for this; any financial risk being carried has to fall within this remit. They are also accountable for ensuring that any risks that break this rule are promptly identified and brought to their attention. Accountability is very clear and ignorance cannot be a credible excuse. Shareholders, regulators and external directors should strictly enforce this accountability. It is amazing to us how often senior management is let off the hook – as they were in the cases of Allfirst, Sumitomo Corporation, Bankers Trust, UBS, and others.

Whilst being totally accountable, the CEO and board must focus on the key risk issues and delegate the specifics to efficient and trustworthy bodies of people within the organization. Several entities external to the company are also integral to a well-run risk management process – regulators, accountants, rating agency and equity analysts. Shareholders today unfortunately get paid the least attention. This will hopefully change as management and external directors start to feel greater scrutiny of their own accountability. The secret is a well-defined process with enforced accountability. We have, unfortunately, found that these are often both sadly lacking.

10.2 ROLES AND RESPONSIBILITIES

In this section we propose a definition of the roles and responsibilities applicable to all participants in the risk management process, starting at the top and flowing down through the whole organization. Assigning responsibility and enforcing it, creates accountability; if management is strong and takes accountability seriously, it creates a far more effective control environment. Failure to drive responsibility from the very top of an organization will undermine the entire process. If the board and CEO do not take the process seriously, why should the CFO, head of risk management, accountants or the risk takers? We also feel that effective governance, centered on these responsibilities, depends heavily on strong communication: communication must flow continuously down the management chain (e.g. communication of risk mandate and principles) and back up again (e.g. communication of top risks, potential problems, issues and disagreements or infractions, and so on). Failure to communicate essential information will soon undermine the chain of command as parties at different levels become, or claim to be, ignorant or uncertain about important risk matters.

Internally, firms must look to their directors, CEOs, CFOs, corporate risk, business and control managers to create and communicate a strong risk control discipline. Our experience is that roles and responsibilities are too often left vague and therefore do not always function as intended. These need to be formalized on paper and enforced through regular employee reviews. New employees also need to be brought into the loop as soon as they join.

The board of directors, or equivalent body, should be aware of, and approve, the risk mandate and principles, the risk framework and the roles and responsibilities of the various participants. They should conduct, at least annually, a review of each of these, focusing particularly on any key issues that have arisen since the last review. Whilst at any point in time being aware of the firm's top 10 risks, the board of directors should delegate the more frequent reviews, analysis of risk and risk issues to a committee of the board – typically the finance committee or an equivalent body. The CEO, CFO and head of corporate risk management should all be present during frequent firm risk reviews (which should include an in-depth analysis of the top 10 risk exposures). The chairperson of the committee, CEO, CFO and head of corporate risk management should agree when the committee gets notified of issues/events between meetings and at what point the full board is made aware of "material" items. A good working relationship between the chairperson of the committee and the head of corporate risk management is obviously crucial. The risk-related disclosure in the quarterly and annual filings with the relevant authorities also needs to be reviewed and signed off by the board committee.

The CEO should firstly define the risk mandate, risk principles and associated risk framework for the company in light of strategy and the many corporate finance attributes discussed in this book. She should propose these to the board committee and board of directors for approval or reaffirmation at least annually. She should also be responsible for communicating the risk mandate and principles throughout the organization and maintaining an independent corporate risk management function (encompassing market risk, credit risk, liquidity and process risks). She should nominate the head of this unit for approval by the board committee and should meet with this individual at least twice a month for a status and issue review. The CEO should at all times be aware of, understand, feel comfortable with, and be able to justify the firm's top 10 risks. She should also expect to be informed immediately of any changes in these top 10 risks and the impact on profitability of events in the marketplace. The CEO should regularly perform spot checks on risk activities with senior business managers or traders to ensure that the organization is always acutely aware of the importance she attaches to the correct management of risk. She should also emphasize risk management in any business reviews. As most disasters tend to be preceded by instances of high profitability or high levels of concentrated risk exposures, she should pay particular attention to such occurrences.

Above all the role of the CEO is to make decisions and ensure they are implemented. The technical risk discipline described in this book is a necessary, but not sufficient, precondition to good risk management. If it is not strengthened by effective decision making at the highest echelons of the company, it will quickly be relegated to a mere bureaucratic exercise. Effective decision making in turn will require that the CEO have a good grasp of the issues at hand and that the process by which information is gathered for decisions to be made yields thorough and balanced views.

Below the CEO many people participate in a firm's risk management. In the same way that there is no finality to the task of risk management, there is also no single failsafe way of avoiding surprises. The best approach is to have as many people feeling ownership of risk management as possible. This helps tremendously by increasing the number of eyes and ears, and checks and balances, along the way.

The CFO should oversee, or work very closely with, the corporate risk management area. The CFO should also know the top 10 risks, albeit in greater detail than the CEO. Additionally, the CFO controls a key risk management function – the finance or accounting division. This finance function needs to be independent of the business units it supports, ensure that positions are marked correctly, that trading profits or losses can be explained by the reported risk profile and changes in business balance sheets, that a transaction entered into the books of the company matches the agreement sent to the counterparty, that any liens or pledges are being appropriately satisfied and marked, and that relevant accounting reserves are taken. Critical in this list is the need to be able to corroborate the explanation of largest profits or losses to the list of top 10 risks reported by each business unit. These are all extremely critical parts of the checks and balances needed, and may require personnel versed not only in accounting, but also in risk. Again, we have too often found the finance function divorced from the reality of being an accountable and vital link in the risk management chain. This must not happen.

The CFO very often also controls the treasury function, an equally critical link. As reviewed in Chapters 1 and 3, risk should be taken in light of firm-wide liquidity dynamics. This means that decisions on the liability side of the balance sheet should not be taken in isolation from the firm's risk profile. The risk appetite sanctioned by the board/CEO naturally leads to a liability structure that has to be reviewed regularly. In addition, treasury, in conjunction with the risk group, must routinely subject the firm to extreme event scenarios to ensure a continued ability to fund the organization under dire straits. Treasury is also responsible for ensuring that the legal structure of the company is taken account of in its analysis.

The head of risk management and the corporate risk management group need to be independent from the business. We would argue that beyond simply being independent they actually need to be of a mindset and stature that lets them stand up to powerful businesses. Every organization rewards pecuniary success and notoriety. This, in turn, drives the power structure of an organization. Very often, however, large losses are preceded by large profitability or publicity. The toughest job of a risk manager is to say "no" to a powerful business with a profitable transaction about to be signed with a very good client. The risk manager needs to be comfortable in so doing, or be able to escalate the issue if there is a disagreement. Needless to say, the risk manager must always appropriately justify the reasons for a decision. Being the head of risk management is typically not a career-enhancing role!

The risk group should be accountable for translating the board/CEO-approved risk mandate into the risk parameters included in the risk limit framework and should be responsible for ensuring that the organization works within these parameters. It should also approve, and sanction, all models used for risk measurement or pricing purposes before they are put to use. Members of the group should also be part of a review of new businesses, large **capital commitments** (e.g. securities/loan underwritings) or very complex transactions. It should work closely with treasury to perform regular disaster scenario analyses on the firm to understand the impact of dislocations on firm profitability and liquidity needs. These findings should be reported to senior management, including the CEO and the board committee. Because such work can easily generate large numbers which look silly and unrealistic, it is also critical to perform regular historical simulations re-enacting actual events such as the 1987 global equity crash, the 1993 or 2001 interest rate bull markets, the 1994 Mexican peso crisis, the 1997/8 emerging market and credit crunch and the 2001/2 dot.com/telecom/loss of confidence in accounting debacle. Large numbers generated by simulating events that people have experienced bring about a greater sense of reality. As noted earlier in the book we have found that the actual numbers generated by disaster scenarios are less useful than the changes that occur from simulation to simulation. Large-scale changes in the composition of the portfolio, and their impact on the risk profile, can sometimes become more apparent through such studies; they are also very helpful in determining the top 10 risks to the firm.

The head of the risk management group, as well as several of its senior members, should have trading expertise. This provides an important practical context to decision making and helps in gaining credibility with the typically tough internal trader community. It is also critical that the group be staffed with very strong credit professionals. As the business of extending credit has expanded from traditional mechanisms such as loans, to more creative, but no less risky, transactions such as repurchase agreements, zero-coupon swaps, credit default swaps, and so forth, the need to evaluate counterparty creditworthiness – and make tough credit decisions – is more complex and important than ever.

We believe that a risk group can quickly become complacent. A great risk management team is always willing to energetically return time and again to analyze that same position, portfolio, client, and so forth – despite having looked at it several times. It is therefore best not to keep senior risk managers in the same role for more than three to five years. Indeed, we believe that a regular transfer of trading personnel in and out of the risk management function allows others to give a fresh look at the issues; it is also a very healthy way to promote a deeper understanding and respect for risk in both the business and corporate risk groups.

Though independent, the risk group becomes very ineffective if it is run as a *policing* function. In the same way that motorists buy radar detectors, a risk profile that is only designed to be in compliance when the radar detector light is on is very precarious. The best way to manage risk is in *partnership* with the business. When it works well the business takes on a self-policing role and treats the risk specialist as a partner and advisor, an integral member of the team. We have found this partnership approach to be very effective. In contrast, when risk managers are perceived as policemen, they tend to get shut out of vital information. This is ultimately counterproductive for the firm.

Risk governance committees can help strengthen the governance and control process, but they should not be seen as vehicles for expediting accountability or "passing the buck!". A risk committee, properly structured and staffed by only the most senior people within the organization, can help the head of risk management, CFO and business leaders codify risk policies and limits under the risk mandate approved by the CEO and board, discuss the firm's tactical risk needs and elevate relevant issues to the CEO. The risk committee can guide the activities of smaller teams focused on reviewing new products, large concentrations or capital commitments, client suitability issues, and so on. In our experience, risk governance committees are only useful when they have an explicit purpose and mandate, are managed with a strong hand, staffed with the most senior business personnel and are used to consider meaningful issues. If they serve to make decisions on behalf of the CEO or board, they often short-circuit the governance structure and can be dangerous.

The business unit is accountable, first and foremost, for policing itself within the risk limits and policies set by the corporate risk management group. As mentioned earlier it is also responsible for delivering accurate and timely risk data as stipulated by the corporate functions. We feel strongly that the collection of risk data should not be the responsibility of the corporate risk function. Making sure risk data comes from the same source that traders, accountants and operations staff look at minimizes reconciliation and timing problems. As noted above, each business unit should, at all times, be able to detail its top 10 risks and defend them. We have found that the best managed businesses are those who set up their own ad hoc risk committees, staffed with traders, that dynamically allocate their market and credit risk limits as opportunities arise. As this discipline takes hold we have also found that many other healthy habits develop!

Internal audit also plays a critical role in ensuring that the risk process is set up as dictated by the board. Independence, strength of character, appropriate staffing, quality of risk data, reliability of marks, frequency of business and risk reviews, escalation of issues and violations are only a few of the items that should be reviewed at least annually, but hopefully more frequently, by the head of internal audit; these should be reported to the board committee. In order to perform this function properly, auditors must have some prior experience with credit, market and process risks.

Externally we have typically found that, with a few exceptions, the risk process is quite weak and not necessarily designed to help stakeholders. Going forward regulators, external auditors, rating agency analysts and equity analysts all have to play stronger roles.

Regulators are rightly keenly interested in risk, but face an uphill battle. They have to attract staff capable of being as informed as their counterparts in banks, insurance companies or fund management groups – at public servant remuneration. We have sometimes had to sit with ex-bureaucrats, policemen and others with no knowledge whatsoever of finance. At other times we have dealt with extremely bright and practical folks, only to see them hired shortly thereafter by a competitor (or our own trading desks!). Secondly, the remit from the politicians is often centered on avoidance of any disasters within a political (read geographical) jurisdiction. The regulated institutions, however, are often multinational cross-border, sophisticated capitalists in search of the cheapest and easiest way to make money. They book transactions based on minimizing capital usage, tax, infrastructure and regulatory oversight. The risk profile presented in any single legal entity or geographical jurisdiction may thus be particularly skewed. Additionally, like Enron, many companies have offshore vehicles, most of which are loosely supervised (if at all!). Without a global purview, the regulator only gets one snapshot of activities, rather than the whole picture. A few regulators have a global mandate. This, however, typically means that a person is sent far away to inspect a member subsidiary or branch office in a land in which the regulator is not versed. As a result, and with very few exceptions, many regulatory agencies are therefore pursuing an incomplete role, staffed with people ill equipped to deal with the complexity of the topic. The public relies on efficient regulation but politicians in many jurisdictions are not allowing regulators to live up to this. Harsh though these words may be, there is a lot of truth to them – truth that is widely known, but not often discussed.

External auditors should include risk as an important part of the sign-off of the health of a company. As noted earlier in the book, risk relative to the liquidity of an enterprise is a critical measure. One would assume that it would be of interest to external auditors, but in our own experience we cannot recollect any substantive discussion with them on the topic. We believe this needs to change radically if auditors are to truly opine on the health of any company to the board of directors and, consequently, the shareholders. This takes on added importance in the wake of recent scandals.

We also believe that the accounting community should look at GAAP, and any changes that it makes, in light of accounting principles *and* the behavioral impact the rules create. For example: derivatives are typically marked to the swap curve, irrespective of the credit quality of the organization; repo transactions are accounted for on accrual basis, yet the same transactions constructed off-balance sheet get marked-to-market; profits on derivative transactions are accrued upfront and employees are paid accordingly, yet the shareholder carries the credit risk, product liability and liquidity impact for the life of the transaction; loans are not marked-to-market, yet credit derivatives (the same risk, but off-balance sheet) are, and so forth. These inconsistencies and rules inevitably have behavioral implications for the industry that may be harmful if not carefully understood, monitored and compensated for.

Rating agency analysts very often take time to ask questions about risk. They typically interact with the treasury function of an organization, which in turn brings in risk personnel to answer a few questions. We believe that in most organizations the treasury function is not sufficiently attuned to the risk and liquidity measures in setting a structure of liabilities for the firm. As a consequence, the rating agencies often only get half of the picture, and are missing an important driver of what they should be most concerned about: the ability to repay debt on time. Again, we have rarely interacted with professionals from the rating community with sufficient practical knowledge of risk.

Equity analysts doing their jobs properly cannot escape the need to ask questions and understand a firm's stance on risk management, risk as part of the corporate strategy, the impact of risk business on earnings per share, etc. They tend, however, to be interested in this topic on a retroactive basis after a disaster (e.g. large loss) occurs. They ought to be asking more questions when the money is rolling in!

Public disclosure by banks and brokerage companies became a hot topic after the LTCM debacle. One thought floated was that banks and brokers had not disclosed enough about exposure to LTCM in particular, and hedge funds in general. Our view is that financial institutions do not disclose enough about their exposures. One proposed solution – forcing a more complex set of unwillingly published numbers into the small print of the filings which appear long after the fact – would not seem to help the average shareholder. Instead, we believe that every quarter each CEO should be required to report to shareholders the firm's risk mandate and top 10 financial risks – however she desires to choose them. She should then report back on these risks on each subsequent filing, detailing returns on risks, losses, changes, and so on. Such a mechanism would create greater clarity for the average shareholder and accountability at a senior level. Fund managers and insurance companies should also be required to report on the top 10 risks of their businesses. We believe that this practice should extend to non-financial industry filings, as many corporations are increasingly taking on credit or investment risks in their businesses (for example, GE, Shell Oil, Enron, Proctor and Gamble, and so on).

Shareholders would greatly benefit from comprehensible disclosures on risk. A bank or investment bank's risk profile is typically mentioned in the footnotes of a regulatory filing or annual report. Understanding it requires the discovery of a new Rosetta Stone! When we were risk managers we certainly never referred to these disclosures, which are driven by regulatory requirements rather than by a desire to get shareholders to comprehend its content. Yet such information is very important. Not only should shareholders need the CEO's risk mandate and top 10 financial risk concerns elaborated in a simple to understand manner, but they should also want to know how the company has performed relative to like-risk assets. For example, if a company is making money by owning an asset class of leases with borrowed money, how would an equally risky credit asset class, leveraged to the same degree, have performed? (In Chapter 3 we mentioned the concept of leverage arbitrage, which companies such as GE have practiced, as an illustration of this point.)

There is no "final destination" in the risk management process, there are only stations along the way. The CEO and board are manning the engine and the rest of the staff have clearly

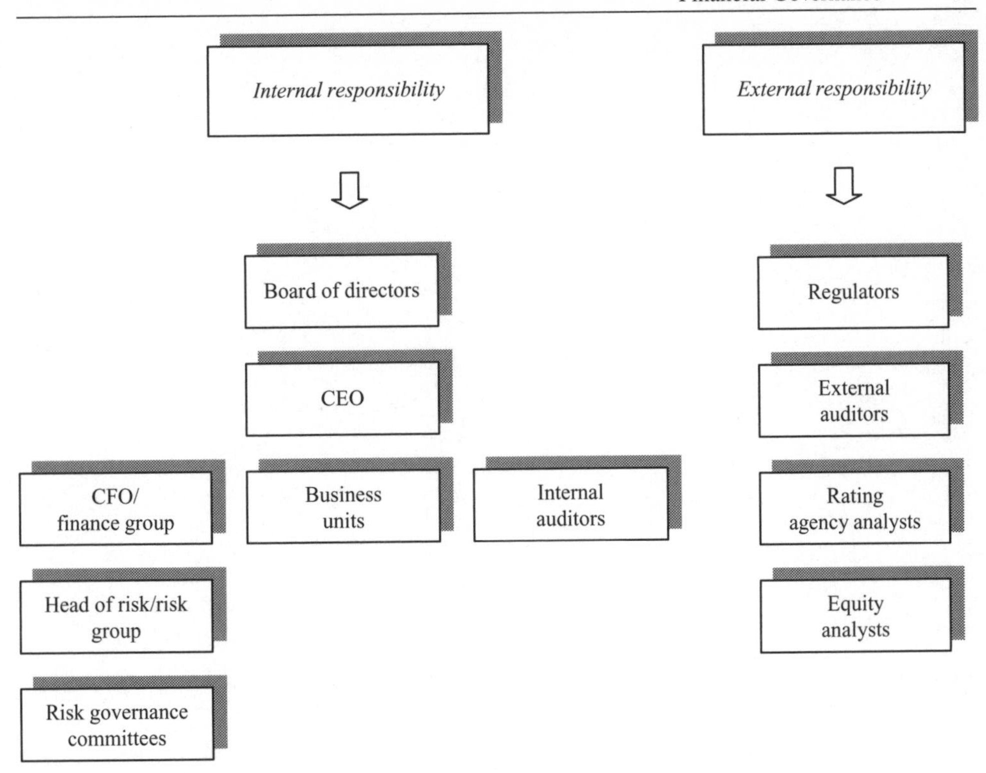

Figure 10.1 Internal and external responsibilities for risk

defined roles (as summarized in Figure 10.1) to ensure that the train runs smoothly. A firm has temporarily succeeded if each successive station is visited with "no surprises" along the way. There are no failsafe mechanisms to ensure that this always happens, however having checks and balances from all angles is the best way to enjoy the journey. The various regulatory, external audit and rating agency "station masters" are currently not adding as much as they could to the safety of the journey, which is a pity. We live in hope that this will one day change!

11 The Risk Framework: Limiting and Controlling Risks

11.1 CREATING A RISK FRAMEWORK

With the risk mandate and principles in hand, a firm needs a way of expressing, and managing, its financial risk appetite. This can be done through a risk limit structure that we refer to as the **risk framework**. As mentioned several times already, it is scientifically impossible today to directly relate a maximum loss tolerance to any action that will indeed guarantee not to ever exceed this maximum loss. The best we can do is surround the problem with a series of proxies. In our view the risk framework is the most important proxy (albeit one that changes over time and differs by institution and types of risks being run). The translation of loss tolerance into the risk framework is not easy – and this is where finance truly becomes an art and the quality and experience of personnel becomes critical.

The risk framework conveys, in common terms, how much exposure the firm in total, and its business units specifically, can take in individual risk classes (e.g. directional interest rate risk, equity volatility risk, credit default risk, asset/liability mismatch risk, and so forth). In our experience a risk framework is most useful for risks that can be quantified in some way, e.g. market, credit and liquidity risks. Those that are more subjective, such as process, model and suitability risks, do not readily lend themselves to the same approach and are better handled through some of the techniques discussed in Chapters 12 and 13. To create a risk framework, a firm needs to develop a process like the one outlined in Figure 11.1.

11.1.1 Computing maximum losses

By computing the P&L arising from various scenarios – which generally involves the selection of hypothetical small and large market moves/events for each type of risk – a firm is trying to determine a possible worst-case loss. As noted in Chapter 6, the maximum loss measure enhances the information provided by the standard VAR measure by ignoring the effects of correlation and assumptions regarding statistical distributions. From a market risk perspective, a worst-case loss does not always come from the largest market movement. For businesses with **optionality** (or gamma, as described in Chapter 2), the worst case might actually be some small or intermediate market move. Accordingly, the concept of a maximum loss centers on taking the worst loss produced by any scenario run for a given risk class. Let us consider two examples to illustrate this concept: a US government bond desk has bond positions (e.g. no options) that create the gains and losses illustrated in Table 11.1 under specific market scenarios. Thus, a 100 basis point drop in rates (across the entire curve) creates a maximum loss of \$5 million.

Assume next that the desk also has government bond options in its portfolio. Its gains and losses might now look like those summarized in Table 11.2. In this case the maximum loss of \$6 million occurs with a 50 basis point drop in rates.

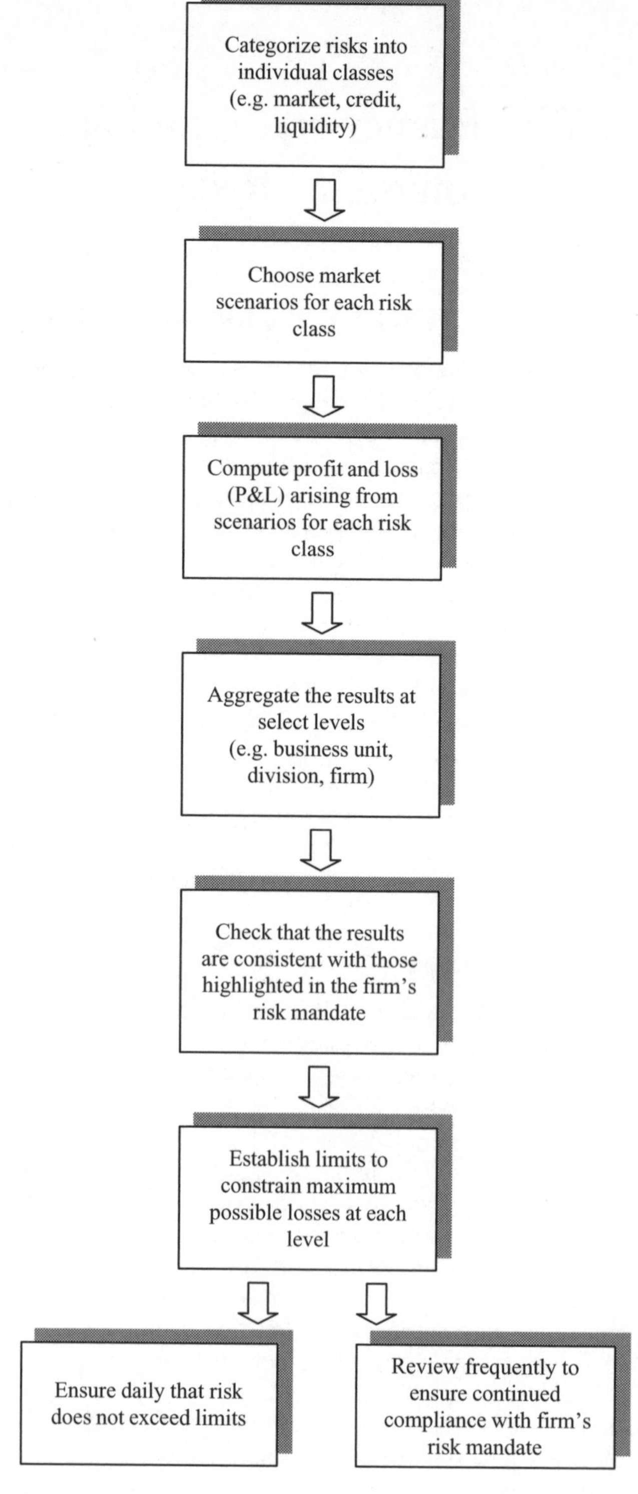

Figure 11.1 Process of creating a risk framework

Table 11.1 Government bond desk market scenario 1

Market scenario change in US Treasury bond yields (basis points)	P&L (thousand dollars)
−100 bps	−$5000
−50 bps	−$2500
−10 bps	−$500
+10 bps	+$500
+50 bps	+$2500
+100 bps	+$5000

Table 11.2 Government bond desk market scenario 2

Market scenario (basis points)	P&L (thousand dollars)
−100 bps	−$5000
−50 bps	−$6000
−10 bps	−$1500
+10 bps	+$500
+50 bps	+$2000
+100 bps	+$55000

The same maximum loss concept can be applied to other market exposures, such as directional equity, currency and commodity risks, volatility risks, credit spread risks, and so on. We have found that it is best to remain flexible by adapting the maximum loss definition to suit the particulars of a given risk class. For instance, in considering the maximum credit spread loss from *emerging market* positions we feel it is appropriate to stress the portfolio on the basis of large price moves rather than large *spread* moves. When *emerging market* assets deteriorate in value they often do so in large price gaps of 5%, 15%, 25% or more – expressing such shocks in more granular credit spread terms (intended to capture "close by" rather than "extreme" moves) does not really make much sense.

Maximum loss can also be determined for credit risks, by computing losses resulting from the failure of an individual counterparty, e.g. counterparty default risk. By analyzing a portfolio of transactions, collateral taken to secure these, and any money assumed to be recovered post-bankruptcy, one can crystallize a maximum credit loss. As noted earlier in the book, in instances where collateral taken to secure a trade is either of poor quality or highly correlated with the counterparty (e.g. the collateral will lose value when the counterparty weakens/defaults), the maximum loss calculation should assign limited (or no) economic benefit to the collateral (e.g. it should not offset the maximum loss).

11.1.2 Aggregating losses

Once individual losses are obtained for a given risk category, the process can be repeated for every other risk category impacting each business. Exposures can then be aggregated by business or risk category. Returning to our example above, scenarios are run for the government bond desk's other risk exposures (e.g. curve risk, volatility risk, volatility curve risk). Scenarios are also run for all other fixed income desks and aggregated to produce exposures by risk class (e.g. all US interest rate risk), all risk exposures by business unit (e.g. interest rate risk, curve risk, volatility risk for all US government bond trading), all risk exposures by division (e.g. all fixed income or equity desks), and so forth. Maximum loss scenarios can then be aggregated and related to the firm's stated loss tolerance. However, as we have noted (and stress once again!), since there is no way to guarantee that markets will behave within these selected scenarios, there is also no guarantee that actual disasters will remain below the stated loss tolerance. Figure 11.2 notes how maximum loss in interest rates can flow from businesses to

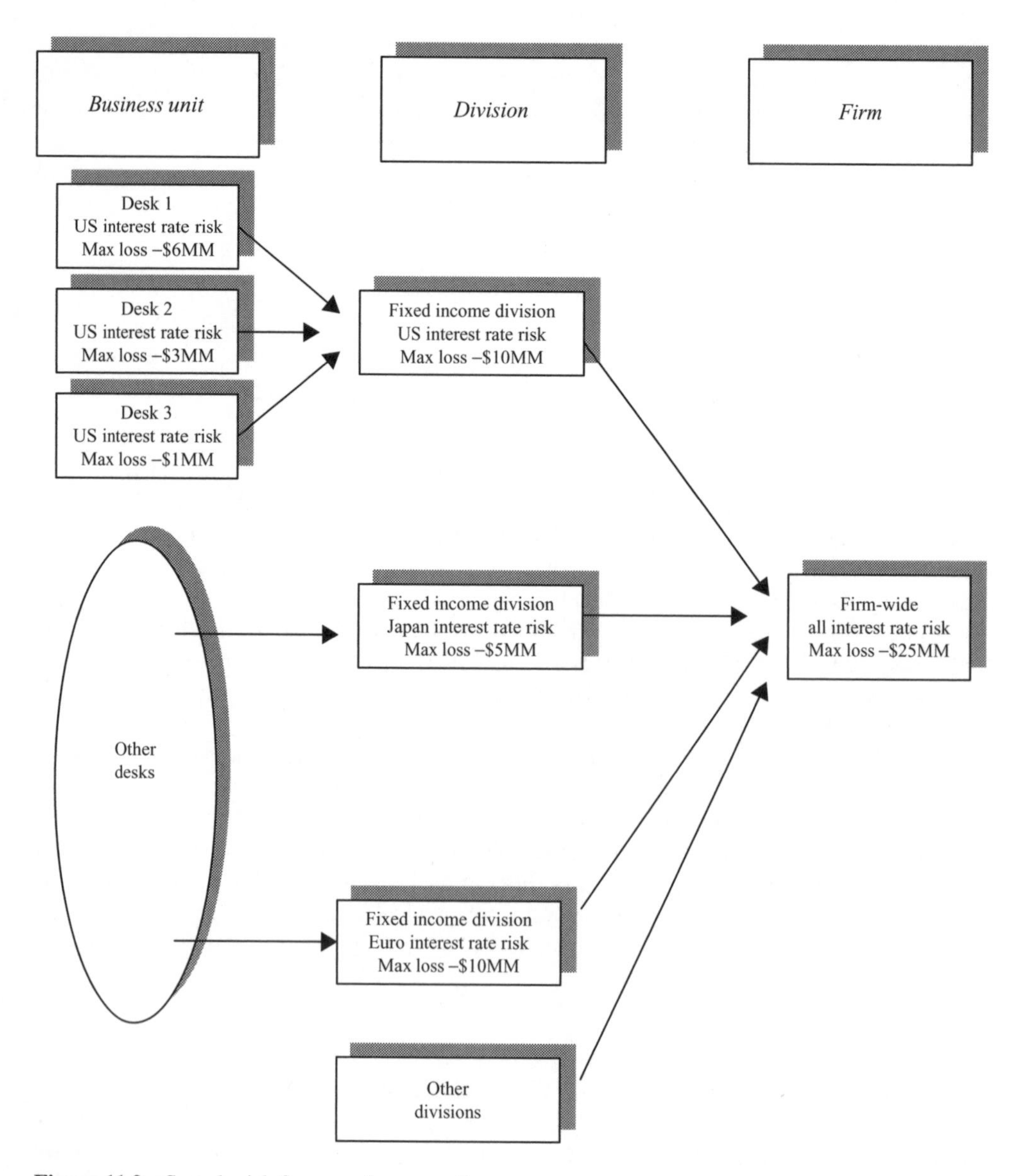

Figure 11.2 Sample risk framework aggregation

divisions and up to the firm in total. The same can be done with all other market and credit risk categories.

From a practical perspective framework limits can be allocated through a "top down" or a "bottom up" approach. The *top down* approach begins with an expression of maximum willingness to lose, say, $100 million. That $100 million might then be allocated to four businesses (say $25 million maximum loss each) and, from there, to the individual risk classes. For instance, Business 1 might take directional equity and volatility risk, Business 2 directional foreign exchange risk, Business 3 credit spread risk and Business 4 directional interest rate risk and curve risk. All four might take credit exposures, too. The $25 million business unit allocation can then be applied to the maximum loss per category. Business 1 might get $5 million for volatility risk, $5 million for directional equity risk and $15 million for credit risk; Business 2 receives its allocations, and so on. Adding these pieces brings the allocation back up to the firm's $100 million risk appetite – the maximum loss it is willing to bear under worst-case scenarios.

Through a *bottom up* approach, a firm starts with the individual risk allocations within risk categories for each business unit and adds them up the chain; here, care must be taken not to over-allocate total risk appetite. If Business 1 wants $40 million and each of the others want $30 million, allocations will have to be reduced to remain within the firm's stated $100 million risk appetite. Remaining within the overall risk appetite is the one inviolable rule!

It is always best to look at limits and exposures *within business units* as well as *across risk classes*. For example, a division comprised of three desks might take interest rate risk in the US, Japanese and sterling markets. Framework limits can be established for *each desk* depending on the type of risk it takes (e.g. US rates only, US and Japanese rates), for *a specific risk class* (e.g. US rates, Japanese rates, sterling rates) and for *the division as a whole* (e.g. all interest rates). Figure 11.3 provides an example of this concept.

11.1.3 Credit risk

Credit exposures can be aggregated and limited through the framework by setting maximum exposure levels per counterparty, ratings category, country and industry – this caps the total amount of *unsecured exposure* that can be extended by the firm. Similar caps can also be placed on any *contingent credit exposure*, e.g. exposure that does not currently exist, but which may arise in the future (such as a drawdown on a revolving credit or commercial paper program, a derivative that "knocks in" (i.e. becomes effective) when particular market levels are hit, and so forth). Letters of credit or guarantees that might be called on to support the financial activities of a weaker counterparty should also be included under contingent exposures, as they represent potential future credit obligations of the support provider.

For example, the framework might set $250 million of unsecured credit exposure and $350 million of contingent credit exposure for every AAA counterparty, and $5 billion and $7 billion, respectively, for all AAA counterparties in aggregate. Similar caps would exist for other ratings groups, by individual company and in total. Since the "treacherous" part of the credit spectrum occurs in the sub-investment grade sector, it also makes sense to limit the aggregate of all *sub-investment grade unsecured and contingent credit exposures* to counterparties rated below the BBB− equivalent. For example, the sum total of all BB+, BB, BB−, B+, CCC and CC unsecured and contingent exposures might be capped at $100 million and $150 million, respectively. A simplified example illustrating unsecured and contingent credit limits for various desks is depicted in Figures 11.4 and 11.5.

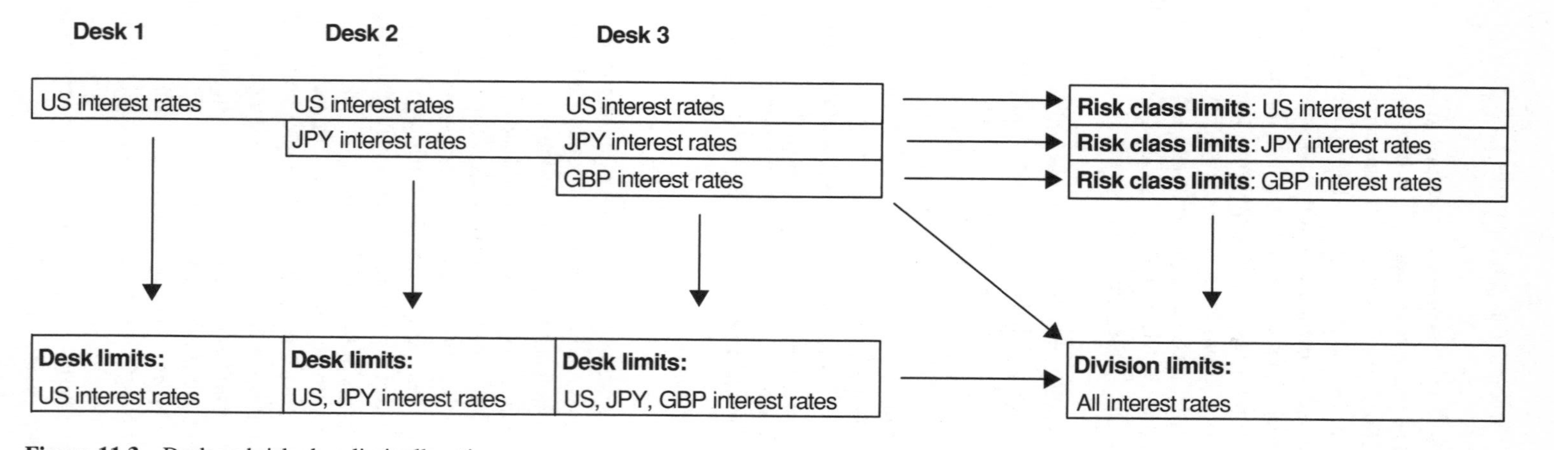

Figure 11.3 Desk and risk class limit allocation

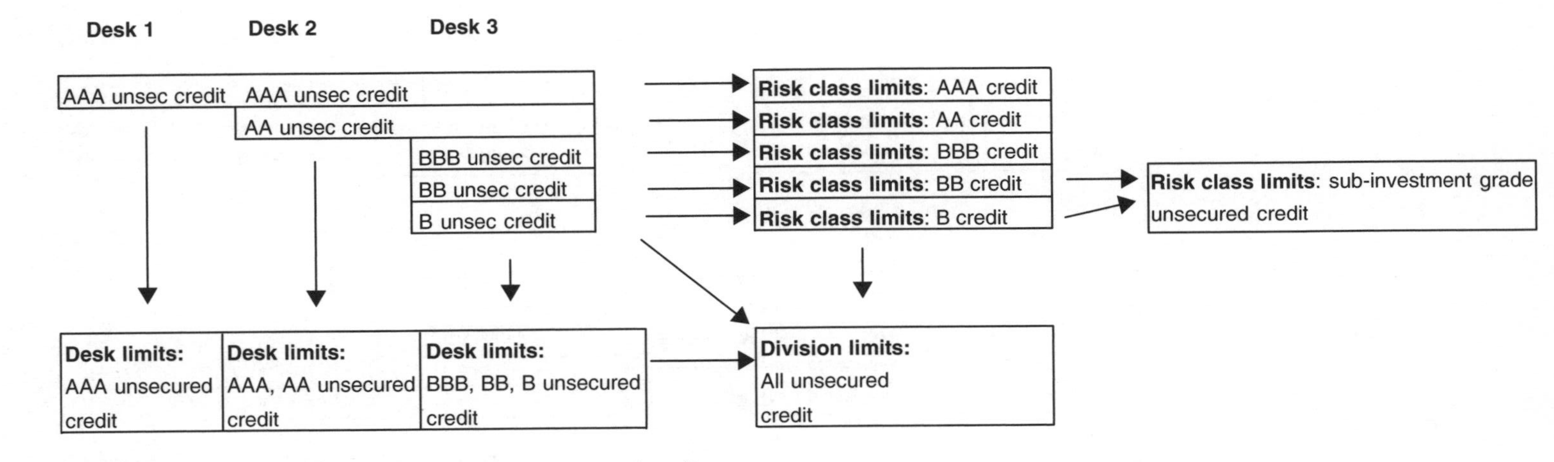

Figure 11.4 Desk and risk class limit allocation: unsecured credit

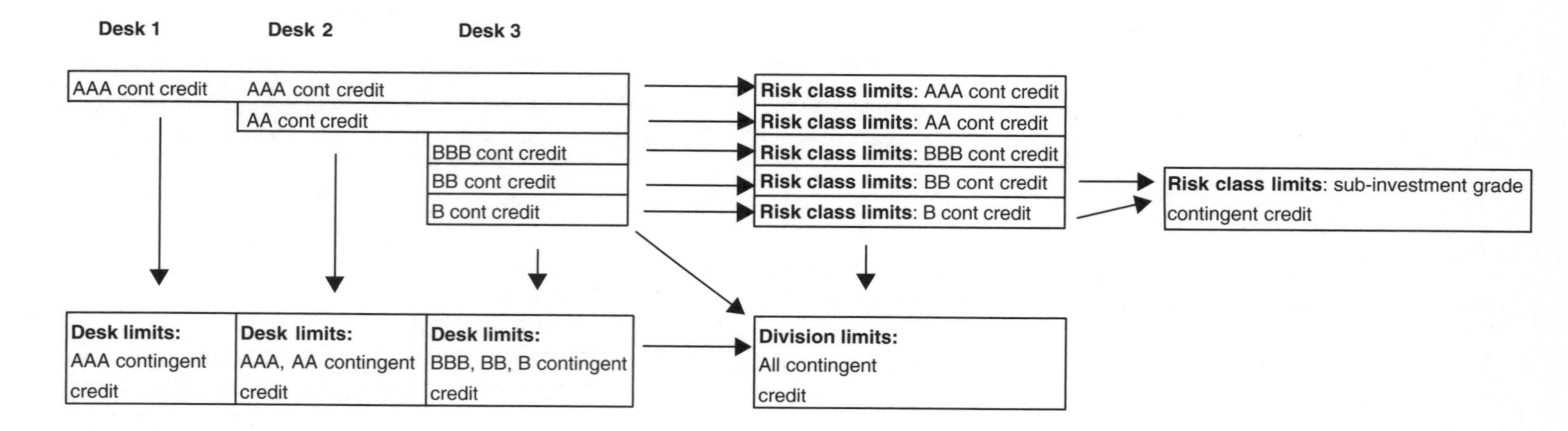

Figure 11.5 Desk and risk class limit allocation: contingent credit

The framework can also be used to limit *long-term credit exposures* by counterparty rating (e.g. any transaction exceeding 12 months). Thus, AA/AAA counterparties might receive 10- or 15-year unsecured credit lines through the framework, while BBB/A counterparties might be limited to five or seven years and borderline investment grade/sub-investment clients to only 12 months. Limiting the term of credit transactions helps keep exposures to counterparties that might be vulnerable to rapid financial deterioration in check. It is worth pointing out that well-rated companies can fall from grace quickly. We have recently been acutely exposed to this through the Enron debacle.

Secured credit exposures can also be limited so that concentrations, and especially correlated concentrations, do not grow out of control. This can be done by setting the maximum amount of a particular security that can be used to collateralize exposures across all counterparties (e.g. $500 million total of esoteric mortgage-backed securities being used to collateralize credit exposures to all clients) and/or the total amount of the free float of a security against which lending can occur; the emphasis here is, of course, on less liquid or lesser quality collateral rather than on highly liquid, risk-free collateral (e.g. US Treasuries, Japanese government bonds). The framework can also be used to limit *correlated exposures* across all counterparties to prevent a build-up of positions that can sour at the same time (e.g. a maximum of $100 million of Turkish bonds being used to collateralize financings for Turkish banks). An example of collateralized limits (per collateral asset and counterparty) is depicted in Figure 11.6.

In Figure 11.7 we illustrate a simple example of secured collateral/counterparty framework limits for exposures that are highly correlated. For ease, we assume in the illustration that Collateral asset 1 (e.g. Turkish bond) is perfectly correlated with Counterparty 1 (e.g. Turkish bank) but not Counterparty 2 (a US bank) or Counterparty 3 (a European investment fund), and that each desk deals only with a single counterparty. Thus, any collateral exposure from Asset 1 carried on Desk 2 in its dealings with Counterparty 2 is counted against the total secured limits granted to Desk 1 (collateral and credit exposure with Turkey/Turkish banks). All other applicable limits described above relating to other counterparties and collateral concentrations remain in force.

11.1.4 Liquidity risk

Since liquidity risks are just as important to consider and limit, we have found that it makes sense to create a separate liquidity risk framework – based on the aggregation of key balance sheet and off-balance sheet items as described in Chapter 3. Though the scenarios and metrics used are different, a liquidity framework helps ensure a firm remains attuned to the asset and funding risks in its operations – and the potential damage they can do.

11.1.4.1 Balance sheet targets

A firm can set *balance sheet targets* through the framework to control the amount of liquidity risk exposure in particular assets. For instance, a bank's management may decide that 10% of the balance sheet will be devoted to "less liquid" risks to meet return targets (e.g. high-yield bonds, emerging market bonds, complex or esoteric structures, and so forth). Accordingly, it can set a 10% threshold through the framework. If illiquid assets rise to 25%, the firm is clearly less liquid and will have less control of its operations in the event of a crisis. Assets often become illiquid gradually. Those that are purchased or underwritten with a view toward subsequent sale may not be sold, and will start to accumulate. A poor market cycle,

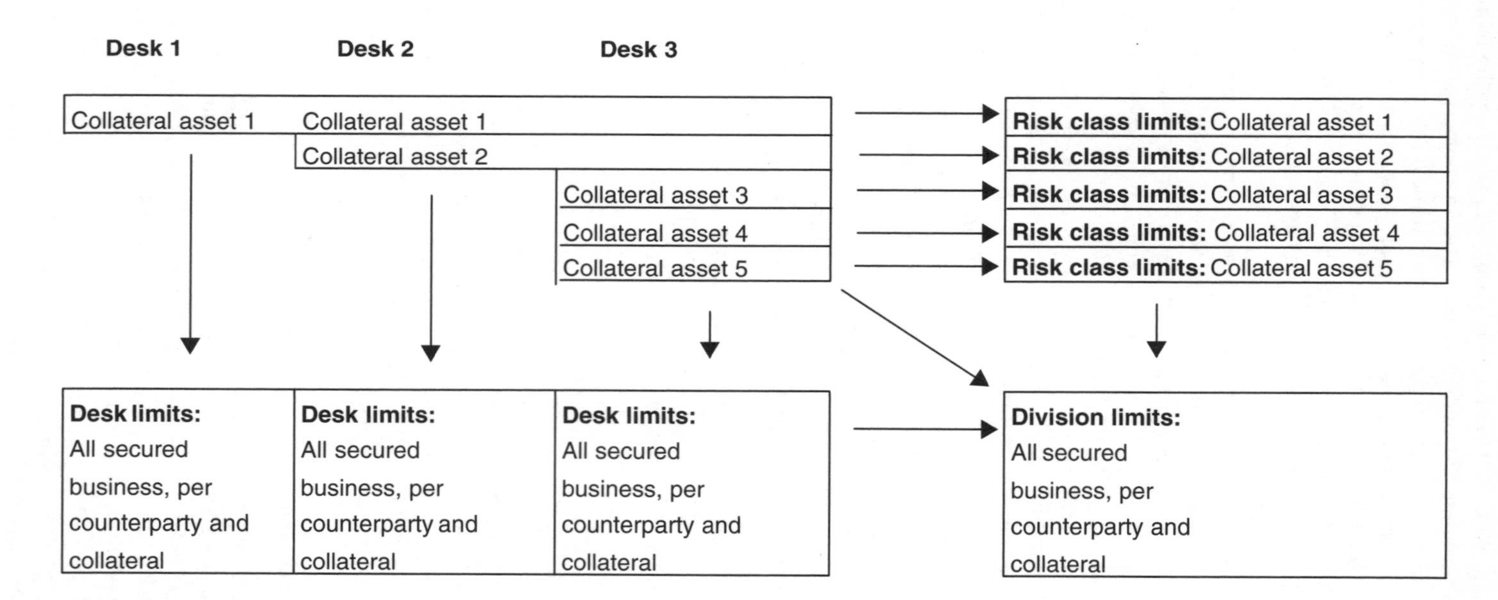

Figure 11.6 Desk and risk class limit allocation: collateralized credit

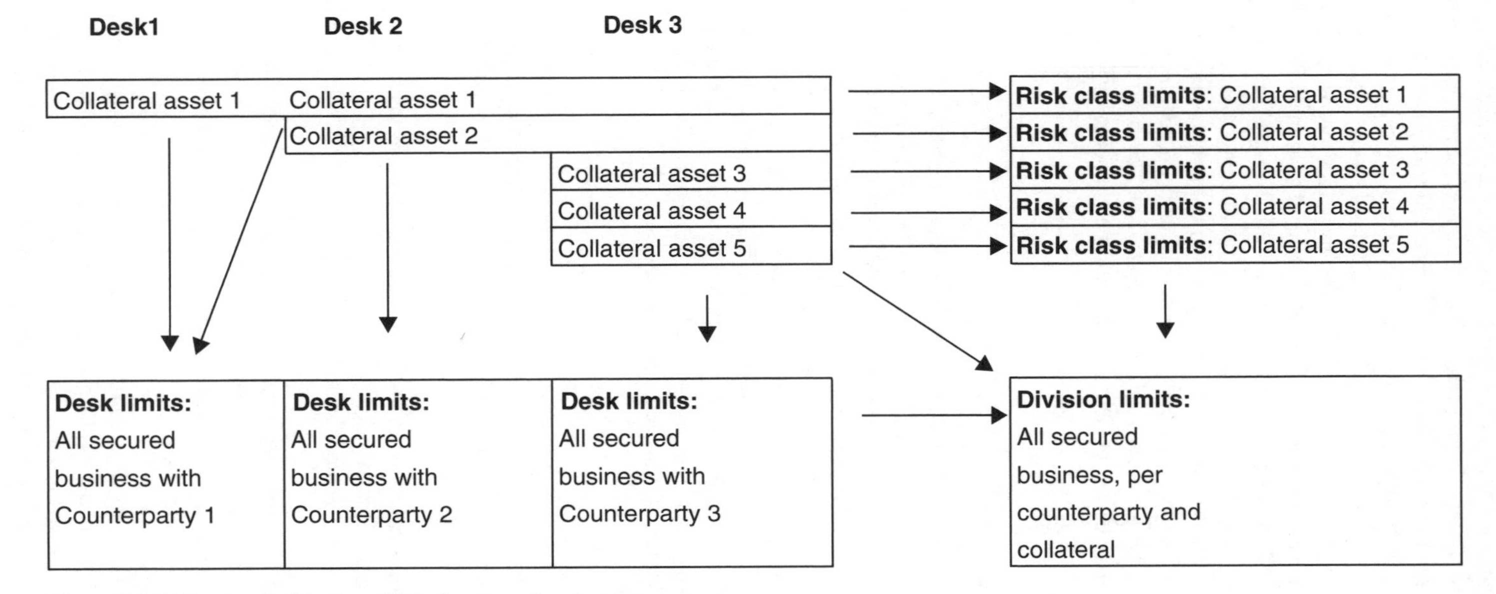

Figure 11.7 Desk and risk class allocation: correlated exposures

changing market dynamics, lack of investor/client demand, or mismarking can all contribute to this accumulation; failure to properly adjust valuations simply compounds the problem. Over time, a bank might realize that its overall asset portfolio is much less liquid than desired and that asset values may not reflect market clearing levels; it is therefore incumbent on management to ensure thresholds intended to cap holdings of "illiquid" assets are defined, communicated, monitored and managed. Management then needs to review the portfolio, its valuations and these thresholds on a regular basis. The framework can also be used to constrain aspects of the *forward balance sheet* as well. Though these limits might be based on somewhat imprecise assumptions about future events, they can serve to keep the firm's future balance sheet construction in check. Such limits might control the maximum allowable growth in total footings, maximum incremental financing requirements at various future points, and so forth. They will also prevent people from "by-passing" balance sheet limits by creating off-balance sheet exposures that will ultimately come back as assets necessitating funding!

11.1.4.2 Concentration limits

As noted in Chapter 3, undue concentrations can create liquidity problems. Using framework *concentration limits* to control the build-up of concentrations can help limit potential problems. For instance, a bank may prohibit positioning of more than \$50 million in any high-yield issuer and \$500 million across all high-yield issuers, and \$200 million in any high-grade corporate issuer and \$2 billion across all high-grade issuers. Positions in excess of these limits would require the review and approval of those in the governance structure – making them aware that by doing so they are potentially increasing the firm's liquidity risk profile. In order to set concentration limits a firm must have appropriate monitoring tools and infrastructure. This generally requires some type of aggregation platform that draws in, and consolidates, identical positions carried in different businesses or locations.

11.1.4.3 Diversified funding

In order to manage funding liquidity risk and reduce the need for sudden asset disposal, the framework should be used to limit *funding concentrations*. This is done by forcing the firm to use standardization around:

- Diversified funding markets (e.g. domestic market, offshore market, loan market, capital market, short-term financing market, secured market);
- Diversified lenders (e.g. domestic and international banks, investment banks, funds, other credit providers);
- A range of instruments (e.g. payables, commercial paper, short- and medium-term notes, bonds, bank loans, equity-linked financings, secured financings, and so forth);
- A range of maturities (e.g. short-term funding, medium-term funding, long-term funding);
- A high percentage of truly committed facilities.

As part of the process a firm should prove to itself that it has enough funds to meet a variety of crisis situations; it should stress its program by considering scenarios that reflect disasters (e.g. withdrawal of a large portion of its funding, availability to access new funds, a spike in interest rates, large, unexpected payments, changes in the forward balance sheet, and so on).

Where necessary it may want to place limits on funding of different legal entities, especially for heavily regulated institutions where "upstreaming" of capital or dividends is sometimes not possible; this can help ensure there is no trouble tapping funds in the right entity, when needed. Moving capital around may also entail other consequences that require careful consideration.

11.1.5 Settling limits at different levels

From a practical perspective we have found that it is helpful to constrain risks at various levels, including firm-wide, divisional and business unit. Different risk limits may apply accordingly.

Firm-wide:

- Total maximum market loss: a summation of the maximum losses across each individual risk class; this has the benefit of not incorporating correlation risk by assuming that correlations will move to their worst possible point.
- Value-at-risk (VAR): as reviewed in Chapter 6, a measure designed to estimate the potential loss across an entire portfolio of market risks, computed to a particular statistical confidence level and liquidation period.
- Total maximum credit loss: a summation of the maximum losses across individual counterparties, ratings, countries and collateral categories.
- Total liquidity targets: a summation of total footings, liquid/illiquid, concentrated and aged positions across relevant balance sheet and off-balance sheet categories. Maximum funding by source, product, market and maturity.
- Individual country exposure: a summation of the maximum sovereign exposure by country subject to sovereign default, currency control or devaluation.

Division:

- Total maximum market loss, VAR, credit loss and liquidity exposure for each risk class in each broad division within the organization (e.g. fixed income, equities, asset management, banking).

Business unit:

- Granular maximum market and credit loss limits across risk classes for each business (e.g. cash equities, US debt derivatives, syndicate, and so on).

A firm operating on a legal entity basis (rather than divisional/business unit structure) should also set its limits accordingly. This is relevant for Japanese banks, for example, which tend to be organized on a legal entity basis.

While our discussion has been geared primarily toward the major risk-taking insititutions – banks, investment banks, securities firms – the proposed framework is flexible enough to be used by non-bank institutions, such as industrial corporations, insurers and fund managers. Relevant adjustments need to be made, of course. For instance, firms that do not follow a mark-to-market convention will find certain measures within the framework, such as VAR, of limited use. Fundamentally, however, many of the concepts we have described above are applicable across industries (and will become applicable to an even wider audience as more industries and firms gravitate toward a mark-to-market convention). Firms that are exposed to risk – regardless of industry – must define a philosophy and tolerance and live within these constraints. The risk framework can be a useful control tool for this. For instance, an energy company that enters into OTC derivative contracts to hedge out commodity risks is taking the same counterparty credit risks that banks normally take. Controlling such credit risks through the credit framework described above is entirely appropriate. Equally, an insurer or pension fund that must meet policy obligations/liabilities through asset streams has to be very sensitive to asset/liability gaps, and can manage its exposures through a risk liquidity framework. Fund managers who have a benchmark hurdle (e.g. treasury yield or an equity index) to meet can likewise construct a framework that limits major deviations from these by limiting concentrations.

11.2 THE COMPLETE RISK FRAMEWORK

To illustrate the concept in its entirety, we present in Tables 11.3–11.5 sample market, credit and liquidity risk frameworks that can serve to crystallize maximum losses. These contain scenarios reflecting both small and large market moves/events and thus provide important information on a range of outcomes – from the very likely/realistic to the very unlikely/extreme. When setting maximum loss limits synchronized with the firm's overall risk appetite, large market moves or credit events equating to "disasters" need to be used; this helps ensure that, even in a "meltdown", the firm is *probably* not going to breach its stated maximum risk appetite. Since every firm is unique, it needs to create the kind of framework that relates to its range of businesses; hopefully, though, these examples serve as a constructive starting point!

Note that credit spreads for emerging market exposures are treated as price movements rather than spread movements. Experience has shown that when emerging market assets start to move by large amounts (which they do!), price measures tend to be far more relevant and accurate than spread measures.

11.3 MONITORING, ADJUSTING AND DEALING WITH EXCEPTIONS

While the framework exists to express and constrain a firm's exposures, it also helps risk managers and business leaders to monitor and manage risks on an ongoing basis. It becomes, in essence, a central means of managing firm-wide market, credit and liquidity risk, and a tool that can be used to alter risk levels as market conditions change. As markets enter new medium-term cycles and it becomes less attractive to take risk, the firm should use the framework to lower its profile in places where it is more dangerous or returns are no longer attractive. Conversely, when it becomes more compelling to take risk, it can use the framework to adjust its profile upward.

We have found that the framework is also a particularly useful way of reviewing exceptions, concentrations or temporary increases in the firm's stated risk appetite. It helps ensure those in the governance structure are aware of, and approve, larger pockets of risk. For instance, if the framework caps unsecured credit exposure to $100 million per BBB counterparty and an attractive opportunity arises to increase that to $150 million, a formal exception process – driven by the corporate risk group – should exist so that the exception is debated and either

Table 11.3 Sample market risk framework

Interest rates: by market	
Developed markets	
Direction	−100 bps, −50 bps, −10 bps, +10 bps, +50 bps, +100 bps
Volatility	−10%, −2%, +2%, +10%
Curve	−25 bps, +25 bps for 1–3 mo, 3–6 mo, 6 mo–1 yr, 1–2 yr, 2–5 yr, 5–7 yr, 7–10 yr, 10–15 yr, 1–20 yr, 20+ yr
Volatility curve	−10%, +10% for 0–1 yr, 1–2 yr, 2–5 yr, 5–7 yr, 7–10 yr, 10–15 yr, 1–20 yr, 20+ yr
Skew	−10%, +10% for at-the-money, 5% out/in-the-money, 10% out/in-the-money
Emerging markets	
Direction	−500 bps, −200 bps, −100 bps, −25 bps, +25 bps, +100 bps, +200 bps, +500 bps
Volatility	−25%, −10%, +10%, +25%
Curve	−100 bps, +100 bps for 0–1 yr, 1–2 yr, 2–5 yr, 5–7 yr, 7–10 yr, 10–15 yr, 1–20 yr, 20+ yr
Volatility curve	−25%, +25% for 0–1 yr, 1–2 yr, 2–5 yr, 5–7 yr, 7–10 yr, 10–15 yr, 1–20 yr, 20+ yr
Skew	−10%, +10% for at-the-money, 5% out/in-the-money, 10% out/in-the-money
Credit spreads: by market	
Developed markets	
AAA–AA	−50 bps, −25 bps, −5 bps, +5 bps, +25 bps, +50 bps
A	−50 bps, −25 bps, −5 bps, +5 bps, +25 bps, +50 bps
BBB	−50 bps, −25 bps, −5 bps, +5 bps, +25 bps, +50 bps
Spread volatility	−50%, −25%, −10%, +10%, +25%, +50%
High-yield markets	
BB	−500 bps, −200 bps, −100 bps, −10 bps, +10 bps, +100 bps, +200 bps, +500 bps
B	−500 bps, −200 bps, −100 bps, −10 bps, +10 bps, +100 bps, +200 bps, +500 bps
CCC	−500 bps, −200 bps, −100 bps, −10 bps, +10 bps, +100 bps, +200 bps, +500 bps
CC	−500 bps, −200 bps, −100 bps, −10 bps, +10 bps, +100 bps, +200 bps, +500 bps
C	−500 bps, −200 bps, −100 bps, −10 bps, +10 bps, +100 bps, +200 bps, +500 bps
Spread volatility	−50%, −25%, −10%, +10%, +25%, +50%
Emerging markets (price)	
BBB	−50%, −25%, −5%, +5%, +25%, +50%
BB	−50%, −25%, −5%, +5%, +25%, +50%
B	−50%, −25%, −5%, +5%, +25%, +50%
CCC	−50%, −25%, −5%, +5%, +25%, +50%
CC	−50%, −25%, −5%, +5%, +25%, +50%
C	−50%, −25%, −5%, +5%, +25%, +50%
Price volatility	−50%, −25%, −10%, +10%, +25%, +50%
Currencies: by market	
Developed markets	
Direction	−5%, −2%, −1%, +1%, +2%, +5%
Volatility	−10%, −2%, +2%, +10%

(*continued overleaf*)

Table 11.3 (*continued*)

Volatility curve	−10%, +10% for 0–1 yr, 1–2 yr, 2–5 yr, 5–7 yr, 7–10 yr, 10–15 yr, 1–20 yr, 20+ yr
Skew	−10%, +10% for at-the-money, 5% out/in-the-money, 10% out/in-the-money
Emerging markets	
Direction	−50%, −25%, −10%, +10%, +25%, +50%
Volatility	−50%, −10%, +10%, +50%
Volatility curve	−50%, +50% for 0–1 yr, 1–2 yr, 2–5 yr, 5–7 yr, 7–10 yr, 10–15 yr, 1–20 yr, 20+ yr
Skew	−10%, +10% for at-the-money, 5% out/in-the-money, 10% out/in-the-money
Equities: by market	
Developed markets	
Direction	−25%, −5%, −2%, −1%, +1%, +2%, +5%, +25%
Volatility	−25%, −10%, −2%, +2%, +10%, +25%
Volatility curve	−10%, +10% for 0–1 yr, 1–2 yr, 2–5 yr, 5–7 yr, 7–10 yr, 10–15 yr, 1–20 yr, 20+ yr
Skew	−10%, +10% for at-the-money, 5% out/in-the-money, 10% out/in-the-money
Emerging markets	
Direction	−50%, −25%, −10%, +10%, +25%, +50%
Volatility	−50%, −10%, +10%, +50%
Skew	−10%, +10% for at-the-money, 5% out/in-the-money, 10% out/in-the-money
Commodities: by market	
Direction	−10%, −5%, −2%, −1%, +1%, +2%, +5%, +10%
Volatility	−10%, −2%, +2%, +10%
Volatility curve	−10%, +10% for 0–1 yr, 1–2 yr, 2–5 yr, 5–7 yr, 7–10 yr, 10–15 yr, 1–20 yr, 20+ yr
Skew	−10%, +10% for at-the-money, 5% out/in-the-money, 10% out/in-the-money

Table 11.4 Sample credit risk framework

Direct/trading credit risk	
*Default risk**	
By counterparty/legal entity*	Sum within each counterparty/legal entity
Loans, securities, deposits	100% of notional, by counterparty/legal entity
Derivatives	5–50% of notional, by counterparty/legal entity
Repos/reverses	1–10% of notional, by counterparty/legal entity
Contingent risk	100% of notional, by counterparty/legal entity
By rating*	Sum across all counterparties/legal entities within each rating category (AAA, AA, A, BBB)
	Sum across all counterparties/legal entities within each, and across all, sub-investment grade categories (BB, B, CCC)
Loans, securities, deposits	100% of notional, by counterparty/legal entity
Derivatives	5–50% of notional, by counterparty/legal entity
Repos/reverses	1–10% of notional, by counterparty/legal entity
Contingent risk	100% of notional, by counterparty/legal entity
By country*	Sum across all counterparties/legal entities within country
Loans, securities, deposits	100% of notional, by counterparty/legal entity
Derivatives	5–50% of notional, by counterparty/legal entity
Repos/reverses	1–10% of notional, by counterparty/legal entity
Contingent risk	100% of notional, by counterparty/legal entity

Table 11.4 (*continued*)

Collateralized credit risk	
By asset held as collateral	Sum across all counterparties/legal entities, 100% of notional underlying all transactions
	Collateral $ max by rating, % of outstanding issue size
By correlated exposures	Sum across all correlated exposures, 100% of notional underlying all transactions
	Collateral $ max by rating, % of outstanding issue size
Sovereign risk	
Default risk	
By sovereign	
Loans, securities, deposits	100% of notional, by sovereign
Derivatives	5–50% of notional, by sovereign
Financings	1–10% of notional, by sovereign
Convertibility risk	
Currency assets	100%
Derivative receivables	100% of receivable
Local equity	100% of position
Settlement risk	
By counterparty	100% of notional on currency, free deliveries

* Can be adjusted for recovery assumptions.

Table 11.5 Sample liquidity risk framework

Balance sheet targets	
Total footings	$ max
Liquid investments/total assets	% min
"Less liquid" investments/total assets	% max
Aged assets over 90 days	$ max
Asset/liability mismatch	max $ gap per maturity: 1–3 mo, 3–6 mo, 6–12 mo, 12–18 mo, 18–24 mo, 2–5 yr, 5–7 yr, 7–10 yr, 10–15 yr, 15–20 yr, 20–30 yr, 30+ yr
Forward balance sheet	
Footings	$ max at 6, 12, 24, 36 mo forward horizons
Funding	$ max at 6, 12, 24, 36 mo forward horizons
Asset concentrations	
Balance sheet positions	
By issuer	$ max per issuer
By issue	$ max per issue
By ratings category	$ max per AAA, AA, A, BBB, BB, B ratings categories
By asset type	$ max per emerging markets, high yield, syndicated loans, equity blocks
Off-balance sheet positions	$ max per off-balance sheet category
Funding diversification	
Funding source (% of funding)	
By instrument type	% max
By market	% max
By lender	% max
By maturity	% max per maturity: 1–3 mo, 3–6 mo, 6–12 mo, 12–18 mo, 18–24 mo, 2–5 yr, 5–7 yr, 7–10 yr, 10–15 yr, 15–20 yr, 20–30 yr, 30+ yr
Commitment	% with true commitments
	% with uncertain commitments
	% uncommitted

approved or rejected by the relevant people in senior management. The process should not be bureaucratic and time-consuming. This is especially important when a firm has to respond to large underwriting transactions (capital commitments) or credit-sensitive deals that require short timeframe responses (e.g. bidding on a large block of shares from an institutional customer, buying a bond deal from an issuer for subsequent distribution to investors or executing a time-sensitive derivative). It must, however, be rigorously enforced. If the framework is a reflection of a firm's risk appetite, then exceptions must be vetted diligently. Exceptions should be kept to a bare minimum and always accompanied by a short expiration. A related issue to consider is how high, within the overall boundaries of the firm's risk appetite, to set limits: high enough that they are never breached, or low enough so that they are close to being breached and require periodic dialog and exceptions? In our view the latter approach is more constructive as it forces continuous dialog between risk takers and risk managers – reinforcing communication and awareness of the risk profile.

In our opinion, the creation and use of such a risk framework is an essential part of any good risk process: it simultaneously places a cap on exposures and concentrations (i.e. a reflection of the firm's appetite), allows easy monitoring of exposures, and explicitely involves executive management when exceptions occur.

12 Automated Management: Automating Discipline on the Front Lines

Part of the management of risk within a corporation can be automated. By this we do not mean that machines will magically perform the work, or that "stuff" will just happen without thinking. Instead, we use this term to refer to the elements in the risk management process that can be institutionalized through the disciplined adherence to well-thought-out rules. By making certain processes and behaviors automated, they become second nature and help to move every person in the organization toward the common goal of creating a properly controlled environment. These rules have to permeate the entire organization – starting from the top. In our experience eight key automated rules can help reinforce sound risk management behaviors. These are illustrated in Figure 12.1.

We have noted several times that risk policies work best when they are not merely imposed, but inculcated into daily discipline and accompanied by a spirit of partnership between the business and control sides of the organization. This remains a guiding principle in the application of these rules. Additionally, they work best when taken to the lowest common denominator within the firm: the closer the rules are to the person pulling the trigger on a daily basis the better!

12.1 RULE 1: STICK TO THE RISK FRAMEWORK

As noted in Chapter 11 a firm controls its market, credit and liquidity risk tolerance by allocating limited risk capacity to each business – we have referred to this as the risk framework, the series of risk limits that are synchronized with the firm's stated risk tolerance. These are set at the top and cascade down within the organization to the lowest possible level. Violations of the risk framework are dealt with through financial penalties and/or disciplinary action for those involved.

In order to efficiently implement the risk framework and make use of this limited resource, each business unit should set up a risk committee to sub-allocate the risk limits given to it by the corporation. For the first time, business units are faced with the reality that risk is a limited resource. As indicated earlier, this creates a "natural" process that ideally results in an efficient allocation of risk toward the most profitable areas – or those with the greatest potential. Naturally, the corporate risk group should participate in this committee and reserve the right to override any decision in order to ensure that risk diversification is guaranteed. Below the committee the command structure of risk approval and oversight should be very well defined and promulgated down to the lowest level (e.g. trader or trading book) with a well-understood chain of command.

12.2 RULE 2: ESCALATE ALL EXCEPTIONS

From time to time there will be transactions that do not fit into the rigid structure of the framework; this might happen because of size or particularity of the structure. These are

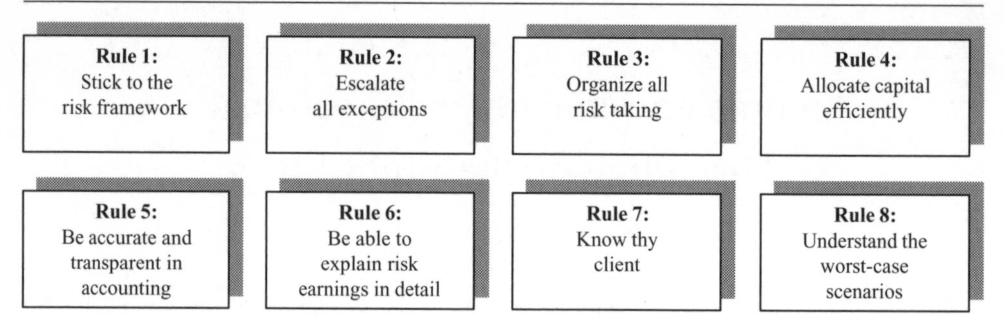

Figure 12.1 Automated rules

concentrated risk exposures and pose an added degree of risk to the organization. Whilst keeping them to a minimum, it is important that if senior management decide to progress with such transactions in "breach" of the boundaries set by the framework, they alone be allowed to make such a decision. A very stringent exception approval and monitoring process must therefore be put in place. We suggest the following guidelines:

- Only the CEO or CFO *and* the head of division *and* head of corporate risk be allowed to make such decisions;
- These be limited to no more than 20 at any one time – so they can realistically be monitored;
- Each approval have a maximum time limit of three months, after which the exposure is again vetted;
- The list of exceptions be reviewed frequently at senior management meetings and with the audit committee of the board.

By following these simple exception rules the senior-most managers are well aware of unusually large pockets of risk, which fall outside the existing comfort zone encapsulated in the risk framework.

12.3 RULE 3: ORGANIZE ALL RISK TAKING

The instruments/risks each trader is entitled to commit the firm to should be well defined, with particular attention being paid to a proper and sound delineation between traders and desks; such "trader mandates" should be properly documented and communicated. Risk takers should stick to their particular area of expertise and not be allowed to drift into lesser known territories (even in tough times!). Those that attempt to play where they do not have the skills or depth of knowledge will, at a minimum, waste scarce corporate resources – and may ultimately expose the firm to large losses. Specialization has the added benefit of hopefully helping to create risk diversification between desks and avoid situations where offsetting positions cancel each other out or identical positions cause risks to be "doubled up". Of course, allowance must be made for the fact that some businesses can generate "residual" exposures outside their domain that need to be managed. However, in most cases these should be passed on internally to the trader/desk primarily responsible for handling that particular risk. Thus, an equity derivative desk, focused on managing the firm's equity derivative risks, may generate residual interest rate and currency risks in the normal course of its business. It should not position or manage these itself, but seek to neutralize them through the relevant interest rate and currency desks. Desks that help their colleagues manage risks should not view cross-desk hedging as an opportunity to gouge by pricing in fat profit margins – pricing should be fair and market-driven. By doing so incentives to trade internally are increased and the use of limited exposure capacity to outside counterparties is minimized.

Desks allowed to commit to large risks should be kept to a minimum. Most institutions do not possess more than a handful of truly skilled risk takers (these are people who are able to consistently make money despite unfavorable odds in situations in which they are *price takers*, and need to be distinguished from jobbers who have odds in their favor either because of better information about market flows and/or by being one of a few *price makers* in a particular product (which gives them better price information and market bid–offer spreads to take advantage of)) – significant risks should be concentrated in their hands. Not only is this more efficient, it also helps everybody focus on what they are good at and enhances transparency to management of large risks. Additionally, if large risks are appearing away from these areas of "risk excellence" something is not right and should be investigated immediately.

12.4 RULE 4: ALLOCATE CAPITAL EFFICIENTLY

Each business unit and each trader should be judged on return on risk capital as well as earnings. Risk capital should, in turn, be charged based on several risk factors: earnings at risk, historical risk-adjusted profitability and its volatility (i.e. the track record), liquidity of the trading strategies and its volatility, process risk, and violations. Capital allocation should be computed at the individual book and desk level in order to be visible to the person actually committing the capital. Aggregation to a higher management level then becomes relatively easy. It is critical to incorporate in the computation the absolute risk measure as well as its volatility over time; this allows the "point in time" measure to be supplemented by historical data. It is also critical not to over-engineer the computational formulas. The more the trading practitioners can relate to the numbers the greater the impact. Simple is beautiful!

A component in the risk capital charge must relate to the process risks described in Chapter 5. We suggest that this be kept simple by having 10 categories of possible process breakdowns (e.g. operations settlement failure, risk of collateral mismarks, legal and documentation risk, quality of risk data, human error, fraud, technology failure, and so forth). The internal audit function of the organization should weigh the importance of each of these categories to the business and rank performance. Capital can then be computed based on this very subjective scoring. Business units very rarely focus on these areas as they are not necessarily easy to quantify, do not appear with regularity or predictability (in the same way credit and market risks do) and are generally considered part of the "back office". As described in Chapter 5, they are, however, real risks that have the potential of creating substantial losses. Imputing them into performance measurement is certainly one way of getting the proper business focus.

As stated in Chapter 2, this book focuses only on so-called "balance sheet" risks. Risk capital allocations alone may underestimate the actual risk to the shareholder. A business that runs very low levels of market or credit risks may have very large and fixed operating costs with relatively vulnerable margins. Thus a risk-based capital usage computation should be supplemented by taking account of "operating" risks. This is, unfortunately, beyond the scope of our book.

12.5 RULE 5: BE ACCURATE AND TRANSPARENT IN ACCOUNTING

Trading desks must not be in control of the computation of earnings. This sounds like "motherhood and apple pie" but is absolutely essential. The finance function is the sole adjudicator of appropriate marks/valuations and is accountable for ensuring they are right. A trader will quickly complain if a position is marked against her, and seldom if it is in her favor. Mismarked positions therefore lead to perverse behavior. Although every institution nominally makes accurate accounting solely the purview of the accountants or financial controllers, when it comes to complex risk and credit portfolios we have rarely seen this being followed. This is because these books are very often too complex for the average accountant to understand. She, in turn, is unlikely to tell her boss of this fact and *de facto* ends up reporting numbers given to her by the desk. Dangerous! From a practical perspective, a firm must upgrade its financial control staff to the point where it is able to keep pace with the intricacies of risk valuation. This may involve the establishment of a more "quantitative-oriented" financial control group that sits between traditional controllers and risk managers. A monthly meeting between finance, business, operations and risk personnel, where marks are reviewed and discussed in detail, is critical. Apart from such monthly mark reviews it is important for the control functions to watch, every day, the valuation of collateral supporting its risk exposures, and make sure that timely collateral calls are made when more security is needed. This simple discipline can end up saving firms a lot of money.

There has to be a very clear statement of accounting policy. Accountants have to produce daily earnings *and* balance sheet statements. They also have to be able to identify risk-related earnings and relate these to changes in the balance sheet – this is critical to ensure that all risks are being accurately captured. On a frequent basis each desk should produce a balance sheet and compare actual earnings to earnings as explained by the changes in balance sheet footings from period to period. While this discipline can be an important check in the process, we have very rarely seen it performed satisfactorily. We also feel very strongly that the same accounting methods have to permeate the whole organization – these should be those shown to the shareholders. Too often organizations complicate matters by producing accounts for the outside world and different, though related, accounts for internal management. In addition to complicating people's lives, this practice greatly reduces transparency and can cause perverse behavior. Earnings must *never* be "smoothed" so as to report less volatility and, in particular, fewer loss-making days. Unfortunately, imposing this rule will allow traders and management less flexibility in managing earnings for shareholders – but we believe transparency is a good discipline!

12.6 RULE 6: BE ABLE TO EXPLAIN RISK EARNINGS IN DETAIL

Earnings are nothing other than the outcome of business risk – including "balance sheet" and "operating" risks. Knowledge of market and credit exposures together with market movements should lead to a fairly accurate estimate of actual "balance sheet" earnings. We refer to this as the "P&L explain" discipline – a discipline that should be conducted by accounting and risk personnel on a daily basis, for every risk book. A small tolerance for differences between actual and estimated earnings should be set by the CFO. Any differences in excess of this have to be explained in detail as they could lead to identifying where risk computations are wrong, earnings are being manipulated or control issues exist – becoming one of the diagnostic tools we discuss in Chapter 15.

Traders or portfolio managers must know their earnings by the end of every day. At the end of every trading day every trader should report "flash" results that, though unofficial, give a reasonably accurate sense of P&L performance. By the following day accounting personnel should independently compute the "official" P&L for the day. Flash and official results should then be compared and any differences explained. A regular occurrence of a large variance between actual results and those reported by traders signifies that there is a problem – this is true for both profits and losses. The accountant or trader may not know what is going on – in a worst-case scenario neither may know! If this persists, the risk book should be closed until the problem can be satisfactorily explained.

Reserves have to be formulaic (e.g. objective, rather than subjective), working within accepted accounting principles. These reserves need to be well defined and computed only by the accountants; traders must never be allowed to take and release reserves by themselves. In establishing reserve rules, allowance needs to be made for the behavioral incentives that these accounting rules can create so as not to unintentionally increase the firm's risk profile.

12.7 RULE 7: KNOW THY CLIENT

Business personnel in client-facing roles, including salespeople, traders, originators and bankers, must manage the internal dimension of client relationships actively. This means they must follow the "know your client" rule mentioned in Chapter 4 – understanding the client institution, its structure and organization, financial needs and risk tolerance, level of sophistication, and so forth. An effective understanding of the client can reduce, or even eliminate, the specter of suitability risk, and permits the firm to operate in a more efficient fashion. Client relationship managers must also be focused and realistic about their prospective client business. While prospecting for new clients is a key part of any business function, originators must be disciplined in the types, quality and quantity of clients they are pursuing – particularly when the firm's balance sheet, risk capacity and reputation are being offered up. Business originators should not hand credit officers a telephone directory of potential clients and request credit facilities for each and every one of them – this is a waste of time and resources, and reflects a general lack of understanding about sane business and risk practices. Rather, originators should carefully consider whom they intend to pursue and, where possible, discuss the relationship in advance with credit officers.

As noted in Chapter 4, a committee consisting of corporate and business unit personnel should review predefined types of transactions, as well as dealings with predefined sets of clients. This should form part of the ongoing governance process and be followed diligently.

12.8 RULE 8: UNDERSTAND THE WORST-CASE SCENARIOS

We introduced in Chapters 6 and 11 a concept of maximum loss scenarios where we "turned off" many of the statistical benefits of diversification to generate a very large, improbable (yet still possible!) "earnings at risk" measure. We believe that it is vital to subject the organization to a discipline of running firm exposures through hypothetical and also experienced disasters such as the equity meltdown of 1987, the Latin American crisis of 1994, the credit crunch and emerging market crisis of 1997/1998, and so forth. It is important to understand the underpinnings of the results as they reveal a lot about the portfolio of risks being held. It is also vital to take the large numbers that these exercises generate, place a limit around them and understand the changes in earnings at risk between exercises. Such scenarios have to be run in conjunction with the treasury and accounting functions to monitor asset and liability impacts on the balance sheet, funding requirements and any regulatory capital issues which may arise.

Efficiently adhering to all these rules will go a long way to fostering a natural tendency toward good risk management behavior. They are, however, very dependent on being supplemented by "softer", harder to measure attributes of an organization which we will discuss in the next chapter. Great infrastructure will also be a critical foundation for success; we review this in Chapter 14. Finally, like every rule there are also limitations that have to be well understood and supplemented for by ongoing diagnostics, experience and common sense. We review these in Chapter 15.

13
Manual Management: Enhancing the Automated Discipline

13.1 SUPPLEMENTING AUTOMATED PROCESSES

In the last chapter we talked about automated risk processes that can help to make risk management become "second nature" within the organization – leading, hopefully, to the creation of a stronger risk culture. Since implementing a rigid and automated structure can reveal drawbacks and flaws, we have found it helpful to supplement the risk process by adding a few less directly quantifiable "manual" controls, as illustrated in Figure 13.1.

13.2 MANUAL CONTROL 1: TOP PROFESSIONALS

Risk takers (traders, originators, bankers, managers), corporate credit and market risk personnel, financial controllers, internal auditors, legal officers and operations specialists are the essential "human element" of the risk control chain. They must have the right mix of professional skills and character in order to strengthen risk control.

13.2.1 Skills

Risk takers must be skilled. Those committing capital bind the firm to risky transactions and must use their authority responsibly. Knowing how to take, manage and unwind risk comes from years of on-the-job experience. Junior risk takers, still "learning the ropes", should be under the close supervision of those with extensive experience. Traders who have not been humbled by the experience of losing a lot of money need close supervision as well. In our view it is good practice for trading and business managers to explicitly limit the positions that can be taken by junior traders or those who have not lost a lot of money at some point during their careers.

A risk-taking firm cannot rely on risk managed by professionals with mediocre skills or limited experience. Understanding the nuances of risk can only be gained through years of experience and training on the front line. Seasoned risk professionals, who have experienced the "one-hundred-year floods" and dealt with turbulent markets, counterparty defaults and other risk-related problems, are essential. They need to be able to make difficult decisions and manage through crises under very high levels of stress, when pressure to do "the right thing" is formidable. Hiring such professionals is not cheap but is, in our view, worth the price – it should be regarded as an investment in the firm's future.

Why hire skilled risk takers and then task inexperienced or underqualified control personnel with monitoring and managing their activities? They will soon be outpaced by traders, which could lead to conflict, problems and losses. We have seen cases where highly seasoned traders, overseen by a cadre of junior risk analysts and financial controllers, impose their will on the control process – demanding greater risk limits, insisting on use of their own position valuations, refusing to sell illiquid positions, and so forth. Inexperienced control personnel, lacking necessary training, experience and confidence, might allow unwise risks or accept

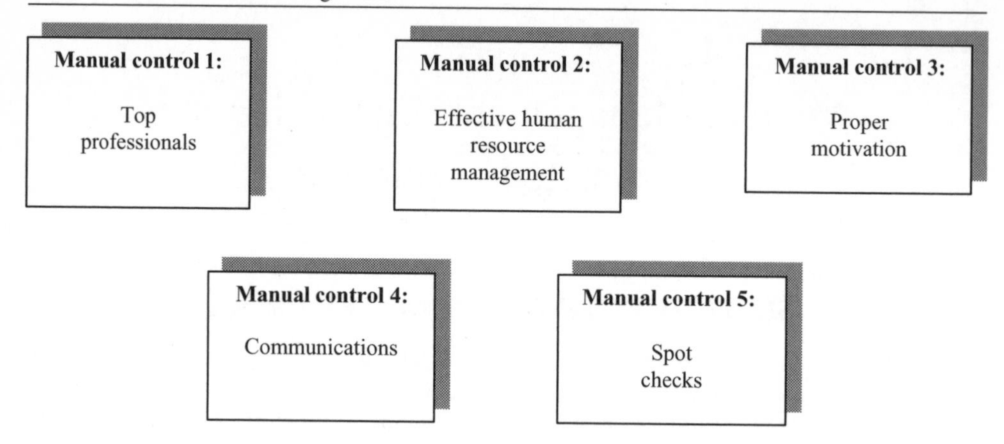

Figure 13.1 Manual management controls

incorrect valuations. The opposite might also occur: inexperienced risk controllers may lack the courage to give traders enough room to make adequate, intelligent and consistent returns for shareholders! Competent professionals are therefore essential in loss mitigation as well as healthy profit generation. The same level of expertise and experience is needed in other parts of the control organization: lawyers, controllers, operations specialists and auditors should also be top-notch.

13.2.2 Integrity and character

Risk takers, risk managers and accounting personnel must be of the highest personal integrity – this is obvious, but is so central to control that it is worth emphasizing. Risk managers and traders have to follow all risk and control directives, and elevate errors, problems or violations – without exception. For instance, a trader marking a risk book for which there are no exchange prices must not be tempted to inflate its value; similarly, a banker bidding on a bond underwriting must not knowingly overprice the deal just to be able to "chalk up a victory" to his name.

Demonstrating integrity means making difficult choices that go against inertia within an organization. In some cases this can even be career-threatening, as "whistleblowers" (or contrarians) are often unfairly branded as working against, rather than for, the team. If they are subsequently proven right they are seldom rewarded! Nonetheless, there is no substitute for doing the right thing and management needs to ensure that there is a culture that encourages this. For instance, a financial controller who notices that a "star" trader responsible for making the firm lots of money routinely overstates valuations in order to bolster P&L must bring this to the attention of the right people, regardless of the "political" consequences.

13.3 MANUAL CONTROL 2: EFFECTIVE HUMAN RESOURCE MANAGEMENT

In order to get the most out of the people working on the front line of risk, it is important that they be managed effectively – this goes a long way toward ensuring a sharp focus on risk taking and risk control.

13.3.1 Staying fresh

Earlier in the book we noted that risk managers, risk takers and other control specialists have to remain fresh and energized in order to add value. Loss of acuity or enthusiasm in any sensitive role can lead to errors, oversights, or larger control breaches. Risk taking, risk management, financial control and operations are high-pressure jobs, and the weight of responsibility and decision making is often significant. Not surprisingly, staying in this kind of role for an extended period of time, not taking "mind-clearing" vacations, and so forth, can lead even the best to "burn out". When this happens, decisions and productivity suffer. A firm should keep its risk personnel fresh by regularly rotating them through departments. This brings in "new blood", new ideas and new perspectives – a fresh pair of eyes on complex risk books can often yield important information!

13.3.2 Managing actively

Supervisors of control officers and risk takers have to manage their people closely. This is especially critical in firms with risk and business representatives spread out geographically. With head office far away, there is a risk of falling into the "out of sight, out of mind" trap. Managers must therefore spend the time and effort to know what their employees are doing – this can help minimize situations like Barings and Allfirst (where distant or disinterested management failed to appropriately question, or care about, what remote employees were doing). The creation of both local and global reporting lines may be required, but a firm still has to be careful as this so-called "matrix" management can lead to lapses if each manager assumes that the other is responsible. Everyone's roles and responsibilities have to be clearly defined and management must be active.

13.4 MANUAL CONTROL 3: PROPER MOTIVATION

A risk process can be made stronger when the economic and professional interests of risk takers and control officers are aligned with firm-wide goals, and when people want to be part of a good organization.

13.4.1 Incentive compensation

Compensating key risk and business personnel based on the firm's medium-term performance (e.g. return on equity, operating income, stock price) is a good way of making sure executives cannot collect large bonuses without meeting corporate goals and delivering shareholder value. Failure to meet corporate targets is typically reflected in a lower stock price and reductions in compensation. (This assumes, of course, that accounting policies are strong and that internal and external auditors are doing their jobs and not permitting any financial shenanigans.) We are proponents of incentives based on *medium-term* earnings goals permeating an organization. With these linkages employees develop a greater sense of ownership, accountability, responsibility and diligence; without them one can never be sure if the employee or manager is acting in the best interests of the company!

Compensating risk takers can be tricky. A bad policy – such as immediately paying out in cash a large percentage of profits from long-dated deals – can encourage the wrong behavior! A more rational policy (e.g. one that limits the amount that can be paid out on deals with tail risk) is advisable. Most remuneration schemes unfortunately tend to be lopsided against shareholders: a trader can assume a large amount of risk in order to generate earnings for shareholders, receive a large bonus if successful (and repeat again the following year); if not successful he posts large losses, receives no bonus, leaves shareholders with the loss and residual exposures and either tries again the following year or leaves the firm for "greener pastures". The firm effectively gives the risk taker a "cheap" option. This is wholly unsatisfactory.

We believe that a proper pay structure must also apply to control officers. Making a control officer's pay a *direct* function of the revenues of the business units is contrary to the best interests of the firm and breaches the independence rules discussed earlier. Control officers should be paid out of medium-term *company* profitability – so there is some incentive to be commercial, and yet they can still ultimately "just say no!".

13.4.2 Leadership and teamwork

Financial compensation is important, yet people seldom work for money alone. They want to be part of an effort that is contributing to the company's progress, be proud of achievements, work with nice people with purpose and – above all – have fun. Business units that are driven by such leaders seem to be better able to control their risks: team members tend to work with diligence, energy and enthusiasm. We have often looked straight to the type of leadership of a business or control unit for a first indication of whether there could be risk issues that need probing! We noted earlier that top management sets the tone for the rest of the company's attitude about risks: business leaders that are enlightened and control-minded inspire their troops similarly, while those that are not can let things slip through the cracks – or, worse, contribute to failures of the risk process.

13.5 MANUAL CONTROL 4: COMMUNICATIONS

Communication is vital in any risk management process. The successful firm promotes regular dialog and debate between risk takers and risk officers. Any communication forum that conveys information, addresses concerns and elevates issues strengthens risk management.

As mentioned earlier, we have found that a regular regimen of monthly business reviews, where business managers and control officers team up to review and discuss key issues (e.g. concentrations, liquidity, risk capital, reserve actions, profit and loss movement, marks, collateral or settlement efficiency, and so forth) is an excellent way of getting to the heart of risk matters. To be useful, these business reviews must allow for open, candid discussion, where everyone can express views without fear of being criticized or challenged; if the environment is uncomfortable, then real concerns will not come to light and the exercise will be for naught. Experienced risk and control professionals have to drive the process so that aggressive business leaders do not use it as a conduit for conveying whatever information they want. No topic should ever be off limits – total transparency must be the operating rule.

13.6 MANUAL CONTROL 5: SPOT CHECKS

A routine of "spot checking" various risk areas and processes can be an effective manual tool that forces risk takers and control personnel to "keep their pencils sharp". Spot checks can take different forms and can help identify risk problems (including many of the process risks discussed in Chapter 5) before they become serious. Some obvious examples include:

- Digging into risk books on a random basis and requiring the sale of a portion of a position to check marks (this is especially effective for large or esoteric positions).
- Checking P&L decomposition estimates versus actuals to help verify the accuracy of reported revenues.
- Requesting internal auditors to review the effectiveness of specific risk policies.
- Having the CEO call lower level trading managers to discuss the status of a particular risk position in order to ensure that people know she is in touch with what is going on.
- Examining whether monthly risk disclosure/valuation reports are being sent to derivative clients when required.
- Reviewing large funding requests being made by trading desks.
- Reviewing marks on collateral (especially after large market moves).
- Reviewing the documentation status on large transactions or with significant clients.

Relying on gut feel is important in the spot-checking process. An experienced risk manager or controller will, over time, be able to tell whether a particular book or desk should be making as much money as it says it is making. If it seems too high, something may be wrong – a spot check can help verify a suspicion. Common sense should also be at work. Again, experienced professionals can quite easily know when something does not make sense.

We believe that by reinforcing the risk process through manual controls, a firm strengthens its overall management of risk. While many of these tools – basic experience, knowledge, motivation, communication, spot checking, and so on – are simply common sense, they should never be forgotten!

14
Nuts and Bolts: Supporting the Process with Essential Tools

If a firm cannot monitor its risk activities it will have trouble making risk decisions, and if executives lack visibility into the firm's risk profile they cannot truly be in control. Monitoring risk across an organization with broad product and geographic scale requires certain underlying infrastructure tools in order to function properly. We call these the "nuts and bolts" and have illustrated them in Figure 14.1.

In our view, an appropriate investment in policies, reporting, data and technology is essential in letting control officers and executives manage the firm's businesses and risks properly.

14.1 POLICIES

As noted in Chapters 8 and 11 a firm's philosophy and tolerance lead to the development of a risk mandate and the risk framework. To be useful risk takers and control officers obviously need mechanisms by which to monitor and control activities within these. From a practical perspective this can be accomplished by implementing appropriate policies.

We believe that practical risk policies, which define specific risk operating rules, should be created for every risk-bearing business. They have to be practical – tied to the realities of doing business – and not simply put in place to satisfy regulators. A policy, drafted by the risk management function and approved by executive management, should outline the specific control requirements and restrictions (including framework limits) a business has to follow to stay within the remit provided through the risk mandate. For instance, if the risk mandate says that the firm will not finance any emerging market bond positions, the trading policy for each group should explicitly indicate that such financing is not permitted. In addition to reiterating the firm's risk principles, a typical policy might include details on:

- Authorized markets, maturities and instruments;
- Methodologies for quantifying exposures;
- Minimum reporting requirements;
- Special details related to settlements or controls.

Some policies might even have a broader, multi-business focus, defining the firm's general posture toward reserves, mark-to-model valuations, aged inventory, settlements and collateral controls, and so on. These, again, should reflect the firm's risk philosophy and principles.

It is also very important that policies be consistent. If care is not taken, different businesses can receive different treatment for identical risk exposures. This leads to internal "arbitrage", and potential control breakdowns. For instance, a repo book might require a 5% haircut on corporate bond financings; a credit derivative book, writing a **total return swap** on the same bond (effectively a corporate credit financing booked in the form of a derivative) might impose a collateral requirement of only 1% – despite the fact that the risk is the same as for the repo! Policies should obviously be created as new businesses come on-line and be updated as they

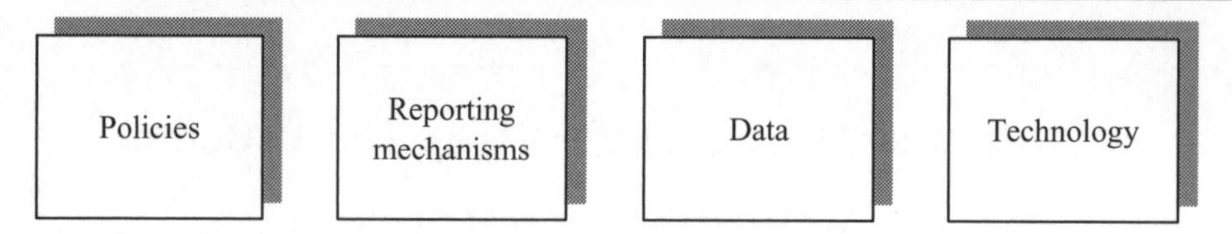

Figure 14.1 Infrastructure tools

change. They should also be presented to new employees at initiation within the company and reviewed at least once a year with all existing employees. Policy manuals should indicate the relevant qualifications required by the company for employees to perform their respective functions. A derivatives trader, for example, should be required to have been trained in option theory, forward curves, derivative accounting, new product and client review procedures, and so forth. It should be pointed out that the standard regulatory requirements (such as Series 7, 8, 24 in the US) might not be relevant or sufficient in this respect.

14.2 REPORTING MECHANISMS

Risk reporting is the "visible face" of risk management. While most aspects of the process occur "behind the scenes", disclosing exposures through a suite of reports brings risk into the limelight. Reporting serves two primary purposes: to inform interested parties about the state of the firm's risks and to ensure that those responsible for taking and managing risk are adhering to the risk framework. Reporting is therefore both a communication and a management tool. It is also an essential part of corporate governance. In order for executives to discharge their fiduciary duties, they have to receive regular information that allows them to understand the firm's risk profile.

Reporting can take various forms. To be effective, we feel that it should include information relevant to the intended audience, delivered with the appropriate frequency, and cover the topic in enough detail so that necessary action can be taken. For instance, executive management and board directors typically require high-level, weekly or monthly summary risk information that describes the state of the firm's risks and highlights the top risks. Extreme detail is usually not a good idea (unless specifically requested) as it adds unnecessary complexity. Business and control managers should receive more detailed daily information. Since they are responsible for the daily management of risk, they need enough information to make trading and management decisions. Traders and risk officers need even more detail than their bosses – they cannot otherwise control the firm's exposures. Trader reports should drill down to position level information and be delivered real-time, intra-day or end-of-day in order to account for changing positions and market dynamics.

We have found that the most useful risk reports, summarized in Figure 14.2, include:

- *Same day risk and P&L "flash" reports*. These are end-of-day trader estimates of how P&L and risk positions have performed during the trading session. Once aggregated these provide management with a fast end-of-day indication of earnings, as well as a pointer toward issues that necessitate immediate attention.
- *Next day end-of-day earnings reports*. The accounting function the next day produces actual earnings and compares these to the prior day flash report. We have found that a process that

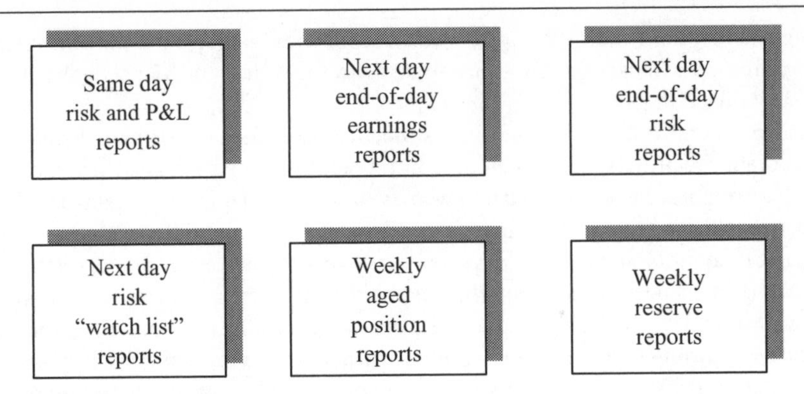

Figure 14.2 Useful risk reports

reconciles flash reports to actual earnings provides an important view of which traders are most familiar with their risk positions, whether the accountants are competent and whether anything is slipping through the cracks.

- *Next day end-of-day risk reports*, reconciling and matching positions against the firm's established risk framework. The report also includes a reconciliation of actual earnings to reported risk data.
- *Next day risk "watch list" reports*, summarizing areas of risk that a firm should be particularly concerned about (e.g. top risk concentrations, framework exceptions, troubled counterparties, collateral or settlement issues, documentary backlogs, risk policy violations, large transactions which have or may get completed, and so forth).
- *Weekly aged position reports*, summarizing illiquid risk positions.
- *Weekly reserve reports*, detailing the credit, market, liquidity, model and operational reserves taken to protect a business.

Risk and control officers need to review such reports every day, watching for large or unusual movements, irreconcilable items, potential limit breaches, and so on. Senior management should similarly see a daily summary of this information.

While many firms aim for real-time risk reporting of all positions, few actually have such capabilities. An individual business, such as foreign exchange, might feature real-time risk capabilities, but a firm in aggregate is unlikely to be able to view its risk that way (especially if it has very broad-based, cross-market world-wide operations). Whilst remaining desirable, for large broad-based institutions or non-financial companies we do not actually believe that having real-time risk information is essential for control purposes. Real-time functionality is expensive and the "value added" is probably only marginal. The money can be spent more effectively by enhancing same-day systems! In practice, end-of-day risk reporting is generally sufficient for control and management purposes. Information compiled and analyzed at the close of business (especially through the "flash reporting" mechanism noted above) gives the firm a reasonably accurate picture of its risks before it enters the next day's trading session. If adjustments or changes need to be made, they can be done on the basis of end-of-day information; adjustments that have to be made during the course of the trading day are likely to occur on a desk-specific basis in any event. In a world of scarce resources, a firm probably gains more from ensuring its data processes are robust than reporting its risks real-time. It is worth reminding ourselves that most large losses and bankruptcies result from a *systemic medium- to long-term build-up* of unacceptably concentrated risk exposures (or fraud), rather than a few transactions booked that day!

External reporting must factor into infrastructure plans. Regulators and shareholders increasingly want specific risk information. A firm operating under the jurisdiction of a particular regulator might have to deliver daily, weekly, monthly, quarterly or annual risk exposure data. Most regulators seem to be requesting increasingly detailed information on firm-wide credit, market, liquidity and process risks (and are likely to become even more demanding in the future as markets become more interlinked and risks become more complex). Reporting to shareholders should, as we have mentioned earlier, be value-added. Communication via quarterly or annual earnings updates should include meaningful information, rather than opaque disclosure that fails to truly reveal any easily comprehensible relevant information. Data infrastructure also needs to satisfy both of these external communities on a timely basis.

14.3 DATA AND TECHNOLOGY INFRASTRUCTURE

Data and technology comprise the backbone of risk infrastructure. We feel that without the right data and technology – featuring sufficient breadth, flexibility and granularity – a firm faces an almost impossible task in understanding, and then managing, its risks.

14.3.1 Data

Data is the primary way of generating information about a firm's risk positions. The data process must be complete, accurate, uniform and flexible. It should also be surrounded by regular audit checks that ensure it is functioning as intended. If the data process is flawed a firm will ultimately lose track of its exposures and be unable to make risk decisions or confirm whether it is adhering to the risk framework. A good data process is also vital to keeping process risk to a minimum.

Data has to be accurate in order to be useful; data errors at the position level lead to bad information at an aggregate or portfolio level, and might then lead to bad risk decisions. Even the simplest error, such as reflecting a position of \$10 million instead of \$1 million, or long instead of short, can radically skew the risk of a portfolio or create fictitious credit exposure. A firm should therefore verify the accuracy of its data through trade-level reconciliation, collateral mark checks, error reports and controller verification. The integrity of the process must be tested/audited regularly as an additional "check and balance".

A data template – effectively a list of required data items – should feature relevant information on a transaction, including details on:

- Business unit,
- Desk,
- Location,
- Trader,
- Notional size,
- Market,
- Underlying product,
- Counterparty/client identifier,
- Rate/yield/coupon,
- Maturity.

It should also include information that touches other control processes, such as:

- Legal documentation status flags,
- Confirmation status,
- Funding rate,
- Collateral detail.

The template might feature pre-computed risk information (e.g. risk sensitivities, desk VAR, and so on), or simply act as the feedstock into risk analytics that compute risk information. Defining the template with as much granularity as possible (but not so much that it becomes burdensome) is a good idea. Once defined, this template should serve as the model for all businesses.

Data uniformity is vital, particularly in large organizations, and using a standard data template is one way of ensuring uniformity. Processes that receive, manipulate, analyze and report back information are far more efficient if they use a common template. Since all businesses have core information they need in order to conduct business, these details should remain consistent throughout the organization. Naturally, businesses have unique risk characteristics and relatively specialized risk reporting requirements, so maintaining some flexibility is important. Uniformity in the data template does not mean rigidity; the best processes can handle new data dimensions, new structures, products, markets and counterparties without breaking down. Uniformity should also extend to data sources. Processes that reference data to perform particular tasks, such as updating market prices, getting transaction or product reference data, computing risk exposures, generating daily P&L, confirming funding requirements, valuing collateral, and so forth, should be drawn from the same reliable underlying source. This leads to greater accuracy, and greater confidence in the results. If the data to compute distinct, though related, processes (e.g. VAR backtesting of P&L) is drawn from multiple sources, there will always be some question as to whether the same trade details are being used; to be absolutely certain, separate reconciliation processes will be required, meaning incremental resources will have to be employed (and still probably won't be able to guarantee with 100% certainty that everything matches perfectly).

Good data leads to good reporting and an accurate picture of a firm's risks. It permits confident decision making. Bad data skews the appearance and magnitude of the firm's risk profile and leads to bad decisions.

14.3.2 Technology

Good technology is the second essential dimension of infrastructure. In today's financial world it is virtually impossible to manage a risk business without proper technology that covers front-end trading, middle-office operations, valuation and risk, and back-end processing. A cohesive platform permits trades to be entered, priced, executed, hedged/risk managed, valued, cleared, settled, reconciled and related collateral or other credit support to be dealt with accurately. If a company cannot perform these functions it is likely to be burdened with incomplete records, misvaluations, settlement errors and large process risk losses; any, or all, of these problems could result in a material misstatement of risk and lead to risk-related losses or bad decisions being made.

A firm's technology platform has to be flexible, scalable and capable of communicating with other internal/external platforms. By sticking to these basic characteristics a firm should be able to handle new, next-generation risk products (as well as large transaction volumes), pass common information between platforms (which is key for firm-wide aggregation) and construct a tree of information such that summary reports are a mere aggregation of easily accessible underlying data. Ideally, every risk-taking unit and desk within a firm would use the same platform; practically, this is sometimes not possible. Therefore, some flexibility is necessary.

Naturally, every risk-taking unit must enter all trades/risk-related business into an authorized trading system – under no circumstances should risk be permitted to live in "off-system" environments that are not linked to settlement processes and "books and records" (the official repository of the firm's accounts). If a firm lets traders use "off-system" technology, it is probably just a question of time before "rogue" traders start writing tickets and putting them in the drawer. Systems that are used for P&L, risk or operations purposes have to be under the direction and control of the information technology (IT) department, not the individual business units. This protects against a situation where a risk taker knowingly, or unknowingly, manipulates pricing or reporting software. A regular audit of all technology platforms is good practice.

Risk analytics embedded in technology platforms (rather than those contained in independent risk and financial control systems) have to be able to provide the market, credit, liquidity and process risk measures defined by the risk management group. For instance, if the firm requires VAR to be computed based on specific parameters, each desk supplying the VAR must adhere to such requirements. The risk management function should independently review and test analytics and approve any changes. If analytic processes to analyze risk exist within the independent risk function rather than the businesses (being fed with predefined data from each business), it is still good practice to benchmark them against third-party models or valuations.

A toolbox containing the right nuts and bolts is vital to effective risk management. Investment in effective risk policies and limits, reporting, data and technology can create a far more secure and efficient environment – leading to more confident risk management. As with any dynamic process, these have to be reviewed regularly and enhanced as needed.

15
Ongoing Diagnostics and Transparency: Knowing if the Risk Process is Working

15.1 ONGOING DIAGNOSTICS

The risk process has to be maintained in good shape if it is to work as expected. Just as an automobile has to be examined and serviced regularly to ensure that it is functioning properly so, too, must the risk process. Risk management has many moving parts. Some of these can break down or become ineffective over time. A regular regimen of *diagnostics* – to re-evaluate different links in the chain and fix what is no longer working – has to be part of the firm's operating culture. By doing so, we believe the firm's controls can keep pace with its changing business activities and, ultimately, that its risks will be kept in check.

15.2 AN IDEAL WORLD

In an "ideal" world a control process always works as intended. That is to say:

- A firm's governance, risk management and infrastructure operate seamlessly to control exposures, limit losses to within tolerable levels and avoid surprises.
- Board directors and executive managers set the tone and attitude toward risk, assume responsibility for losses and are always kept fully apprised of all the firm's exposures, including the top 10 risks.
- The independent risk function is a tough, but value-added, partner that works with businesses to avoid "bad" risks and support "good" ones.
- The independent finance and treasury functions are also tough and competent in fulfilling their respective roles in the risk process.
- Other control groups or processes are similarly in command of legal, client and operational exposures.
- Risk takers are intimately familiar with their positions, have full knowledge of policies and limits (which they adhere to diligently), know how to manage crisis situations and consult regularly with control officers.
- Capital resources in support of risk activities are allocated efficiently and profits and losses associated with such activities fall within the firm's overall corporate finance attributes and business strategy.
- Infrastructure is robust, flexible and reliable: data is of the highest quality and the technology platform can handle a broad range of products (analyzing, aggregating and communicating the firm's risk profile efficiently).
- Senior management has confidence in its risk takers, risk managers and sales-people, and knows that they will operate with professionalism and integrity.
- Despite all of this, the firm sticks to a strong liquidity profile to be cautious and spends a lot of time analyzing and reacting to "rainy day" scenarios.

The end result is a controlled environment, where surprises do not occur. Unfortunately, few, if any, firms live in this ideal state. Different parts of the risk control process might not always work as intended, or might become outdated as the environment changes. Looking for clues as to what might not be working properly can lead to the discovery of problems; once uncovered, a cure can be prescribed.

15.3 CLUES, CAUSES AND CURES

We need to always start from the premise that no risk control process is "ideal or perfect". Analyzing potential flaws and solutions to these should be ingrained in the culture of the organization and regarded as a corporate mantra. Though looking for problems formally falls on the shoulders of internal and external auditors, in our view this is not enough: every employee must be on the lookout for, and be encouraged to point out, warning signs that the risk process may not be working or is being abused in some way. Actually finding problems involves some detective work. Clues can often be discovered in the behaviors and actions of managers, executives and traders: if they do not understand or care about the firm's exposure, there is a good chance that something is not working right. Clues can also be found in the numbers: a **profit and loss explain process** is a good starting point. If a firm does not understand how money is being made or lost, it probably has some blind spots in need of attention.

In the section below we highlight common clues that "all is not well" and some of the potential causes. We also consider possible remedies. When a patient is ill and a diagnosis has been made, a prescription for cure follows. The same should occur with a flawed risk control process. In some cases these remedies can be simple, such as clarifying a risk policy or upgrading a software package. In other instances they are going to be much more complicated and expensive, such as developing a new technology platform or recruiting a team of experienced risk professionals. Whatever the remedy, a firm must follow up diligently on issues it uncovers. It is of little use to identify a weakness and then fail to propose a solution or follow through.

Our list below is not, of course, comprehensive or complete. Many other kinds of problems can arise, so always stay on the watch!

15.3.1 Governance

Proper governance sets the firm's tone and attitude toward risk. If top management does not understand, or support, a strong risk process, then the rest of the firm will not take it seriously either. Getting it right, and keeping it right, at the senior-most levels is therefore vital.

- *Clue:* ***Senior management does not understand the firm's risks – even its largest exposures.***
- *Causes:* Senior managers may not believe that risk matters are important enough to spend time on or may lack the skills needed to understand the firm's risk exposures. Also, risk reporting at senior levels may not clearly express the firm's exposures.
- *Cure:* Make sure that the board of directors and executive management are fully aware of their accountability for risk throughout the firm and that they have a thorough understanding of the firm's risk businesses, how risk exposures can be generated and the impact risk can have on financial results. Stress this especially for the top 10 risks, and ensure that risk reporting clearly exposes these. Demonstrate, through stress scenarios and other relevant analyses, the actual financial losses that can occur. Ensure senior management acknowledges that these results, if they were to occur, fit within their risk tolerance. Conduct regular risk education seminars for executives and ensure that risk reporting for senior managers is

simple but comprehensive. This is intended to solve the governance issues highlighted in Chapter 10.

- *Clue:* ***Senior management refuses to take responsibility for the firm's risk process and exposures.***
- *Causes:* Senior managers may be uncomfortable with, or unaware of, the firm's risk activities; they may not want to place themselves in jeopardy by accepting control of an area they do not fully understand. Alternatively, they may try to avoid knowledge of these on the working assumption that this obfuscates accountability.
- *Cure:* Make sure all senior managers are educated on risk matters until they are comfortable; then make sure that the firm's governance structure clearly assigns accountability to senior managers. This is intended to address the accountability issues highlighted in Chapter 10.

- *Clue:* ***Business units influence risk control managers.***
- *Causes:* The corporate risk function has a direct reporting line into the businesses, or those generating revenues determine compensation. Board members and senior executives fail to understand the need for independent risk control, do not perceive the potential conflict of interest or have simply not promulgated this principle throughout the organization.
- *Cure:* Make sure the risk function and associated risk and control committees remain independent – with no compensation, performance review or reporting responsibilities linked to the business units. Ensure that the board and senior managers enforce this and promulgate its importance throughout the organization. This is intended to solve the independence issues highlighted in Chapter 10.

- *Clue:* ***The firm's approach to risk taking and its tolerance for risk-related losses are unclear.***
- *Causes:* Managers do not understand their business lines, are unaware of how they make or lose money, and are uncertain how risk impacts their operations. Senior management cannot relate its loss tolerance and capital resources to risk activities and may even fail to understand the nature and magnitude of the firm's risks. Business leaders tend to chase the "latest deal" without regard for the firm's strategic views on risk.
- *Cure:* Make certain that the board considers, defines and communicates a risk philosophy and tolerance and that it adheres to these objectives diligently. Broadcast the mandate and related framework and principles to all relevant parties on a continuous basis. Ensure that these are appropriately inserted into each risk policy manual and regularly signed off on at each business level. This is intended to solve the risk tolerance and framework issues highlighted in Chapters 8 and 11.

- *Clue:* ***Inappropriately large or new risks are routinely taken.***
- *Causes:* Senior management does not set appropriate limits to constrain exposures or is routinely willing to exceed them in order to capture new business. The firm may lack a framework to limit risk concentrations or allocate risk-based capital, and/or does not measure returns earned against risks taken. It may also lack a formal process to consider new products.
- *Cure:* Ensure that the firm has instituted a risk framework based on the risk mandate and a proper capital allocation process that is well understood and properly implemented; measure returns generated on a risk-adjusted basis to demonstrate the relative profitability (or lack thereof!) of all risks – including those that are particularly large or new. Report regularly to senior management and board members on the risk profile, the top 10 risks and outstanding risk issues so they have a thorough understanding of the largest positions. Sensitize them to the financial damage the positions can entail under various scenarios and ensure that they

sign off on these. Institute a new product process to ensure proper vetting of new risks. This is intended to solve the framework limit issues highlighted in Chapter 11.

- *Clue:* ***Large losses surprise management regularly.***
- *Causes:* The risk framework or limit structure is ineffective (e.g. too liberal, too imprecise) or risks are not being identified or measured properly. Additionally, the capital allocation process may not be working properly (allowing too much "mispriced" risk to be put on the books).
- *Cure:* Make sure that limits are based on the firm's absolute tolerance levels and scenarios that reflect worst cases; also make sure that the limit structure does not permit risks to go unchecked (e.g. nothing is slipping through the cracks). Enforce a capital allocation process and optimize the allocation of capital so that desirable risk-adjusted returns are being earned. This is intended to solve the framework and capital allocation issues highlighted in Chapters 8 and 11.

- *Clue:* ***Policies, procedures and limits intended to control businesses are violated without penalty.***
- *Causes:* Senior management is not capable of controlling business managers or risk takers. The corporate risk management function may not have any authority or management support.
- *Cure:* Make sure the corporate risk function is given authority to act on behalf of the firm when it comes to risk matters. Impose penalties (including economic penalties or other disciplinary action, e.g. firing for cause) for violators of control policies – without exception – and make examples of these. Ensure that internal auditors actively review and report on breakdowns in the process. This is intended to solve the policy/infrastructure issues highlighted in Chapter 14.

- *Clue:* ***Mediocre risk takers, managers and controllers appear in many parts of the organization.***
- *Causes:* Senior managers are not hiring the best talent possible or do not believe that spending on the necessary resources is justified. Underperformers are not "managed out" of the organization, but are permitted to continue working in potentially sensitive roles.
- *Cure:* Insist on hiring only the best risk takers, risk managers and control officers throughout the organization, at all times. Make sure senior management and the board are aware of the need for top talent and the difficulties that can arise with underperformers. Manage all underperformers out of the firm through regular, rigorous reviews. Do not let "dead wood" accumulate! This is intended to solve the personnel and professional skill issues highlighted in Chapter 13.

15.3.2 Identification

Flaws in identifying risks can cause important exposures to be ignored and might lead to "surprise" losses from unexpected sources.

- *Clue:* ***Risks are frequently misidentified.***
- *Causes:* Business and control managers lack the skills to understand new products, or do not devote time and resources to the effort. Appropriate forums for reviewing and discussing new products or business initiatives may not exist or may be staffed only by junior personnel (e.g. new product committee). Data underlying transactions may be incomplete or wrong, and technology platforms may not be able to aggregate exposures properly.

- *Cure:* Make sure that risk professionals have the skills and experience to judge the risks of products, market, structures, processes and counterparties. This should include capturing all SPVs and subsidiaries within an organization (in a complex organization, these can sometimes be missed). Create and enforce a new product committee that permits products/transactions to be dissected, analyzed and discussed constructively. Make sure that standard data templates are used for each business, and that technology platforms are capable of, and are delivering, a proper aggregation. This is intended to solve the common identification and new product review issues highlighted in Chapters 2 and 11.

15.3.3 Measurement

Flaws in measurement can lead to a misstatement of the firm's risk exposures.

- *Clue:* ***The firm loses money on basic or complex risks or hedged positions.***
- *Causes:* Business and risk functions do not have the quantitative expertise needed to evaluate the risks of transactions/products, or may not understand the firm's risk positions. Analytics software to compute exposures may be wrong and/or data might be corrupt.
- *Cure:* Ensure that risk professionals with the right quantitative skills are involved in the process (e.g. reviewing new products, evaluating analytics and algorithms used to price and quantify risk exposures, etc.); upgrade personnel where necessary. Make certain that *all* mathematical pricing/risk algorithms are reviewed for accuracy and that proper data templates are employed. This is intended to solve the professional skill, analytics and data issues highlighted in Chapters 13 and 14.

15.3.4 Reporting/monitoring

Weakness in reporting and monitoring mechanisms creates difficulties for those trying to understand and manage the firm's risk exposure. If a firm cannot accurately report its risks, it may not truly be in control of its exposures.

- *Clue:* ***The firm cannot explain its P&L properly.***
- *Causes:* The firm lacks the technical infrastructure to decompose business activities and resulting gains/losses accurately, fails to understand the critical importance of relating P&L to risk exposures or does not understand its businesses. It may also mean that P&L is being "smoothed". This is serious, as it also means that the firm lacks a diagnostic tool to be able to find out if other control problems exist.
- *Cure:* Develop a thorough P&L explain process as a matter of priority and promulgate its use throughout the firm. If the technology does not yet exist to properly support the process, institute a manual one with additional resources. Also, make sure that accounting policies are completely transparent and cannot be manipulated. This is intended to solve the P&L explain and accounting transparency issues highlighted in Chapters 9, 10 and 12.

- *Clue:* ***Daily P&L "flash" results do not reconcile to actual earnings.***
- *Causes:* The firm's P&L explain process is not working properly (e.g. maybe it lacks granularity or misses important components) or is being manipulated in some way. It might also mean risk takers or the accountants do not really understand how money is being made or lost.
- *Cure:* Re-examine the P&L "flash" process in detail and determine whether something is missing. Make sure that those taking risk and those "counting the beans" can explain how

money is being made or lost and have them prove it. This is intended to solve the accounting transparency and valuation issues highlighted in Chapters 9, 10 and 12.

- *Clue:* ***Timely reporting of risks is not possible.***
- *Causes:* The firm's technical infrastructure is inadequate or "disorganized" and yet risk taking is liberally permitted across many markets. Alternatively the discipline of timely risk reporting by traders is not instituted or enforced.
- *Cure:* Upgrade the technology platform so that it is flexible enough to generate reporting for all relevant parties (managers, executives, regulators, investors); if necessary, make use of "off-the-shelf" software to provide some reporting relief. Insist on organized risk taking across products and regions. Enforce the discipline of risk and P&L reporting by traders and finance personnel by the end of the day and next day, respectively. This is intended to solve the risk-taking mandates and data infrastructure issues highlighted in Chapters 12 and 14.

- *Clue:* ***Risk reporting is often inaccurate.***
- *Causes:* Technical resources are inadequate, business units are not able (or required) to adhere to a common data template, analytics are wrong, and/or "off-system" risk exposures are allowed.
- *Cure:* Develop and enforce a common data template and do not permit any risk positions to reside outside an authorized trading and reporting system (e.g. one with links into firm-wide processes). Perform regular checks to ensure that the problem has been resolved. If the problem is not resolved, cut back trading to a point where everything is under control. This is intended to solve the reporting infrastructure issues highlighted in Chapter 14.

- *Clue:* ***Risk reporting appears suspicious or nonsensical.***
- *Causes:* Risk data may be flawed or incomplete, or the technological infrastructure may not be able to compute or aggregate with precision. Alternatively, risk takers may be manipulating risk information to give a different picture of risk.
- *Cure:* Make sure the data and technology requirements for each business are well defined and thoroughly reviewed and that all code used to generate risk reports is under the control of an independent function (e.g. audit, risk management, financial controllers). If this does not resolve the issue, cut back trading until it is clearly under control (and rebuild it once the reported numbers match). This is intended to solve the data infrastructure and independent valuation issues highlighted in Chapters 9, 10 and 14.

15.3.5 Ongoing management

Weakness in the daily management of risk exposures, and in the personnel responsible for taking or overseeing risk, increases the chances that losses will occur.

- *Clue:* ***Large profits are not investigated.***
- *Causes:* Top management rewards large producers without understanding how they make money or questioning how potentially large gains are related to risks. Management prefers to keep its "head buried in the sand" when times are good and merely show good results. In addition, the accounting function may not be strong enough to delve into the real source of P&L, and the P&L explain process may not be working adequately.
- *Cure:* Insist on a thorough explanation of any gains or losses above a predefined amount, every day. No manager should be satisfied until the nature and source of all large gains is well understood. Make sure that the infrastructure is robust enough to deliver the information regularly and on a timely basis, and that the financial control function is appropriately staffed.

Once profits and losses have been explained ensure that the results fit into the firm's stated risk mandate and that executive management is comfortable with this. This is intended to solve the P&L explain, governance and accounting transparency issues highlighted in Chapters 9, 10, 12 and 14.

- *Clue:* ***Unusual cash movements, payments or obligations occur – but are not questioned.***
- *Causes:* Risk takers may be funding obligations that are not known to others in management or control – that may be indicative of large risk exposures now, or in the future.
- *Cure:* All requests for funding must be analyzed and approved by those outside of the business function; businesses cannot be allowed to have a free call on the firm's treasury without justification. Business managers should explain large or unexpected payments to risk and treasury managers before any payments are authorized (risk managers must ensure that these always relate to risk that fits into the risk mandate). This is intended to solve the funding issues highlighted in Chapter 3.

- *Clue:* ***Operational risk losses occur with frequency.***
- *Causes:* Coordination between front- and back-office processes may be broken. Back-office and settlement personnel may be inexperienced and might be given too much authority for their relative level of market knowledge. New account, securities transfer and/or collateral procedures might be unclear (or non-existent). Additionally, technical infrastructure supporting business activities may not be able to cope with high volumes or might require too much manual intervention.
- *Cure:* Ensure a smooth and efficient link between front- and back-office processes. If needed, institute a "middle-office" group to make sure nothing can fall between the cracks. Staff the operational function properly, and ensure that the ability to transmit cash/securities/payments is done at a proper level of seniority and experience. Make sure that all operational policies related to new accounts, wire transfers, collateral management, etc. are in place and being followed. Determine where weak links in the technology infrastructure supporting operational processes exist (e.g. lack of scalability) and implement alternate technical or manual solutions – with proper audit controls. This is intended to solve the process risk issues highlighted in Chapter 5.

- *Clue:* ***Exceptions to the framework are permitted with frequency and/or are carried for a long time.***
- *Causes:* Business managers and risk takers have figured out that the risk function is a "paper tiger" that will approve continuous extensions to the risk profile. In addition, executive management may not take an active interest in the exception process, or are willing to support risk requests blindly.
- *Cure:* Enforce the risk framework process by only allowing a certain number of exceptions at any time, and by limiting the length of those exceptions to defined time horizons – without any possibility of extension! Ensure that senior management is regularly informed of the worst-case scenario of every exposure contained within framework limits as well as those granted on an exceptional basis. This is intended to solve the framework and limit exception issues highlighted in Chapters 11 and 12.

- *Clue:* ***Illiquid, complex, leveraged, aged or concentrated positions are permitted to grow without constraint.***
- *Causes:* Business and control managers do not fully appreciate, or are ignoring, the damage such exposures can create, the technical infrastructure cannot track or aggregate positions, the risk limit structure is too liberal, positions are deliberately or mistakenly misvalued.

- *Cure:* Implement a risk framework process to control exposures, concentrations, aged inventory, and so forth. Ensure that this fits into board and CEO-approved risk tolerance and that there is awareness and discussion about the worst-case scenario for these positions. Fix the technology platform as a matter of priority (particularly if risk aggregations are involved). Upgrade or reinforce the independent financial control function, insist on periodic liquidations of positions to prove marks. Make sure that policies, new product/commitment and client suitability committees are being used appropriately. This is intended to solve the framework, governance and liquidity issues highlighted in Chapters 3, 9 and 11.

- *Clue:* ***Business managers permit aggressive risk-taking behavior to proceed without check.***
- *Causes:* Prudent management of risk is not a corporate imperative, senior managers are not in control of their risk takers (and do not understand their capabilities and personalities) or they fail to appreciate that aggressive behavior can lead to financial losses.
- *Cure:* Put stronger business managers in charge of "aggressive" risk takers or reassign those that are overly aggressive to areas where they can add value but not commit capital. This is intended to solve the personnel management issues highlighted in Chapter 13.

- *Clue:* ***Accounting and financial policies lack transparency.***
- *Causes:* The accounting department may not be qualified to understand the complexities of the business or may be understaffed; risk takers and business leaders may intimidate junior accountants. Reserve and mark adjustments may leave too much leeway lower down in the organization. Additionally, the accounting team may lack the independence and integrity needed to question the businesses.
- *Cure:* Put strong and experienced financial controllers in key accounting positions, and support their efforts. Insist on clear, documented financial and accounting policies for key areas such as reserves, valuations and markdowns; make sure that reserve/valuation decisions are made at an appropriate level and receive proper visibility. Occasionally mandate the sale of part of large concentrated positions to verify prevailing marks. This is intended to solve the financial transparency and personnel skill issues highlighted in Chapters 9, 10 and 12.

- *Clue:* ***Legal documentation backlogs are significant, and permitted to increase without constraint.***
- *Causes:* Managers do not understand the financial damage legal and process risk can create. The legal department may be understaffed or inexperienced, and/or technical resources supporting legal and operational processes may be insufficient to track the status of documentation.
- *Cure:* Constrain business activities when documentary backlogs exist and ensure awareness of documentary status at all times. Staff the legal and operational functions appropriately. This is intended to solve the process and legal risk issues highlighted in Chapters 4 and 5.

- *Clue:* ***Clients routinely enter into highly leveraged transactions or complain about the risks they are being given or the losses they are sustaining on transactions.***
- *Causes:* The firm is operating without proper sensitivity to client requirements, and is unaware of, or unconcerned about, how clients fare in transactions. Business management may be following a *caveat emptor* policy in its dealings, interested only in trying to make as much money as possible for the firm (or themselves!). A formal client suitability review process probably does not exist.
- *Cure:* Establish a client suitability review forum with proper representatives from the business, risk management, legal and financial control functions. Create minimum standards for

disclosure and downside exposure. Make sure client strategy edicts are driven from the very top of the firm! This is intended to solve the suitability issues highlighted in Chapter 4.

- *Clue:* ***Confusion exists about reporting lines and management structure; communication breakdowns occur with frequency.***
- *Causes:* The firm operates a complex geographic/product/client/legal entity split that lacks clarity and fails to assign ultimate responsibility. Individual managers may be trying to "grab P&L" by taking over product or market responsibility that is not rightly theirs, thereby creating confusion. Internal politics and time-zone differences may be complicating the situation.
- *Cure:* Minimize matrix reporting relationships. When these cannot be avoided, be "crystal clear" in assigning management responsibilities for products and clients. Internal rules for trading, risk control and financial accounting have to be very simple in order to avoid confusion about accountability; clearly document all such roles and responsibilities. This is intended to solve the manual management issues highlighted in Chapter 13.

15.3.6 Infrastructure

Shortcomings in a firm's infrastructure process can lead to errors that impact the entire risk chain.

- *Clue:* ***Technology cannot accommodate the firm's risk exposures.***
- *Causes:* The firm is utilizing outdated legacy systems that cannot handle the firm's existing business including "next-generation" products.
- *Cure:* Upgrade the firm's infrastructure platform; make sure that it is built on a flexible foundation and that it contains short-, medium- and long-term technology plans for enhancement; assign accountabilities and deadlines to ensure proper progress. Slow or close down business and business development until the results are clearly visible. This is intended to solve the infrastructure issues highlighted in Chapter 14.

- *Clue:* ***Bad risk data is prevalent and data used to compute risks and valuations is derived from multiple sources.***
- *Causes:* Control managers do not impose minimum data standards (e.g. templates), fail to collect data from all desks or do not reconcile data records. System platforms may be outdated and unable to handle data requirements and a central data repository may not exist.
- *Cure:* Establish firm-wide minimum data standards for all risk-taking businesses, institute a standard data template and route all control data (risk, financial, legal, settlements) through a central data repository (with clear accountability!). Check the various data sources for consistency. This is intended to solve the risk data issues highlighted in Chapter 14.

- *Clue:* ***Manual mechanisms are used to value, compute and aggregate risk positions, thereby increasing potential problems.***
- *Causes:* The firm does not invest in technology and/or business development is outpacing the underlying infrastructure supporting it (forcing manual solutions to be used).
- *Cure:* Begin upgrading the technology platform to one capable of handling leading edge products. In the meantime, curtail business until greater volume and new products can be handled in a more controlled environment. This is intended to solve the technical infrastructure issues highlighted in Chapter 14.

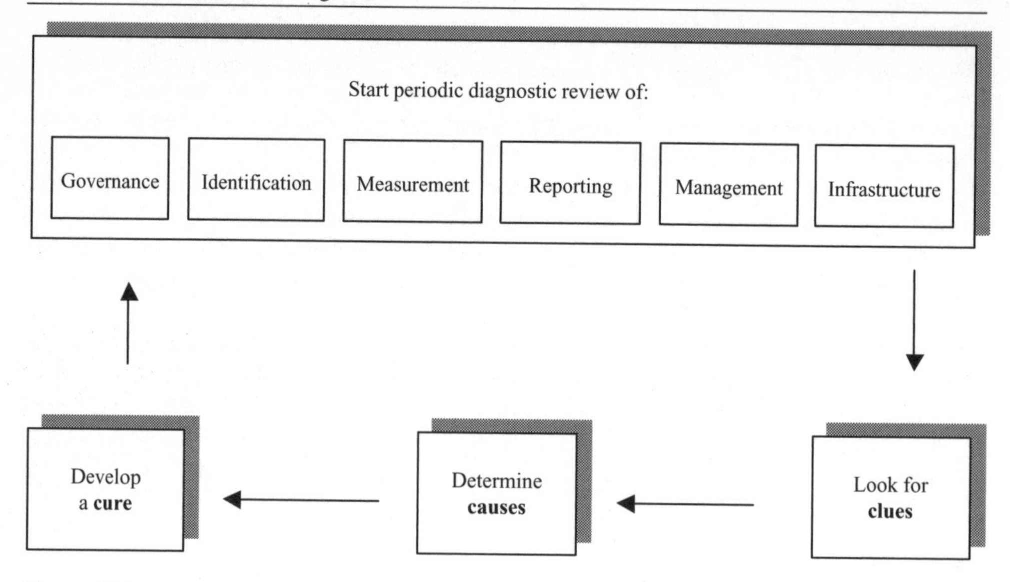

Figure 15.1 The diagnostic review process

- *Clue:* ***The firm cannot determine the nature/amount of collateral it is holding or the precise counterparties it is dealing with.***
- *Cause:* The firm lacks the technical tools to properly track transaction information.
- *Cure:* Create basic tools for tracking collateral and counterparties. Curtail business until this is in place. This is intended to solve the data and systems issues highlighted in Chapter 14.

The weaknesses we have highlighted above are only examples of some of the flaws that can hurt a firm; many others can, unfortunately, surface. Accordingly, the organization should never stop reviewing its risk controls and must make sure that diagnostics become a regular part of the risk awareness program. Whenever a major problem occurs (e.g. a very large or unexpected loss, a breakdown in information or process, a significant violation, misreporting of critical data, and so on), a firm is well advised to curtail business and conduct a "post mortem" to determine what went wrong – and to fix the problem! Figure 15.1 summarizes the continuous diagnostic process a firm can adopt as part of its checks and balances.

15.4 TOWARD GREATER TRANSPARENCY

Throughout the book we have focused on creating transparency and keeping things simple. One of our strong beliefs is in the clarity and accountability created by the simple requirement of having people focused on thinking about, expressing, defending and backtesting the top 10 "balance sheet" risks of their relevant part of the organization. After all, at the end of the day, if properly identified, it is amidst these top risks that the seeds of large failures are sown! As stated before, these top 10 risks need to be kept specific and not so broad that accountability is avoided, they have to be signed off by the management of each unit and fit into corporate strategy. If they do not, this needs to be acted upon immediately. Not doing so is being negligent. Not correctly identifying one of the top 10 risks that subsequently leads to a problem is an equally greater failure!

A CEO must therefore regularly review with the board her top 10 "balance sheet" risks. Board members, the CFO, the head of corporate risk, the head of internal audit should all be present, equally versed on the topic and equally accountable. The chief regulator, rating agency analyst and external auditor have to similarly be on top of these disclosures and feel comfortable. The behavior of focusing on the top 10 risks should then be made to naturally flow down throughout the organization, with similar reviews, discussion and debate.

In the same light, we believe that shareholders ought to be able to ask questions, and receive intelligent answers, regarding the firm's risks – in order to form an opinion on how these will affect their investment decision. The key people inside and outside the company ought to be able to regularly answer such a demand and respond to other key questions. For illustrative purposes we have listed a few of these below (others can, of course, be developed to suit the needs of a specific organization – but the themes are likely to be similar).

15.5 TEN QUESTIONS THE BOARD MEMBER OR CEO OUGHT TO BE ABLE TO ANSWER

1. What are your top 10 "balance sheet" risks? Explain and justify them.
2. Are you accountable for, and comfortable with, your "balance sheet" risk and liquidity profiles?
3. Do you receive sufficient "balance sheet" risk information to fulfill your responsibility and have you invested sufficiently in your risk infrastructure?
4. Have you promulgated throughout the organization financial risk principles (e.g. such as the eight cardinal risk principles)?
5. Have you created and empowered an independent corporate risk management function, and do you meet with them regularly?
6. Are your CFO and finance team strong and able to correctly and independently mark your books?
7. Do you have a risk culture that encourages differences of opinion to be voiced? How many disagreements have you had to adjudicate on?
8. How much could you lose under a disaster scenario and can you explain how this fits within the company's tolerance for loss?
9. Have you any areas of excessive profitability? Please explain why this is occurring?
10. Have you had any large losses and what lessons did you learn from such experiences?

15.6 TEN QUESTIONS THE CFO OUGHT TO BE ABLE TO ANSWER

1. What are the firm's top 10 "balance sheet" risks? Explain and justify them.
2. Are you accountable for, and comfortable with, your risk versus liquidity profile?
3. Are you accountable for, and comfortable that the numbers you are reporting accurately reflect economic performance?
4. Is your finance team strong and able to correctly and independently mark your books?
5. Do you receive sufficient information about "balance sheet" risk to be able to fulfill your role?
6. Are you comfortable that your public financial risk disclosures are clear, complete and transparent to shareholders and creditors?

7. How much can you lose in a disaster and what would be the implications for the corporation in terms of funding and capital?
8. Are your liabilities sufficiently diversified in terms of investors/lenders, maturities and covenants to withstand a disaster?
9. Are you comfortable with your ability to explain trading results from your "balance sheet" risk profile and are reserve policies transparent?
10. Have you entered into any transaction(s) that would materially affect the forward balance sheet and net worth of the company? If so, how?

15.7 TEN QUESTIONS THE HEAD OF CORPORATE RISK OUGHT TO BE ABLE TO ANSWER

1. What are the firm's top 10 "balance sheet" risks? Explain and justify them.
2. What are your trading credentials?
3. Have you had any "surprises" and what were the causes/remedies?
4. Do you feel that you can go against, or above, a business unit to deal with a disagreement about risk or trading personnel? Do you have proper support from the CEO/board to do the job effectively?
5. How much could you lose in a disaster?
6. How often do you sit down and review firm risk with the CEO, CFO and representatives of the board?
7. Do you receive sufficiently accurate data to do your job?
8. Are you in control of all models used for client, mark or trading purposes?
9. How long have you been doing this job and do you still feel fresh?
10. Without going overboard do you have sufficient resources to fulfill your role?

15.8 TEN QUESTIONS THE HEAD INTERNAL AUDITOR OUGHT TO BE ABLE TO ANSWER

1. Is the corporate risk management function truly independent from the business?
2. During audits do you check that there are properly written practical financial risk procedures that are enforced?
3. Do these include a strong delineation of who can trade which products, as well as a clear command structure of risk and escalation procedures that take account of possible absences?
4. Is there a strong discipline of risk control in the post-transaction process?
5. When did you last audit the corporate risk function and provide a report to the board, and what was the conclusion?
6. What audits have you performed reverting to recent risk problems, and what were the conclusions?
7. Are procedures to reconcile transactions to the actual books of the firm effective?
8. Are you comfortable that disaster recovery and business interruption plans are operational and sufficient?
9. Are you comfortable with the strength of the finance department's marking process and that collateral, special purpose vehicles and multiple legal entities are adequately handled?
10. Do you have personnel able and equipped to handle the complex topic of "balance sheet" risk?

15.9 TEN QUESTIONS THE PRIMARY REGULATOR OUGHT TO BE ABLE TO ANSWER

1. Are you regulating the whole company or only a portion of the company?
2. What is the business of the company and how do they make their money?
3. What are the top 10 "balance sheet" of the company?
4. Do you feel comfortable with the risk versus liquidity profile of the company?
5. Are you comfortable that you get sufficient "balance sheet" risk information in order to fulfill your role?
6. Are you familiar and comfortable with the risk principles promulgated within the company?
7. Are you comfortable with the command structure of risk and the independence of the risk function?
8. Are you comfortable that the board and CEO are sufficiently on top of the firm's risks?
9. Do you feel that the financial risk disclosures are clear, accurate and transparent to shareholders and creditors?
10. Are you comfortable with the company's ability to withstand an isolated or general dislocation in the market place?

15.10 TEN QUESTIONS THE HEAD EXTERNAL AUDITOR OUGHT TO BE ABLE TO ANSWER

1. What is the business of the company and how do they make their money?
2. What are the top 10 "balance sheet" risks of the company?
3. Do you feel comfortable that the results accurately reflect economic performance?
4. Do you feel comfortable with the risk versus liquidity profile of the company?
5. Are you comfortable that you receive sufficient and accurate risk information to fulfill your role?
6. Do you feel that the "balance sheet" risk disclosures are clear, accurate and transparent to shareholders and creditors?
7. Are you comfortable with the company's ability to withstand an isolated or general dislocation in the market place?
8. Are you comfortable that the company has uniform accounting and risk standards throughout the organization capturing, in particular, all subsidiaries, collateral and special purpose vehicles?
9. Has the company entered into transactions that would substantially alter its balance sheet in the future? If so how?
10. Do you feel that the risk process in place and quality of personnel are up to the complex task of keeping the company away from unpleasant financial risk-related surprises?

The hope at the end of the day is that through a greater focus on ongoing diagnostics and improved transparency, the shareholder is able to discern the 10 aspects of "balance sheet" risk that most affect an investment. This is certainly not possible today, but we believe that it can become possible – with some work and commitment!

Conclusion: Can there be Heroes?

Which CEO and board will be the next to trip up? Which regulator or auditor will be "guilty by association"?

Snowboarding the Himalayas is dangerous without a guide. But few guides have the experience required, and none are perfect. Common sense must therefore prevail, and the more you actually know about the mountains and snow conditions, the better your chances of survival.

Translated into financial lingo, we believe the next victims of unwelcome financial avalanches will be the CEO, board, supervisory regulators and auditors who:

1. *Allow business to be conducted without risk controls;*
2. *Permit the existence of weak risk controls; and or*
3. *Fail to make decisions based on common sense.*

Throughout this book we have built a case for strong "balance sheet" risk control. We have explained some of the risks and measurement tools at our collective disposal. We have also proposed a framework for effective control. It is not perfect, and is certainly not the only one that can be built. What should be clear, however, is that operating without some formal risk control process, or implementing a faulty one, is unacceptable. Regardless of the specific risk process in place, you should always remember that we have presented a methodology, not a universal remedy for everyone. Each organization is different and adequate allowance must be made for this fact.

As we have discussed earlier, any risk discipline, however good, is a necessary, but by no means sufficient, precondition to good risk management. To be effective the risk process must be accompanied by strong decision making based on complete, unfettered and thorough information – together with a healthy dose of common sense.

Human beings have a herd instinct that is reinforced by capitalism. Organizations tend to hire people who are similar in nature and who are often concerned with behaving like their colleagues or competitors. A few years ago, herds of bankers were falling over each other to lend to, or raise capital for, telecommunications companies. At the time these were perceived as attractive investment opportunities. It took courage not to join in these festivities by pointing out that many of these companies were overvalued "works in progress" with no predictable cash flows. Those who did, and were right, suffered the wounds of the slings and arrows from investors, analysts, competitors, clients and colleagues. These people have all long been forgotten. Effective risk management must therefore take account of the sociological reality that decisions are often made by people more concerned with perception than shareholder interests.

It, therefore, ultimately falls on the shoulders of CEOs, board members, regulators and auditors to understand, and accept, that the buck stops with them. There are heroes only *after the damage has been done*. Given this unfortunate reality, risk decisions must be driven from the highest echelons of the command structure, where common sense and a healthy dose of skepticism will also prevail.

Safe snowboarding!

Glossary

We have tried to keep technical jargon to an absolute minimum in this book, but have had to fall back on certain "commonly used" financial terms in a few chapters; this section features simple definitions of these terms.

10K the term for the annual report filing all US-registered public companies must file with the Securities and Exchange Commission.

10Q the term for the quarterly report filing all US-registered public companies must file with the Securities and Exchange Commission.

Aged assets assets held for sale that have been carried on the books for a long period of time; aging may be indicative of misvaluations.

Analytic measures methods of measuring the riskiness of positions that can be computed through relatively straightforward mathematical formulas (e.g. duration, or bond price sensitivity).

Arbitrage financial dealing, investing or structuring intended to take advantage of market discrepancies in order to generate risk-free (or low-risk) profits.

Asset/funding liquidity risk the risk of loss arising from an inability to fund a position, leading to the forced sale of assets at less than expected. A subcategory of liquidity risk.

Asset liquidity risk the risk of loss arising from an inability to realize expected value on assets when needed. A subcategory of liquidity risk.

At-the-money option an option where the market price is precisely equal to the strike price.

Authorization risk the risk of loss that comes when an individual commits the firm to a transaction he or she is not authorized to approve. A subcategory of process risk.

Backtesting a process of reviewing past profit and loss performance to determine how it accords with results suggested by value-at-risk (or other risk) models.

Basis risk the risk of loss due to adverse changes between two similar reference assets.

Business recovery risk the risk of loss arising from a temporary disruption in business activities due to lack of accessibility to physical infrastructure. Not as damaging as disaster recovery risk, and generally firm-, business- or product-specific. A subcategory of process risk.

Call option a financial contract giving the purchaser the right, but not the obligation, to buy a specific asset at a predetermined strike price.

Capital commitment a financial transaction, such as an underwriting of securities or loans, where the lending institution uses its own capital to fund the transaction – with a view to subsequent distribution or syndication to other investors or lenders.

Chinese Wall the name given to the mandatory separation in financial institutions between functions that actively call on clients and arrange deals (e.g. bankers) and those that are privy to non-public information related to those clients (e.g. research).

Collateral assets (e.g. cash, securities, letters of credit, physical property) taken to secure, or protect, a credit exposure.

Collateral risk the risk of loss arising from errors in the nature, quantity, type or specific characteristics of collateral securing a transaction or from price risk related to the value of the collateral. A subcategory of process risk.

Committed funding financing from a bank that cannot be withdrawn, requiring a bank to fund its client regardless of the market environment or borrower's financial condition. Funding facilities with a material adverse change clause or contingent trigger cannot be regarded as committed.

Concentration risk the risk of loss arising from a concentrated position – large position in a single asset or risk exposure.

Contingent credit risk the risk of loss arising from a potential credit exposure that could appear in the future (e.g. drawdown on a bank line or commercial paper program). A subcategory of credit risk.

Contingent triggers financial covenants in a credit agreement requiring a borrower to undertake certain actions (e.g. lower debt, sell assets, issue equity) if predefined events occur (e.g. rating downgrade, breach of financial ratios).

Convertibility risk the risk of loss arising from an inability to convert local currency into hard currency (e.g. US$, euros, yen) and/or to repatriate hard currency back to a home country. A subcategory of sovereign risk.

Correlated credit risk the risk of loss arising from credit exposure that increases precisely as a counterparty's ability to pay declines, or when collateral taken as security deteriorates in tandem with a counterparty's ability to pay.

Correlation the price relationships that exist between assets.

Correlation risk the risk of loss arising from a change in the historical relationships, or correlations, between assets. A subcategory of market risk.

Credit risk the risk of loss arising from non-performance by a counterparty on a contractual obligation. Credit risk can be subcategorized into direct credit risk, trading credit risk, correlated credit risk, contingent credit risk, settlement risk and sovereign risk. Also known as default risk.

Curve risk the risk of loss arising from changes in the shape of the maturity profile of interest rates, volatility or other asset classes.

Default risk see credit risk.

Delivery versus payment (DVP) a common settlement practice in the financial markets, where securities are delivered to the purchaser once payment has been received. If securities are released prior to payment, a settlement risk exposure is created.

Delta a measure of an asset's price sensitivity to a small change in market prices; often used as an indicator of directional risk.

Derivative a financial contract, such as a swap, forward, future or option, which derives its value from an underlying reference asset or market (e.g. equity, interest rate, currency, commodity, credit).

Devaluation reduction in the value of a currency through market selling pressures of government intervention.

Direct credit risk the risk of loss due to counterparty default on a direct obligation (such as a loan or deposit). Unlike trading credit risk, where the value of the contract may be in favor of the counterparty and thus generate no loss, a direct credit risk will always result in a loss for the lender. A subcategory of credit risk.

Directional risk the risk of loss arising from a movement in market prices.

Disaster recovery risk the risk of loss arising from a disruption in physical infrastructure, which prohibits use of real estate, technology and communications; the disaster may be firm-specific, regional or system-wide. A subcategory of process risk.

Documentation follow-up risk the risk of loss coming from documentary requirements governing specific financial transactions that have not been completed. A subcategory of process risk.

Double leverage borrowing at multiple levels within the company, e.g. at the holding company and through a primary subsidiary.

Duration a measure of a bond or swap's price to changes in interest rates. The greater the duration, the more sensitive the price.

Equity volatility the level of turbulence in the equity markets, often measured through implied volatility of options.

Fails to deliver financial transactions that are not settled properly, e.g. securities/monies are not received or sent according to instruction. Fails are commonly used as a measure of operations error risk.

Forward balance sheet a depiction of a firm's balance sheet in the future based on its off-balance sheet activities, commitments and contingencies.

Front-office error risk the risk of loss due to trade ticket/input errors by front-office personnel. A subcategory of process risk.

Funding liquidity risk the risk of loss arising from an inability to rollover existing funding or to secure new funding to meet expected or unexpected payments. A subcategory of liquidity risk.

Gamma a measure of an asset's delta sensitivity to a large change in market prices; as with delta, gamma is often used as an indicator of directional risk.

Generally Accepted Accounting Principles (GAAP) a body of accounting rules, adopted by many public companies, that is intended to provide uniform treatment of activities impacting the balance sheet, income statement and cash flows. GAAP is used in the US and various other countries.

Governance a formal process/structure, designed to protect shareholders, that ensures a company's executives and directors are responsible for particular duties and that they are discharging their duties appropriately.

Haircut a discount taken on security held as collateral against an exposure; the haircut is typically a function of the price movement and liquidity of the security – i.e. the more volatile and/or less liquid the security, the greater the haircut.

Hedge an offsetting position taken in a financial instrument (e.g. security or derivative thereof) intended to protect the underlying position. In a properly constructed hedge, a loss on one position should be offset by a gain on the other, for a net result of zero.

Implied volatility the volatility imputed from the market price of an option. See also volatility.

In-the-money option an option where the market price is above the strike price (call option) or below the strike price (put option), meaning the contract has immediate economic value if exercised.

International Accounting Standards (IAS) like GAAP, IAS are used to promote uniform treatment of financial dealings impacting the balance sheet, income statement and cash flows. IAS rules are widely used outside of the US.

Inverse floaters securities with a coupon that is structured as the reverse of a normal coupon. Thus, when interest rates rise, the inverse floating coupon declines, and vice versa. The reverse payment often adds leverage to the structure, making them far more sensitive to changes in rates.

Key-person risk the risk arising from the departure of one person, or a small team of people, critically responsible for a vital function within the firm (e.g. revenues, technology, operational support).

"Know your customer" rule a process where originators/bankers are made responsible for understanding a client and its financial needs (e.g. financial position, financial sophistication, risk appetite and profile, and so forth). The rule is designed to make sure that a financial institution conducts appropriate business with the right client base.

Legal risk the risk of loss arising from failures in the legal process, including lack of appropriate documentation (e.g. guarantees, netting agreements, bank agreements etc.) or enforceability in contracts, and so on.

Leverage the use of borrowings to magnify the potential returns, and risks, of a given investment strategy.

Leverage arbitrage an arbitrage scheme intended to take advantage of a misperception between a company's credit rating and its actual financial activities/condition. This most often occurs when a highly rated company uses its credit rating to borrow, and then invest, very large amounts of funds in investments that will lead to an overstatement of the available rating of the company.

Linear instrument a financial instrument or transaction, such as a stock, forward or future, that provides a unit payoff for a unit move in the underlying asset.

Liquidation the process of selling assets or collateral in order to cover a payment or counterparty credit exposure. Collateral liquidation may occur when the counterparty is unable to post additional collateral on a transaction, or when it defaults on a transaction.

Liquidity risk the risk of loss due to an inability to sell an asset at carrying levels, fund a position or payment, or both.

Long position an owned, or purchased, position in an asset.

Marked-to-model the process of valuing a position based on mathematical models rather than market prices. This type of valuation occurs when the transaction is very unique (e.g. long-dated, complex payout, etc.) and true market prices are unavailable.

Market risk the risk of loss due to an adverse move in the market value of an asset – a stock, bond, loan, foreign exchange or commodity – or a derivative contract linked to these assets. Market risk can be subcategorized into directional risk, curve risk, spread risk, basis risk, volatility risk and skew risk.

Material adverse change (MAC) clause a covenant in a loan facility or funding commitment that permits the lender to withdraw financing in the event of a severe market dislocation or difficulties with the borrower. MACs can make otherwise "committed" banking facilities disappear.

Maximum loss a measure indicating how much a firm might lose across a portfolio of risks by ignoring the "beneficial" effects of correlation.

Model risk the risk of loss arising from flaws in, or erroneous assumptions related to, mathematical models or analytics used to value financial contracts.

Netting the process of condensing a portfolio of credit exposures with a counterparty into a single payment or receipt. In order to be effective, netting must be legally documented through an appropriate agreement, and recognized by the relevant legal system where dealing is taking place.

Non-linear instrument a financial transaction, such as an option, that features a payout that varies with changes in the market movement of the underlying asset. For example, while a small change in the underlying will lead to the same small change in the contract value, a large change in the underlying leads to an even larger change in the contract.

Off-balance sheet activities financial transactions that are not fully disclosed/carried on the balance sheet, including funding commitments, derivatives, special purpose vehicles and non-consolidated equity ownership.

Operational risk see process risk.

Operations error risk the risk of loss due to operational mistakes, such as late or misdirected payments or mishandling/misdirecting securities. A subcategory of process risk.

Option a financial contract giving the purchaser the right, but not the obligation to buy (call option) or sell (put option) a specific asset at a predetermined strike price.

Optionality see gamma, non-linear instrument.

Out-of-the-money option an option where the market price is below the strike price (call option) or above the strike price (put option), meaning the contract has no immediate economic value if exercised.

People risk the risk of loss arising from the departure of key individuals (or teams) that possess a great deal of knowledge and expertise related to the business, and who are not immediately replaceable. A subcategory of process risk.

Pin risk the risk of loss arising from a large option position (or many small ones) trading near the strike price at maturity. A small move above/below the strike price can dramatically change the hedging requirement and potentially induce large losses or gains.

Potential credit exposure a statistical methodology for computing the potential credit risk that might arise over the life of a dynamic (e.g. fluctuating) contract, such as a derivative or repurchase agreement.

Process risk the risk of loss arising from control/process inadequacies including disaster recovery risk, business recovery risk, people risk, front-office error risk, operations error risk, software error risk, authorization risk, structured product risk, authorization risk, regulatory compliance risk, documentation follow-up risk and collateral risk.

Profit and loss (P&L) explain process a method of decomposing daily earnings/losses and relating them to starting risk positions, intra-day activity and market movements to determine the true source of earnings.

Put option a financial contract giving the purchaser the right, but not the obligation, to sell a specific asset at a predetermined strike price.

Recoveries amounts received by creditors after bankruptcy proceedings have taken place (e.g. senior, unsecured creditors might recover 30–50 cents per dollar of exposure after proceedings).

Regulatory compliance risk the risk of loss arising from failure to comply with regulatory rules related to authorizations, authorized dealing personnel/business lines, reporting, and so forth. A subcategory of process risk.

Repurchase agreement (repo) a financial transaction involving the sale, and future repurchase, of securities for cash. Through the exchange, the repo party is effectively borrowing money while the "reverse repo" party is acting as lender.

Reverse repurchase agreement (reverse repo) a financial transaction involving the purchase, and future sale, of securities for cash. Through the exchange, the reverse repo party is lending money while the repo party is borrowing it.

Risk-adjusted return on capital the return earned on capital allocated to any risk-bearing position in direct relationship to the amount of risk being taken; risk-adjusted capital permits the true return of different risk positions to be compared on an equal footing.

Risk framework a set of risk limits used to constrain various classes of risk exposures. The framework can be used as a limit structure and risk/exceptions monitoring tool.

Risk mandate a firm's risk operating guidelines, defined to include its risk philosophy and risk tolerance.

Risk philosophy a formal expression of a firm's view on risk, including its corporate goals as related to risk, the focus of its risk activities, and the expectations of stakeholders regarding the firm's risk activities.

Risk tolerance a quantitative expression of a firm's view on risk, generally based on the amount it is willing to lose on risk business, how much it is being paid to assume risk, and the financial resources it has at its disposal.

Scenarios hypothetical "what if" computations that reveal the potential profit or loss arising from a particular market shock. Scenarios are widely used to understand how portfolios of market, credit or liquidity risk react under particular stress situations, e.g. the 1987 stock market crash.

Settlement risk the risk of loss due to failure by a counterparty to make a payment of cash or securities after it has received securities or cash; this risk is commonly encountered in certain securities markets as well as the foreign exchange market for short periods of time. A subcategory of credit risk.

Short position a sold, or borrowed and sold, position in an asset.

Software error risk the risk of loss arising from mistakes in, or manipulation of, programming code used to value or process risk-related transactions. A subcategory of process risk.

Sovereign risk the risk of loss arising from an action by a sovereign nation, including default, currency inconvertibility/controls or devaluation. A subcategory of credit risk.

Special purpose vehicles (SPV) separate legal entities that are often structured away from a firm's main operations (and often carried off the balance sheet). These SPVs can be used for a variety of purposes, including securitizations, funding of projects, booking of derivative transactions, and so forth.

Spread risk the risk of loss due to adverse changes between two reference assets with a common link – such as a risk-free asset and a risky asset pegged to the risk-free asset.

Statistical measures methods of computing the risk of positions by employing statistical distributions to estimate the potential future market state of asset prices. Commonly used for computing value-at-risk and potential credit exposure.

Straddle an option strategy where the purchaser buys a put option and a call option with the same strike price; this permits the purchaser to gain in the event markets are volatile – regardless of market direction.

Strike price the market level at which the option begins to create value for the holder.

Structured product risk the risk of loss arising from a complex, multi-leg transaction that requires considerable oversight and maintenance. This most often occurs with structured derivative transactions that cannot easily be accommodated in existing technology platforms or within the legal set-up of available documents. A subcategory of process risk.

Style drift a term given when an investment fund (e.g. hedge fund, mutual fund) starts to deviate from its original investment focus/expertise in the hope of achieving better returns.

Subjective measures judgemental methods of measuring the riskiness of positions that can be used when no analytic or statistical method seems appropriate (e.g. process risks from settlement problems).

Suitability risk the risk of loss arising from clients claiming financial injury on transactions (e.g. derivatives, financings, leveraged structures) with supposedly "unsuitable" characteristics (e.g. too much risk, too little disclosure, ineffective hedge, etc.).

Swap a financial contract where two parties agree to exchange periodic cash flows based on some underlying reference asset or market.

Swap spreads the differential between an interest rate or currency swap transaction (embodying the credit of bank counterparties) and a risk-free benchmark (e.g. a government bond). A widening spread indicates a worsening credit and vice versa.

Theta the risk of loss associated with the passage of time. Since time is a wasting feature of an asset, any position with time value (e.g. a purchased option) loses money at a rate estimated through theta. Also known as time decay.

Time decay risk see theta.

Total return swap a derivative contract where one party receives the gain or loss on a reference asset (e.g. the "total return") in exchange for a periodic funding payment. The economic impact of the transaction is similar to that found in a repurchase agreement transaction.

Trading credit risk the risk of loss associated with counterparty default on a financial transaction that changes in value (e.g. a derivative, financing). Since the credit exposure is dynamic, it is possible that no loss will occur even if a counterparty defaults. A subcategory of credit risk.

Ultra vires financial dealing that is outside the authorization scope for an organization. This is particularly relevant for government municipal and tax-exempt entities, which often have specific charters/mandates on authorized activities.

Value-at-risk (VAR) a statistical measure of a firm's market risks that estimates how much might be lost in a given time period. VAR, which is often used to measure entire portfolios of risk, requires assumptions related to the liquidation or holding period, the shape of the statistical distribution and the correlations between assets. See also maximum loss.

Vega the risk of loss associated with changes in volatility. A long option loses value by an amount estimated by vega as volatility declines; a short option loses value by an amount estimated through vega as volatility increases.

Volatility the relative measure of a position to changes in implied market movements. Vega captures losses due to changes in volatility.

Volatility skew the difference in volatility between out-of-the-money put and call options; in some markets puts trade at a higher volatility than calls, reflecting the fact that buyers and sellers value insurance more highly on the downside than on the upside. See also volatility smile.

Volatility smile a comparison of an option's implied volatility to its strike price; in some markets out-of-the-money options trade at a higher volatility than at- or in-the-money options, under the assumption that the "disaster scenario" is more common than financial theory normally predicts.

Yield curve the relationship between interest rates and maturities, typically expressed as a plot of one against the other.

References

Many excellent references, covering some of the financial and risk concepts we have discussed in this book, are available. We have found the following to be among the most useful:

Altman, E. (1993), *Corporate Financial Distress and Bankruptcy*, 2nd edition, New York: John Wiley & Sons.

Banks, E. (1997), *The Credit Risk of Complex Derivatives*, 2nd edition, London: Macmillan.

Banks, E. (2002), *The Simple Rules of Risk*, Chichester: John Wiley & Sons.

Chew, L. (1996), *Managing Derivative Risk*, Chichester: John Wiley & Sons.

Cox, J. and M. Rubenstein (1985), *Option Markets*, Englewood Cliffs, NJ: Prentice Hall.

Das, S. (1994), *Swaps and Financial Derivatives*, 2nd edition, Sydney: Law Book Co.

Fabozzi, F. and T. Fabozzi (eds) (1995), *The Handbook of Fixed Income Securities*, 4th edition, Chicago: Irwin.

Fridson, M. (1995), *Financial Statement Analysis*, New York: John Wiley & Sons.

Gastineau, G. (1992), *Dictionary of Financial Risk Management*, Chicago: Probus.

Hale, R. (1983), *Credit Analysis*, New York: John Wiley & Sons.

International Swap Dealers Association (1998), *Credit Risk and Regulatory Capital*, Washington, DC: ISDA.

Jorion, P. (1997), *Value-at-Risk*, Chicago: Irwin.

Matten, C. (1996), *Managing Bank Capital*, Chichester: John Wiley & Sons.

Ong, M. (1999), *Internal Credit Risk Models*, London: Risk Books.

Risk Books (ed.) (1995), *Derivative Credit Risk*, London: Risk Books.

Siegel, J. and J. Shim (1987), *Dictionary of Accounting Terms*, New York: Barron's.

Smithson, C. (1998), *Managing Financial Risk*, 3rd edition, New York: McGraw Hill.

White, G. *et al.* (1993), *The Analysis and Use of Financial Statements*, New York: John Wiley & Sons.

Index